ESSENTIALS OF ASIAN COOKING

WILLIAMS-SONOMA

ESSENTIALS OF ASIAN COOKING

GENERAL EDITOR
CHUCK WILLIAMS

PHOTOGRAPHY
TUCKER + HOSSLER

RECIPES
FARINA KINGSLEY

TEXT
THY TRAN

Contents

In 1960, when I opened The Mandarin, my restaurant in San Francisco, most Westerners knew little about Chinese food other than the Americanized versions of Cantonese dishes they had come to enjoy. Now, nearly fifty years later, it's hard for me to imagine that I once had to describe to my customers what pot stickers were, or minced squab in lettuce cups, or mu shu pork, or hot-and-sour soup. Times have certainly changed.

In those days, it was also difficult to obtain many of the ingredients for my restaurant, like Sichuan peppercorns, sesame paste, and even Asian eggplants. Now I don't have to travel to ethnic markets in the city's various neighborhoods. I can find whatever I need at my nearby grocery store. As well as having better access to ingredients, many Westerners are well versed on specialties from Chinese regions such as Sichuan, Guangdong, Shanghai, and Beijing. They also understand the nuanced but distinct differences among other major Asian cuisines, Thailand compared with India, for instance, or Vietnam with Indonesia.

Whether you're an armchair traveler or an avid global cook, a novice or an expert, *Essentials of Asian Cooking* will lead you on a journey that is both inspirational and informative. It begins with a culinary tour of the rich cuisines of fifteen countries, from Japan to Indonesia, the Philippines to Pakistan. The book then takes you into the kitchen where you'll find authentic recipes that are precisely and clearly written. Helpful photographs illustrate stir-frying, making spice paste, working with wonton wrappers, and other techniques. All of these resources will enable you to confidently make your favorite Asian dishes at home.

From appetizers to sweets—and including everything in between—the recipes in *Essentials of Asian Cooking* range from the simple and familiar to the more complex and perhaps less familiar. So the next time you have a taste for Asian food, instead of going out, taking out, or ordering in, try opening this invaluable and practical book. That's what I'm going to do.

The World of Asia

East Asia, South Asia, Southeast Asia—these storied regions are home to a splendidly varied mix of cultures. Yet these distinctive communities have also crossed national boundaries, sharing their traditions, including what goes on their dinner tables, with their neighbors.

The boundaries of Asia vary according to context, with some definitions extending the borders of Asia to the Red Sea, the Bosporus, and the Urals. These pages, however, focus on just three major geographic regions of this vast landmass: the Indian subcontinent of South Asia, the wide expanse of China and its eastern neighbors, and the tropics of mainland and maritime Southeast Asia. The contours of the mountains, rivers, and oceans that make up these diverse areas shape their climates, cultures, and cuisines.

Arab traders, while attempting to navigate the Indian Ocean, were the first to notice the seasonal, alternating winds of the monsoon. Bringing hot, moist air and heavy rain to South and Southeast Asia for several months a year, the monsoon ensures tea, rice, tropical fruits, and aromatic spices such as pepper and cardamom will thrive.

Ginger flavors foods both savory and sweet.

Holding back the monsoon from the cold, dry steppes of central and northern Asia, the towering Himalayan mountain range rises between China and the subcontinent. Its melting snow feeds the great rivers of Asia, including the Indus, the Brahmaputra, the Yellow, the Yangtze, and the Mekong. Their slow-moving, silt-laden waters have long provided fish for the table and rich, irrigated soil for staple crops in India, China, and mainland Southeast Asia.

The archipelagoes of maritime Southeast Asia arc thousands of miles east toward the Pacific Ocean. Indonesia and the Philippines include thousands of islands within their borders. Seafood and spices, especially nutmeg, clove, and cinnamon, have long been essential to the economy and the cuisine of the region.

ANCIENT CIVILIZATIONS

The fertile basin of the Yellow River and the floodplains of the Indus Valley were the sites of Asia's earliest settlements. By the fourth millennium BCE, Chinese farmers were cultivating rice, millet, mung beans, and soybeans, and farmers on the subcontinent were harvesting wheat, barley, legumes, dates, oranges, and sugar. From these ancient cradles of civilization rose the two largest countries of modern-day Asia: China and India. Their early advances in agriculture, science, government, and religion would have lasting influence throughout the region.

Their traditional integration of food and medicine also shaped their neighbors'

customs, and those early practices continue today. Herbalists in China still call for the careful balancing of the five flavors—sweet, salty, sour, spicy, and bitter—and Ayurvedic healers in India strive for the harmony of pungent, bitter, and astringent against sweet, sour, and salty. Spices play an especially important role. Ginger, cinnamon, cumin, turmeric, cardamom, and many others have ancient medicinal uses in addition to imparting flavor to favorite dishes.

THE ROLE OF RELIGION

Religion has long influenced local tables as well. Among the hundreds of religions practiced in Asia, Hinduism, Islam, and Buddhism inspire the largest number of followers. Even in this modern era, with its increasingly pragmatic approach to cooking, meals in Asia reveal deeply rooted spiritual, moral, and philosophical beliefs. At the central market in any of its bustling cities, a shopper will find Muslim butchers selling halal lamb, traditional herbalists displaying packets of dried spices mixed in precise proportions for restorative soups, dried bean curd sheets shaped into mock duck breast for vegetarian gourmands, and special sweets for placing on the altar at a nearby temple or before a miniature spirit house maintained at home.

The sacred texts of Hinduism, the world's oldest religion still practiced today, established well-defined codes for choosing, preparing, and consuming food. Certain simple items, such as grains, legumes, vegetables, dairy, and nuts, are considered purifying for the mind and body. Hinduism's reverence of the sacred cow, Islamic prohibition against eating pork, and Buddhism's call not to harm living creatures all have deep influence on the food served at Asian tables. This spectrum

Lemongrass gives many Southeast Asian dishes, including jasmine rice, a citrusy scent and taste.

RICE: THE CONTINENT'S ESSENTIAL GRAIN

Rice, more than any other food, unites the countries of Asia. Rice plants are highly local in color and flavor. Red rice is prized in Kerala and Bhutan, Vietnamese diners look forward to seasonal jade green rice, and Thai cooks enjoy purple-black rice in sweet dishes. All Asian rice stems from one species of grass, *Oryza sativa*, though two major cultivars of the plant define distinct culinary traditions: *indica*, known as long-grain rice, and *japonica*, or short-grain rice.

■ Long-grain rice, which grows in warmer climes, has slender grains that cook to a dry, fluffy texture. The elegantly thin, long basmati rice of India and Pakistan has a pronounced nutty flavor, and the jasmine rice of Thailand and Vietnam is appreciated for its flowery aroma.

■ Short-grain rice thrives in cooler, mountainous regions. Plump and pearly, its cooked grains are moist, slightly sticky, and notably shiny. It is a staple in Korea and Japan.

■ Sticky rice, which can be either short grain or long grain, is especially rich in starch. Also known as sweet or glutinous rice, it is often used for making desserts because its kernels readily absorb ingredients like coconut milk and sugar. In parts of Laos, Cambodia, and Thailand, sticky rice is a staple of daily meals.

Highly versatile, rice is also ground into flour for making noodles, paper-thin cakes, crackers, and various sweets, and is pounded into delicious chewy confections.

of practice accounts for highly developed vegetarian cuisines and for the many traditional dishes that have been adapted for a diverse array of believers.

By the end of the sixth century, Buddhism had traveled from India to China. Not long after, Japanese monks studying in China returned home with a new religion—Zen Buddhism—and with valuable tea leaves and innovative techniques for making soy sauce, miso, and wheat noodles. This movement of religions followed earlier trade routes. Arab traders carried Islam to the island kingdoms of Southeast Asia, and the rulers of Cambodia, Burma, Laos, and southern Vietnam erected temples to the Hindu gods of Shiva and Brahma. The complex, spice-infused cuisines of Southeast Asia reveal these ancient ties.

CULINARY EXCHANGE

Tributes and gifts to distant rulers were among the first ways food moved from one part of Asia to another. The best-quality rice, tea, spices, wild game, and even fresh fruits were presented at distant imperial courts. The famed

Silk Road was instrumental in spreading and melding the flavors of traditional cuisines. Consisting of many interconnected routes that linked the Mediterranean to eastern China, it allowed the exchange of art and ideas along with spices and silks.

China's storied history reaches back to before written language. By the time cooks and diners began recording their recipes, the Middle Kingdom had already developed some of the world's most important foods. From native soybeans came soy sauce, tofu, and fermented bean pastes. Rice and wheat became staples, along with the many types of noodles made from them. Also developed were woks for stir-frying, bamboo trays for steaming, cleavers for deft slicing, and chopsticks for eating. Traders and immigrants carried these ingredients and equipment with them to new lands. Roast duck in Bali, fried spring rolls in Manila, and rice noodles in Vietnam—the flavors of China had traveled across Asia by the seventh century.

Arab spice traders plied the waters of the Indian Ocean and South China Sea for

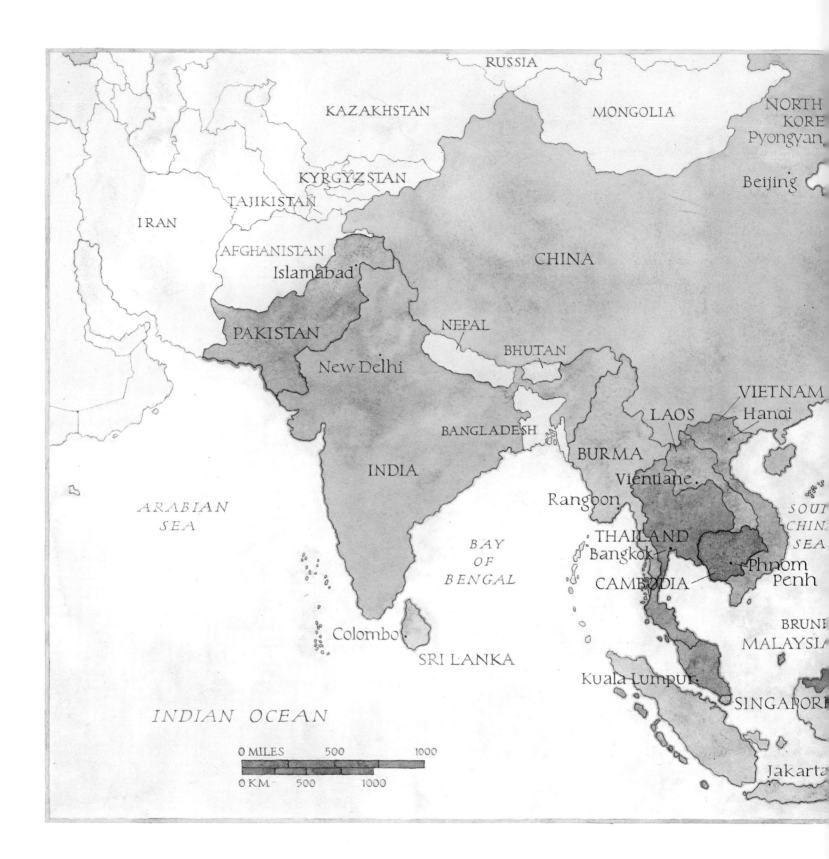

centuries, moving their cargo around the area. By the sixteenth century, Portuguese explorers had introduced a wealth of ingredients to the Asian pantry. As they sailed from Goa to Malacca to Nagasaki, their ships unloaded the first chiles, corn, tomatoes, potatoes, and peanuts ever seen in these ports. Locals readily incorporated the new foods, and it is difficult now to imagine Thailand without its chiles, India without its potato masala, or Indonesia without its peanut sauces.

Starting in the early 1600s, European colonists also dramatically influenced Asia's cuisines by bringing large communities of workers from other lands. Hong Kong, Shanghai, Singapore, Saigon, Calcutta, Jakarta, and Malacca were all colonial ports where foods were traded and flavors were blended and refined. To this day, these cities are renowned around the world for their vibrant cuisines. Much more numerous than the traveling merchants of previous centuries, waves of soldiers, government clerks, and agricultural laborers intermarried and settled in their new homes. The Straits Chinese of Malaysia, the Spanish mestizos in the Philippines, the Portuguese of Macau, and the Tamil community in Singapore all created unique cuisines still enjoyed today.

Asian food continues to change. Voyages that once took years now require only hours, and as travel becomes easier, foods evolve ever more quickly. Cantonese chefs, inspired by trips to Vietnam and colleagues from Japan, add exciting dishes to the traditional lineup found in dim sum teahouses. Families in New Delhi and New Jersey once separated by immigration can now visit each other to trade recipes. And travelers exploring the remote hills of Laos or the burgeoning cities of China can return home with new foods to share.

The Countries

The flavors of Asia have evolved over centuries, steadily pushed along by shifts in empire and migration. As a result, many new ingredients and techniques have been folded into local kitchens. But Asian cooks have never sacrificed old and rich traditions.

CHINA

Regional Traditions

The kitchen of China boasts a long history and a wealth of ingredients, both native—soybeans, millet, cucumbers, peaches—and adopted—beef and wheat from western Asia, various vegetables and fruits from central Asia, peanuts from Africa, spices from South and Southeast Asia and much more. Geography and tradition have helped define how this bountiful pantry is put to use throughout the country's vast and varied landscape.

The country's culinary traditions can be divided into four major geographic regions: the rolling steppes of the north, the coastal cuisine of the east, the mountainous river provinces of the west, and the fertile deltas of the south. In the cold north, breads, noodles,

Soy sauce originated in China centuries ago and has since spread throughout Asia.

and dumplings made from wheat rather than rice are staples. Mongol rulers introduced use of the hot pot, in which thin slices of meat and various vegetables are cooked in a flavorful broth at the table. Muslim communities began settling in Beijing by the late seventh century, and their halal dishes with lamb, mutton, and beef, known as *qingzhen cai*, are an integral part of northern cuisine.

Shanghai, the country's largest port, anchors the east coast. An influx of Europeans that began in the mid-1800s and ended a century later contributed an international flavor, especially to desserts. But the city is best known for its slow-simmered dishes, its wine-infused foods, and its smoky, sweet flavors. *Hong shao*, or "red cooking," a local technique now found throughout the country, calls for simmering pork, poultry, fish, or tofu in soy sauce along with rice wine, rock sugar, ginger, and spices.

Cantonese cuisine, at home in Guangdong Province, is the pride of the south. Oyster sauce, hoisin sauce, sesame oil, dried scallops, and a light hand with ginger, green (spring) onions, and five-spice powder reflect a subtle palate. The region's temperate climate and fertile floodplains ensure an abundance of vegetables and rice paddies, with such greens as spinach, pea shoots, young mustard, and watercress especially favored. Fish and shellfish from the South China Sea and a network of rivers star in local dishes, and steaming and stir-frying are the favored cooking methods to preserve delicate textures and flavors.

Cantonese *yum cha*, or dim sum as it is more popularly known in English, is the custom of enjoying numerous small plates and tea in the early morning or at midday.

The western province of Sichuan defines the fourth major cooking school. Copious amounts of dried red chiles and crushed Sichuan peppercorns, a spice native to the area that induces a numbing effect on the tongue, distinguish the cuisine. Complex spice mixes along with pungent bean pastes give local dishes their famously heady flavors.

Foods in China invariably carry symbolic significance. Many ingredients represent good luck or prosperity, and dishes that contain them appear at festive occasions. Diet also plays a central role in traditional Chinese medicine. Cooks follow time-honored traditions when using strong aromatics, dried spices, and preserved ingredients, always carefully balancing the unique properties of the foods.

Culinary Signature: Soy Sauce

Used in China for more than twenty-five hundred years, the best soy sauces are made by mixing soybeans with wheat, allowing the mash to ferment, pouring off the richly flavored liquid, and then letting the liquid age and mellow. Known as *jiang you*, soy sauce appears in two basic styles: Light or thin soy complements seafood, chicken, soups, and stir-fries. Dark soy, with its thicker body and deeper flavor, is used to season red meat, stews, and glazes.

Other Specialties

Dongpo rou Pork belly simmered in soy sauce, rice wine, and ginger and then steamed until meltingly tender
Peking duck Named for the imperial capital, this whole roast duck is prized for its crisp skin
Xihu cu yu Named for the famed West Lake

of Hangzhou, this classic dish features local grass carp, gently poached and then drizzled with a sauce flavored with black rice vinegar

Mapo doufu Home-style dish made of tofu, minced beef or pork, spicy bean paste, and Sichuan peppercorns

Xiaolongbao Shanghai's popular steamed pork-filled dumplings and soup broth

Lo han jai Vegetarian stew that highlights dried ingredients, such as mushrooms, lotus seeds, mung bean noodles, bamboo shoots, golden lilies, and tofu skins; traditionally served as the first meal of Chinese New Year

Chow fun Common southern dish of wide, silky rice noodles tossed with thinly cut vegetables, meat, or seafood; known as *chaofan* in Mandarin

Lo mai gai Popular southern dish of glutinous rice cooked inside lotus leaves with sausage, chicken, salted egg, black mushrooms, and peanuts; *nuo mi ji* in Mandarin

Choy sum Cantonese term for flowering, dark green cabbage with flat, narrow leaves, often steamed or stir-fried with garlic slices; called *caixin* in Mandarin

Youtiao Deep-fried long savory pastries that are served with rice porridge or hot soy milk for breakfast

Hong dou tang Sweet soup of red beans served for dessert at banquets

JAPAN

Artful and Subtle

During the more than two and a half centuries of the Edo period, when Japan closed itself off to the outside world, the country's cooks developed a distinctive, refined style that emphasized visual appeal and the integrity of natural flavors over complex sauces or intricate cooking methods. Their mastery of such gentle techniques as steaming and poaching and of raw preparations helps preserve the flavors and textures of fresh, seasonal ingredients.

Beginning in the sixth century, Buddhist clergy prohibited consumption of all meat from four-legged animals for over a thousand years. But with increasing Western influence in the late nineteenth century, beef slowly became part of the traditional diet, and today, the tender, highly marbleized Kobe beef of Hyogo Prefecture is famous around the world. Still, seafood and soybeans remain the most important sources of protein in this island nation. In the sixteenth century, Portuguese traders popularized a new cooking method, deep-frying, which eventually led to such popular dishes as tempura, potato croquettes, and *tonkatsu*, breaded pork cutlets.

Everyday cooking relies on numerous ways of enjoying fish, squid, shrimp (prawns), seaweed, and the country's distinctive silken tofu. Miso paste, made by fermenting soybeans, is an essential, nutritious component of simple soups, marinades for broiled fish and meats, and a wide range of salads and pickles.

Culinary Signature: Dashi

Cooks in Japan have mastered the preparation of dashi for use in a multitude of soups and sauces. The delicately flavored broth is traditionally made with squares of *konbu*, or dried kelp, and feather-light shavings of dried bonito (tuna) and then is carefully strained. Other dried ingredients, such as shrimp, anchovies, or mushrooms, sometimes provide variations on flavor.

Other Specialties

Sunomono "Vinegared foods"; raw or lightly blanched vegetables or raw or cooked seafood tossed with vinegar- or lemon-based dressing

Sashimi Raw fish and shellfish, ranging from

Flakes of dried bonito, or tuna, season Japanese broths and dipping sauces.

sea bream and tuna to yellowtail, squid, and clams, expertly cut and served with soy sauce and wasabi for dipping

Hokke-yaki Grilled mackerel served with grated daikon and fresh citron

Shabu-shabu Traditionally, thinly sliced beef (modern versions of the dish use seafood and poultry) and vegetables cooked in hot broth at the table

Yakitori Small pieces of chicken threaded onto skewers, basted with a sweet soy sauce–based marinade, and grilled; popular bar food to accompany beer or sake

Chawan mushi Savory steamed egg custard flavored with small pieces of meat, seafood, and/or vegetables

Nori-maki Rice and simple savory fillings, such as raw tuna, egg omelet, cucumber strips, or pickled plum, rolled inside sheets of toasted nori (seaweed) and sliced into bite-size pieces

Okonomi-yaki Thick, savory pancake served with a sweet brown sauce and mayonnaise

Unagi-no-kabayaki Charcoal-grilled eel brushed with a sweet teriyaki-like glaze

Soba Buckwheat noodles served hot in broth or chilled with a dashi-based dipping sauce

Mochi Rice that is pounded to a smooth, chewy dough and then formed into various confections filled with sweet red bean paste, black sesame seeds, or fruit jam

THE KOREAS

Big Flavors, Rising Smoke

Like their neighbors in Japan and China, Koreans boast a historical court cuisine, but it is their bold-flavored home-style dishes, laced with green (spring) onions, garlic, ginger, and chiles, that set their cuisine apart. Red chile paste and fermented soybean paste are key pantry ingredients, and sesame seeds, gingko nuts, and pine nuts add distinctive texture and richness to foods.

At home on a peninsula subject to both hot, humid summers and long, harsh winters, Koreans enjoy a healthy mix of refreshing chilled dishes and comforting hot stews. The word *kimchi* is most commonly associated with salted napa cabbage seasoned with garlic and

Eggs are stirred into hot soups and broths and are added to hearty noodle dishes.

chiles, which is served as a condiment and used as an ingredient. But *kimchi* is actually a generic term for scores of different preserved vegetables, flavored with everything from brined shrimp (prawns) to ginger, that vary by region and also by season.

Cooking over charcoal at the table is common, with beef ribs, or *kalbi*, the most popular choice for the grill. Pork, chicken, squid, and other meats and seafood are also treated to a garlicky and sometimes spicy marinade and then seared over a smoky fire. Little side dishes, known as *banchan*, are part of every meal. A generous spread may include over twenty different *banchan*, from braised soybean sprouts to wilted spinach, dried fish to fried tofu, preserved garlic stems to pickled sesame leaves. Even a quick daily meal typically includes at least three or four.

Culinary Signature: Chiles

Korean food is famously spicy. The liberal use of hot chile powders and pastes tints many dishes bright red. Fine shreds of dried red chile, known as *silgochu*, appear as garnishes. Milder, fresh green chiles, large enough to be served as a vegetable, are often stuffed with minced fish, shrimp, or beef.

Other Specialties

Naengmyon Chilled summer soup of buckwheat noodles, shredded meat, and thin slices of Asian pear and cucumber in clear broth

Bulgogi Thinly sliced beef marinated with soy sauce, sesame oil, garlic, and green onions, often grilled at the table and then wrapped in lettuce leaves with chile bean paste for eating

Dolsot bibimbap Rice, beef, vegetables, and egg stirred together quickly in a hot stone bowl

Sundubu chigae Hearty stew of soft tofu

and spicy broth with small amounts of pork, seafood, or mushrooms

Chap chae Chewy, translucent mung bean or potato starch noodles stir-fried with assorted meats and vegetables

Pajan Small, crisp egg pancakes with green onions, seafood, and sliced vegetables, served with soy dipping sauce

VIETNAM

Fertile Deltas

Before spilling into the sea, the wide, lazy Mekong winds through southern Vietnam, depositing rich brown silt along its banks and floodplains. In the north, the Red River forms an equally fertile delta. Many of the country's food sources—irrigated rice paddies, canals with freshwater fish, abundant market gardens and orchards—depend on these waters. With their penchant for raw greens and herbs, Vietnamese diners, especially in the south, often wrap meat or seafood, crisp vegetables, and herb sprigs inside tender leaves of lettuce or translucent rice paper.

Vietnam's proximity to Thailand, its long history as a Chinese tributary state, and its recent status as a French colony are evident in its cuisine. Green papaya and fish sauce, rice noodles and five-spice powder, and pâté and French bread sit side by side in the Vietnamese kitchen. The long coastline ensures a steady and diverse supply of saltwater seafood, and beef, introduced by Mongol soldiers in the thirteenth century, remains popular long after the invaders retreated.

Culinary Signature: Fish Sauce

Nuoc mam, or fermented fish sauce, is made by layering tiny anchovies with salt, letting the fish age in wooden vats, and then pouring off the clear, amber, pungently salty liquid.

Varieties of rice differ from region to region, and each often has a distinctive color and flavor.

It is the cornerstone of the Vietnamese kitchen, used like salt in nearly every savory dish and as the base of a wide variety of dipping sauces, dressings, and condiments.

Other Specialties

Banh xeo Thin, crisp folded crepe made from rice flour and filled with pork, shrimp (prawns), and bean sprouts; a southern specialty
Bun cha gio Cold rice noodle salad topped with matchstick-cut cucumbers, fresh herbs, roasted peanuts, and fried spring rolls
Pho bo Beef broth infused with star anise ladled over beef slices and rice noodles; a northern specialty
Goi Salads made with finely sliced cabbage, lotus stem, or other vegetables, tossed with shrimp, squid, or shredded chicken or duck
Banh cuon Translucent steamed rice noodle wrappers filled with pork, shrimp, or mushrooms and topped with fresh herbs

Bo luc lac Quickly seared tender beef cubes served over watercress
Banh mi French baguette sandwiches filled with roast pork, grilled chicken, or pâté; cucumbers; pickled carrots; chiles; and cilantro (fresh coriander)
Che Variety of sweet soups or drinks that feature colorful mixtures of red or yellow beans, coconut milk, fruit, and nuts

LAOS

Highland Cuisine

The lush mountain ranges of the tiny, landlocked nation of Laos are home to over sixty distinct hill tribes. Here, as in other highland cuisines in Southeast Asia, glutinous long-grain rice is the staple, and eating the sticky rice out of hand is standard. The Laotian table features freshwater fish and a variety of dishes based on finely minced meats.

Most important, though, are plates piled high with fresh herbs and raw vegetables, such as watercress, tender spinach, young mustard, crunchy long beans, and thinly sliced cucumber. Laotians traditionally alternate bites of grilled fish or spicy sausage with rolled packets of herbs and vegetables.

Cooks rely heavily on black pepper, chiles, shallots, and ginger for seasoning dishes. *Bong chaeo*, a favorite table condiment, is a specialty of Luang Prabang, the ancient highland capital. This popular chile sauce uses a uniquely Laotian ingredient, thin strips of dried buffalo skin, to add texture and savory flavor.

Culinary Signature: Fresh Herbs

Herbs and delicate greens are cultivated in neat rows along fertile riverbanks, and small raised garden beds appear at the front gate of many homes. Nearly every meal comes with neatly tied bunches of fresh mint, dill,

holy basil, and/or cilantro (fresh coriander). Whole leaves are stirred into soups, and tender sprigs brighten meat and rice dishes.

Other Specialties

Laab Dish of finely minced chicken, pork, beef, or duck dressed with fish sauce, lime juice, shallots, and mint
Khao chi Sticky rice pressed into patties, dried in the sun, and then grilled or deep-fried to make crisp, crackerlike rounds
Ua no mai Bamboo shoots stuffed with ground (minced) pork
Khao poon Golden noodles made from fermented rice, tossed with chile-garlic oil or stir-fried with pork and egg
Pa fok Minced fish that is wrapped in banana leaves and steamed until done

CAMBODIA

Land of Lakes and Rivers

Tonle Sap lies at the center of Cambodia and of its cuisine. Hardworking fishermen pull nets laden with freshwater fish from the monsoon-swollen waters of this sprawling lake and the many rivers that flow toward it. The larger ones are simmered in soups, or scraped and pounded into a smooth paste. The smaller ones are either fried or split and grilled until the skin is deliciously crisp.

Simple stir fries and rice noodle soups reflect Chinese, Thai, and Vietnamese influences. Ancient links between India and Cambodia's Khmer empire can be tasted in the country's many-hued *kreong*, complex pastes made from herbs and spices that are the foundation for a large array of curries, soups, and stews. Heady amounts of clove, cinnamon, cardamom, nutmeg, turmeric, and star anise marry their warmth to such brightly flavored aromatics as lemongrass, lime, shallots, and galangal.

Culinary Signature: Freshwater Fish

Nearly three-quarters of the protein in the Cambodian diet comes from fish, and it appears in some form at nearly every meal. Catfish is simmered in coconut milk or stir-fried with copious amounts of ginger, pomfret is deep-fried, and elephant fish is steamed with dried lily buds. Even the tiniest fish are used: packed with salt into ceramic jars, they become *prahok*, a pungent paste that adds depth to sauces and dips.

Other Specialties

Nom banchok somlah Khmer Hearty rice noodle dish with a jade green sauce made from minced lemongrass leaves

Amok Fish steamed in banana leaves with a turmeric-based sauce

Saiong jayk mien snoul Small chicken or pork sausages rolled in banana blossom petals and deep-fried until crisp

Saich moan char trop Smoked eggplant

Dried seaweed seasons broths, soups, and sauces.

(aubergine) stir-fried with chicken

Sankya lapov Dessert custard steamed inside a small pumpkin

THAILAND

Colorful Curries

Drawing on influences from early Indian migrants, Thai cuisine highlights fish, meat, and vegetables in complex curry sauces. The curries fall into three basic families: yellow (*gaeng penang*), enriched with coconut milk; red (*gaeng phet*), spiked with dried chiles; and the spiciest of the trio, green (*kaeng kiow wan*), heavily laden with fresh green chiles and finely shredded lime leaves. Each sauce, regardless of color, is distinguished by its reliance on fresh aromatics over dried spices. Thai cooks, whether making curries or not, regularly reach for garlic, galangal, lemongrass, shallots, fiery bird's-eye chiles, and *nam pla*, or fish sauce.

Sticky rice, grilled chicken or pork sausages, fresh salads, and a liberal use of lime juice are hallmarks of the northern highlands. The narrow southern provinces, surrounded by the sea and bordering Malaysia, are home to richer, sweeter, more pungent dishes flavored with coconut milk, fresh turmeric root, shrimp paste, and dried spices. In the south, beef and seafood are preferred over pork.

Chinese culinary traditions are filtered throughout the country, as evidenced in such typical dishes as fried rice, stir-fried noodles, hot noodle soups, and *jok*, rice porridge with minced pork or beef, an echo of the *congee* of southern China.

Culinary Signature: Galangal

A member of the ginger family, galangal is pounded into nearly every Thai curry paste, and slices of galangal add a piney citrus flavor to many soups. The rhizome possesses smooth, ivory skin with dark rings, a dense texture, and a sharper, hotter, more pungent flavor than fresh ginger.

Other Specialties

Som tam Salad of shredded green papaya, tomatoes, and long beans with spicy fish sauce dressing

Tom yam gung Light soup of shrimp (prawns), tomatoes, and mushrooms in a spicy-tart broth infused with tarmarind and lemongrass

Yum pra mik Spicy squid salad partnered with lime dressing

Gaeng phet phed yang Roasted duck with pineapple in red curry

Nam prik Spicy, smoky condiment made from dried red chiles, dried shrimp or anchovies, shallots, and shrimp paste that have been roasted in oil and then blended together

Kai pad krapow Chicken stir-fried with generous amounts of holy basil

Pad thai Rice noodles stir-fried with tofu, shrimp, bean sprouts, eggs, and garlic chives

Khao niaow ma muang Sticky rice cooked in coconut milk and topped with mango slices

BURMA

Culinary Crossroads

Nestled among India, China, and Thailand, Burma, officially known as Myanmar, absorbed and then smoothly blended the flavors of its three neighbors. Mild curries and noodle soups, chickpeas (garbanzo beans) and dried shrimp paste, ghee and coconut milk—the Burmese pantry harbors ingredients culled from kitchens that run in a swath from the subcontinent to southern China.

Unique to Burmese cuisine is *thoke*, a composed presentation of numerous finely chopped ingredients served as an elaborate one-dish meal, a vegetable side, a midday snack, or a postmeal digestive. Each *thoke* highlights a special ingredient, such as pickled ginger, fermented tea leaves, or pomelo. Dried shrimp, toasted yellow peas, sesame seeds, fried garlic, green peppers (capsicums), lime juice, and green chiles are typically among the other ingredients.

Culinary Signature: Chickpeas

Burmese cuisine reveals its Indian roots in the frequent use of chickpeas. They are simmered whole in curries, pressed and fried into fritters, or ground finely to thicken soups and sauces. Chickpea flour, tinted gold with turmeric, even replaces soybeans as a base for tofu.

Other Specialties

Mohinga Hearty rice noodle soup with fish, chickpea fritters, banana stems, and a thick broth infused with lemongrass and ginger

Panthe kaukswe Chicken curry with noodles

Poodi Potatoes simmered in yellow curry and served with flaky flatbread

Pe taw bat htamin Rice cooked with butter and lentils

Goorakathee kyawjet hin Thinly sliced chayote simmered in a broth of dried shrimp, turmeric, and black pepper

PAKISTAN

Tandoori Cooking

Pakistani cuisine reflects both historic ties with India and ancient trade links and cultural exchange with the Middle East. The country's predominantly Muslim communities have raised meat cookery to an art. Halal lamb, mutton, goat, and chicken star in finely spiced curries, *biryani* (meat-laced rice flavored with spices), kebabs, and, most famously of all, *tandoori* cooking, a tradition originally adapted from the Persians. This style of cooking is now a specialty that has become popular around the world. The word *tandoori* is derived from tandoor, a deep, round, charcoal-fueled clay oven that gives yogurt-marinated meats and buttery naan their distinctive smoky, seared finish.

Culinary Signature: Lamb

Pakistanis have invented or refined numerous ways to serve lamb. Whole legs of lamb are sprinkled only with salt and cooked on stakes over hot coals. Spicy chunks of the meat punctuate flavorful rice for *biryani* or simmer in long-cooked curries. Sausages made of seasoned minced meat are shaped around skewers and grilled.

Other Specialties

Rogni naan Leavened wheat flatbread sprinkled with sesame seeds

Chapli kebab Minced beef or lamb flavored with cumin and onions and cooked on a large, round griddle

Shabdeg Celebratory stew of lamb or mutton, turnips, and onions cooked overnight

Nihari Rich, spicy beef curry garnished with shredded ginger, raw radish, fried onions, and fresh lemon

Falooda Sweet drink of milk and rose syrup garnished with basil seeds or tapioca pearls

INDIA

Diverse Cultures, Diverse Kitchens

A country with sixteen hundred dialects, eight major religions and scores of minor ones (each with its own culinary restrictions), and a landscape that encompasses arid plains, snow-peaked mountains, and lush jungles can be expected to boast astonishingly varied cuisines. And India doesn't disappoint.

Indian cooks fry fresh okra in a highly fragrant spice paste to make a dry curry.

Muslim rulers once based their courts in the north, and to this day, their Persian-inspired cuisine defines the region's classic flavors. Many of the well-known foods of India are from the Mogul period: rich, meat-based curries, *pullao* (rice) extravagantly studded with nuts and raisins, vegetable-filled samosas, and frozen *kulfi* (ice cream–like dessert) with saffron and rose water.

Wheat and dairy are northern staples. Plain unleavened roti (soft, round bread), leavened and filled naan, flaky *paratha* (whole-wheat/wholemeal bread), and crisp, cumin-studded puri (deep-fried whole-wheat bread) are just a few of the many local breads. *Paneer*, a fresh cheese, is an important source of protein; yogurt lends its acidic creaminess to marinades, curries, drinks, and *raita*, a cooling condiment flavored with fresh herbs or vegetables; and butter and ghee (clarified butter) are used.

In the east, Bengalis are famous for their fish and shrimp curries flavored with mustard seeds and poppy seeds and use pungent mustard oil in their cooking. They are also sweets makers and have mastered delicate, milk-based desserts such as tender balls of *sandesh* and custardy *mishiti doi*. In the west, Goa's history as a Portuguese port can be tasted in *caldeirada*, a seafood stew, and *vindaloo*, a fiery, sweet-sour curry with red chiles and vinegar. In southern India, coconut oil is used for frying and sautéing, and rice reigns at the table, where it is ground, fermented, and spread into a thin crepe, steamed into a fluffy cake, or served with spicy-tart sauces, chutneys, and pickles.

India's curries depend on layers of spices and aromatics. A dry masala is a mixture of dried spices, with garam masala, a warming blend of such seasonings as cinnamon, cumin, cloves, nutmeg, and cardamom, among the most common. A wet masala is a thick paste of such fresh ingredients as grated coconut, turmeric, ginger, and chiles. In southern India, cooks add a final layer of flavor: typically black mustard seeds, cumin seeds, and curry leaves, fried in oil and drizzled over a dish just before it comes to the table.

Culinary Signature: Pulses

Pulses, from tiny lentils such as red *masoor* and black *urad* to plump yellow chickpeas (garbanzo beans) and smooth, green mung beans, line the shelves of every Indian kitchen. They are used whole or split, and some are ground into flour for making batters, fritters, and desserts. These nutrition-loaded dried legumes are vital to a healthful, balanced diet, especially for the country's sizable population of strict vegetarians.

Other Specialties

Rasam Thin, tart soup based on tamarind or tomato water; particularly common in the south

Gosht korma Lamb simmered in a mild, creamy sauce thickened with yogurt, poppy seeds, and ground nuts

Biryani Basmati rice flavored with spices, layers of yogurt-marinated meat, and a finish of saffron and fried onions; specialty of Muslim communities

Saag paneer Cubes of *paneer* cheese cooked with spinach or mustard greens

Dhansak Persian-inspired curry of lentils, pumpkin, eggplant (aubergine), spinach, and lamb or chicken, traditionally served over brown rice

Molee Rich, spicy fish curry; specialty of Kerala, on the southwest coast

Upama Coarse semolina roasted and then cooked with ghee, nuts, black mustard seeds, and curry leaves

Dosa Large, thin, crisp crepe that is made from fermented rice and *urad dal* (lentils); specialty of the south

Bel puri Popular street snack of puffed rice, tiny cubes of potatoes, green mango, onion, crushed puri, and mint and tamarind chutneys

Rossogollas Dumplings made from sweetened curds, filled with nuts, and served in rose water syrup; specialty of Bengal

Kheer Creamy rice pudding flavored with cardamom and almonds

Sevian payasam Dessert soup made from toasted vermicelli, cashews, raisins, and milk

SRI LANKA

Spicy Curries

The small, tear-shaped island of Sri Lanka, lying only 30 miles (50 kilometers) from the tip of India, draws heavily from the culinary traditions of its large northern neighbor. Cooks often simmer fish or vegetables in a red *kari* based on dried chiles, in a golden sauce colored with turmeric, or in a pale curry thickened with coconut milk. The most iconic Sri Lankan curry is a masala of deeply roasted spices that gives the sauce a distinctive brown-black color and an intensely rich flavor.

Local cooks are known for their generous hand with chiles—grinding twenty to forty chiles for one meal is not uncommon—and their repertory includes some of the spiciest dishes of the subcontinent. Once known as Ceylon, the island was an important source of tea for the British, and today it remains one of the world's largest producers and exporters of tea.

Culinary Signature: Coconut

Coconut trees flourish in Sri Lanka's hot, humid climate. The grated meat appears in rice and roti (flatbread), the clear water

Lentils, central to the Indian diet, appear in curries, stews, and other mainstays.

of young fruit makes a refreshing beverage, and the thick milk of mature nuts enriches both sweet and savory dishes. To make *pol sambol*, the ubiquitous table condiment, grated coconut is ground with chiles, onions, garlic, and lime juice.

Other Specialties

Kiritbath Rice cooked in unsweetened coconut milk and served with a chile relish

Mallung Chopped seasonal greens cooked with coconut and red onion; served as an accompaniment to rice

Kadju Young cashew nuts curried with a mixture of onions, coconut milk, turmeric, fenugreek, and chiles

Hoppers Bowl-shaped pancakes made from rice flour and coconut milk; served for breakfast, often with an egg or a dollop of coconut cream at their center

Pittu Lightly roasted rice flour mixed with grated coconut and then steamed inside a length of bamboo

MALAYSIA

Married Flavors

Early Arabic, Indian, and Chinese merchants and later European trading ships all depended on Malaysia's straits and safe harbors for passage to the lucrative spices of Indonesia. The popularity today of *biryani* (rice laced with meat and spices), flatbreads, egg and rice noodles, coconut-milk curries, and strong coffee with toast reveals the enduring culinary contributions of each successive wave of visitors.

Chinese merchants, in particular, settled with deep roots. The men married local Malay women, and their descendants, known as Straits Chinese or Peranakan, flourished in trading cities such as Malacca and Penang.

In Malaysia, Indonesia, and Singapore, chiles and other seasonings are blended into a pungent sauce, or *sambal*, for flavoring foods such as shrimp (page 171). *Sambals* are also a popular table condiment.

Nonya cooking, named for the women in these communities, is known for its elaborate spicing and for its unique blend of Chinese techniques with Malay ingredients. Liberal use of coconut milk, lemongrass, turmeric, and chiles transformed Chinese soy sauce, tofu, rice, and noodles.

Workers from southern India added their specialties based on rice batters, such as *idli* (steamed rice cakes) and *dosa* (large, thin, crisp pancakes), and immigrants from nearby Indonesia brought their grilled *satay* (skewered meat) and spicy *sambals* (spice condiments). Many Malaysian recipes begin with the pounding of *rempeh*, an aromatic paste of lemongrass, ginger, garlic, chiles, dried spices, and rich, thickening candlenuts. Beef and pork do appear in local specialties, but chicken and fish are most often featured in a country where Muslims, Buddhists, and Hindus have exchanged culinary traditions freely and generously.

Culinary Signature: Lemongrass

Long, slender, pale stalks of this grass are used as an herb to add citrusy flavor to broths and spice pastes. Crushed and tied into knots for a bouquet garni, finely minced, or pounded smooth in a mortar, lemongrass complements other everyday aromatics of the Malaysian kitchen, such as lime and ginger.

Other Specialties

Laksa Spicy rice noodle soup with regional variations, with two of the most popular being a tart tamarind broth and a coconut curry broth

Curry puffs Small, flaky deep-fried turnovers filled with curried chicken and potatoes

Popiah Crepelike wrappers rolled around a filling of daikon, egg, Chinese sausage, fried tofu, chopped peanuts, lettuce, bean sprouts, and hoisin sauce

Bak kutthe Pork ribs simmered in broth with ginseng, star anise, and black pepper

Satay, grilled poultry or meat served with peanut sauce, likely originated in Indonesia.

Nasi lemak Rice cooked with coconut cream and served with spicy condiments such as anchovy *sambal* and *achar* (pickle)

Char kuey teow Wide rice noodles stir-fried with egg, shrimp (prawns), bean sprouts, Chinese chives, chiles, and dried shrimp paste

Sambal belacan Ubiquitous condiment of fresh chiles, dried shrimp paste, and lime juice

Onde-onde Round, sweet rice dumpling filled with syrupy palm sugar and rolled in freshly grated coconut

SINGAPORE

Hawker Fare

Singapore's famed open-air food markets have fed the island nation's residents since England first established a trading post here in the early nineteenth century, a crucial entrepôt along Asia's maritime trade route. Hawker stalls (now formerly known as food centres) have joined their ranks. Workers and merchants from China and southern India added their favorite ingredients to the cuisines of their Malay and Indonesian neighbors. Today, spicy curries, stir-fried noodles, lamb-filled flatbreads, and grilled *satay* (skewered meat) with a spicy *sambal* (condiment) all vie for space on the Singaporean table.

Culinary Signature: Pandanus

The long, narrow leaves of the fragrant pandanus plant, also known as screw pine, add a flowery fragrance and subtly sweet flavor to rice, chicken, curry sauces, custards, and cakes. They can be pounded and squeezed for their juice, which lends a recognizable green tint to desserts, or they can be tied into loops for infusing liquids.

Other Specialties

Hainan chicken rice Poached chicken served with rice cooked in clear soup, cucumber slices, and ginger oil, chile sauce, and dark soy sauces for dipping; adopted from China's Hainan Island

Fish-head curry Indian-inspired dish of a large fish head simmered with tamarind, tomatoes, okra, coconut milk, and spices; served with rice on a banana leaf

Murtabak Dough skillfully stretched until paper-thin, folded around a savory filling such as ground (minced) lamb, egg, or onions, and cooked on a griddle until crisp; an Indian-Muslim specialty

Black pepper crab Whole crabs coated with a buttery sauce flavored with generous amounts of crushed peppercorns, garlic, and ginger

Beehoon Thin rice noodles stir-fried with cabbage, bean sprouts, shrimp (prawns), egg, and soy sauce

INDONESIA

Spice Islands

The famed Moluccas, with their treasured groves of cinnamon, clove, and nutmeg trees, lie among the Indonesian archipelago's nearly eighteen thousand islands. The spice harvest from these narrow, mountainous isles is combined with coconut milk for richness, chiles for searing heat, and aromatic ingredients to create scores of distinctive dishes throughout the country.

Distinct culinary variations are found from island to island. Abundant vegetables and fiery curries characterize Sumatran cooking, and Javanese dishes carry sweetness from *gula jawa*, the local palm sugar that tastes of caramel and molasses. Hindu settlers on Bali established pork as a popular meat, distinguishing that island's cuisine within the predominantly Muslim country. Early Chinese merchants and traders added their own techniques and foods to the Indonesian kitchen, including stir-frying, soybeans, daikon, and noodles.

Culinary Signature: Lime

Indonesian cooks mix the juice of the common, smooth-skinned Persian lime into many dishes. But they use the native kaffir lime, too, adding its thick, bumpy peel to curries and marinades to infuse them with a flowery, citrusy brightness and its glossy, double-lobed leaves whole in soups or stews or thinly shredded as a garnish.

Other Specialties

Nasi kuning Celebratory rice tinted yellow with turmeric and flavored with lemongrass

Rendang Beef slowly simmered in coconut milk, spices, and chiles until the sauce is reduced to a thick, concentrated glaze

Satay Thin slices of chicken, mutton, pork,

or rabbit threaded onto skewers, grilled over coals, and served alongside a sweet-spicy peanut sauce

Galeg A vegetarian curry made with young jackfruit, coconut milk, coriander seed, galangal, and candlenuts

Soto ayam Soup of turmeric-infused broth ladled over rice vermicelli, shredded chicken, and hard-boiled egg and garnished with celery leaves and fried shallot

Rojak Fresh fruit served with peanuts, sugar, and chile

Spekkuk A buttery, many-layered cake laced with cinnamon, nutmeg, and cloves

Bandrek Beverage infused with ginger and spices, served warm or iced

PHILIPPINES

Spanish Infusion

The Philippines, lacking a native imperial court, has preserved its rustic, rural food traditions. Over time, local ingredients such as milkfish, hearts of palm, *patis* (fish sauce), and heady *bagoong* (fermented shrimp paste) melded with Chinese soy sauce, noodles, and rice. Fish and pork anchor Filipino cuisine, and many dishes carry a sour flavor from the addition of coconut vinegar, the native *calamansi* (lime), or tamarind.

The Spanish, much more than other Europeans, left their mark on the food of their colonies. In the Philippines, cooks adopted dried salt cod, corn, annatto seeds, baked breads, empanadas, *longganisa* (pork sausage), and *tocino*, sweet cured pork belly reminiscent of bacon. Little round yeast-raised rolls, known as *pan de sal*, are popular with butter, jam, and cheese for breakfast. Later in the day, hot chocolate and a selection of sweet and savory snacks are served for *merienda*

(midafternoon snack). The country's many desserts are a testament to the Filipino sweet tooth.

Culinary Signature: Tamarind

The curved pods of this large shade tree hold one of the most important ingredients of tropical Asia, lending a fruity tartness to soups, glazes, dips, and chutneys. It is sold in many forms, from whole pods to packed bricks to a convenient concentrate, but Filipinos especially appreciate the unripe pods, which they use to impart sourness to palate-cleansing soup broths.

Other Specialties

Sinagang Soup of tart tamarind broth and dark greens, served alongside rice and meat and fish dishes

Kinilaw Small pieces of fish "cooked" with lime juice or coconut vinegar

Pancit Thin rice noodles stir-fried with pork, shrimp (prawns), and thinly sliced vegetables

Adobo Pork or chicken braised in vinegar, soy sauce, sugar, and lavish amounts of garlic, black pepper, and bay leaf

Lumpiang sariwa Soft, pale crepe filled with shredded heart of palm, chicken, egg, daikon, peanuts, and lettuce and served with garlic dipping sauce

Lechon Roast suckling pig with crisp skin, accompanied by a dipping sauce thickened with pork liver

Halo halo Shaved ice drizzled with sweetened condensed milk and topped with young coconut, tapioca pearls, fresh jackfruit or mango, red beans, or purple yam

Bibingka Coconut rice cake, resembling custard, that is sweetened with palm sugar and cooked in banana leaves

Pork or chicken is cooked slowly on the stove top in sweet and sour flavorings, including vinegar, soy sauce, and sugar, to make the Philippine specialty called adobo (page 224).

Tea Service

First sipped by early Buddhist monks to keep themselves alert during meditation and long considered a medicinal drink by nobility, tea became an important offering at weddings and religious ceremonies. Today, hot tea is the most common accompaniment to food in Asia.

After water, tea is the most commonly drunk beverage in the world. Thousands of types exist, from ethereal silver needle to earthy Pu'er. All come from one species, *Camellia sinensis*, a small evergreen tree native to China's cool, misty mountains. Clippings were carried to every Asian country, where they took root and, as a result of the local climate, cultivation techniques, and drying, rolling, and fermenting methods, produced an astonishing array of flavors and colors.

Teas can be clear, light infusions with fresh, green, grassy flavors or deep, rich brews that call for a touch of milk and sugar. Green teas go well with subtle flavors, light dishes, and foods that highlight fresh ingredients. Versatile oolongs bridge a medium range of flavors, from seafood and quick stir-fries to grilled chicken and braised noodles. Dark, fully fermented, smoky teas pair well with rich, intensely flavored dishes, such as stewed pork, roasted duck, and spicy lamb.

Darjeeling, Assam, and Ceylon are black teas typical of India and Sri Lanka. Originally developed for serving European style with milk, they create robust, malty infusions that complement desserts and savory pastries.

BREWING TEA

The best flavor comes from loose-leaf tea, but high-quality teas are increasingly available in convenient bags. Black teas are brewed with fully boiling water, but slightly lower

ASIAN TEAS

Type & Characteristics	Examples	Steeping Temperature & Time
GREEN Large, green, unfermented leaves that steep to clear, pale yellow-green infusions with delicate, fresh aromas and raw, grassy flavors.	China: Long Jing (Dragon Well), Ho Chin (Pine Needles), Lo Chu Cha (Gunpowder); Japan: Sencha, Genmaicha, Matcha; Vietnam: Dalat	185°–195°F (85°–90°C) 15 seconds to 4 minutes
WHITE Pale, white-green, lightly fermented leaves covered with fine, white hairs that steep to clear, pale yellow infusions with delicate, sweet flavors.	China: Pai Hao Yin Chin (Silver Needle), Pai Mu Tan (White Peony), Shou Mei (White Eyebrow)	175°–185°F (80°–85°C) 15 seconds to 1 minute
OOLONG Semifermented leaves shaped by hand into a wide variety of forms that steep to bright yellow infusions with fresh, rich, lingering flavors.	China: Ti Quan Yin (Monkey-Picked Iron Buddha), Single Stem, Gold Oolong, Jasmine Oolong; Japan: Sofu; Vietnam: Pleiku	195°–205°F (90°–95°C) 10 seconds to 2 minutes
BLACK Known as red tea in China, fully fermented leaves with rich, complex aromas and flavors. Dark leaves create strong, pungent, slightly bitter infusions with hints of smoke, pine, fruit, or nut flavors.	China: Qimen (or Keemun), Yunnan, Lapsong Souchong; India: Darjeeling, Assam, Nilgiri; Sri Lanka: Ceylon, English Breakfast, Earl Grey	205°–212°F (95°–100°C) 3 to 5 minutes
PU'ER Fermented after roasting, leaves are sometimes pressed into bricks or cakes for aging. Generally, the older the tea, the richer the flavor. Dark, red-brown infusions are robust yet mellow, full bodied with hints of musk and smoke.	China: Pu'er, Liubao, Liu-an	205°–212°F (95°–100°C) 10 seconds to 3 minutes
SCENTED Leaves are combined with fresh flowers to absorb fragrance. Dried blossoms may also be added.	Jasmine Pearl, Rose, Orchid, Osmanthus, Broken Black, Gardenia	185°–212°F (95°–100°C) 30 seconds to 3 minutes

temperatures are better for green teas because of their more delicate leaves (to approximate the cooler temperatures, bring water to a full boil and then add some cold water). For the best taste, start with cold water and avoid heating it beyond the boiling point. The ratio of tea leaves to water depends on the type of tea and personal taste, but 1 teaspoon per cup (8 fl oz/250 ml) of water is a good general rule. More important Is the steeping time. High-quality tea leaves will give several infusions, and each successive brewing requires slightly more time, from mere seconds for the first one up to several minutes for the fifth or sixth (steeping times in the chart at left are for first to last infusion).

SERVING TEA

Chinese *gongfu cha* and Japanese *chado* ceremonies, with their artful teaware and time-honored rituals, formalize tea service for special occasions. But everyday tea drinking is relaxed and informal. Traditional teapots are made of pottery or porcelain, often decorated with flowers, animals, or calligraphy. Look for pots with removable, perforated baskets for the leaves. In Asia, tea is usually sipped from small cups, and keeping a guest's cup full is the duty of an attentive host. A *gai wan,* a traditional single-serving Chinese tea set, has a cup, a saucer, and a lid that is used to gently push aside floating tea leaves as you sip.

JAPANES SAKE AND KOREAN SOJU

Sake has been brewed in Japan for over two thousand years. Made from rice that has been inoculated with yeast and *koji* mold spores, it typically has an alcohol content of 13 to 18 percent. Brides and grooms sip sake at their weddings, and religious ceremonies often include it. Most important of all, it is a beverage enjoyed often among friends and business colleagues.

How much the rice kernels are polished, what methods are used for fermenting and aging, the decision to fortify with distilled alcohol or filter through cotton cloth—these are only a few of the factors that determine the many classifications and grades of sake. It can be crystal clear, milky white, or golden amber. Most sakes are crisp, but some have a creaminess in the mouth, and a few are carbonated to evoke the bubbles of Champagne.

Traditionally, sake is not served with rice because it is made from the grain. Avoid pairing it with heavy or spicy foods, choosing instead fresh or lighter, fruitier dishes. While some sake can hold up to gentle warming, premium bottles should be served slightly chilled to highlight their smooth, delicate flavors.

Korean *soju* is also made from rice, but unlike sake, it undergoes distillation to create a beverage with up to 45 percent alcohol content. It appears at festive gatherings, where toasting guests and elders is a venerable tradition.

Similar to vodka, *soju* is generally clear and neutral in flavor. This quality makes it popular as a base for various cocktails, especially mixed with fruit juices and citrusy sodas.

Asian teas range from rich, strong brews to simple infusions enhanced with spices.

SPICES, HERBS, AND AROMATICS

Asia's vibrant, diverse cuisines draw their unique flavors from specific combinations of both dried and fresh ingredients.

Dried Spices

Cardamom, whole

Cayenne, ground

Cinnamon, sticks and ground

Cloves, whole

Cumin, ground

Nutmeg, whole

Peppercorns, black and white

Saffron

Seeds, coriander, cumin, fennel

Star anise

Turmeric, ground

Spice mixes

Five-spice powder

Garam masala

Madras curry powder

Fresh Herbs

Cilantro (fresh coriander)

Dill

Holy basil

Lemongrass

Mint

Fresh Aromatics

Galangal

Garlic

Ginger

Green (spring) onions

Onions

Shallots

Asian Flavor Essentials

Asian dishes depend on a good balance of spicy, salty, sweet, and sour flavors. Once you become familiar with how to achieve these four basic taste sensations, you can experiment and create new versions of your favorite dishes, sauces, marinades, and condiments.

SPICY

Long before Portuguese trading ships carried chiles throughout Asia, spicy heat was added to dishes with Sichuan peppercorns, Javanese long peppercorns, or the seeds of the Japanese prickly ash tree. Of course, the common peppercorn in all its forms—fresh green, dried black, and polished white—was also a widely used seasoning.

When chiles arrived from the Americas, Asian cooks eagerly adopted them. Indians use both fresh green chiles and dried red ones, especially the slender cayenne pepper. Thailand's fiery cuisine depends on the tiny but powerful bird's-eye chile. Korean cooks add ground dried red chiles to pickles, soups, and stews. Chile-garlic paste, chile oil, smooth Sriracha sauce, and chunky *sambals* are popular condiments that cross borders. In Japan, where chiles have had limited influence, pungent grated wasabi root is common.

SALTY

Many Asian cooks employ salty sauces and pastes in addition to salt. Fermented preparations are especially popular for the rich, savory meatiness, known as *umami* in Japan, they add to many dishes.

In northern Asia, soy sauce is made from soybeans fermented with wheat and then aged. As it moved from country to country, China's soy sauce was modified to fit local preferences. Japanese cooks use a light soy at the table and tamari, a stronger-tasting version with little or no wheat, for long cooking. In Indonesia and Malaysia, a thick, sweet soy called *kecap manis* and a thick, salty soy called *kecap asin* serve as condiment and seasoning. Southeast Asian cuisines depend on fermented fish and shrimp pastes for salty flavors.

Other common salty ingredients are fermented black beans used in Chinese cooking, miso paste in Japan, and dried shrimp used all across Asia.

SWEET

Sugarcane was first domesticated in India, but Indians prefer the richer, deeper flavor of palm sugar, known as jaggery or *gur*. Formed into cubes, cones, or disks, or simply dried into lumps resembling rocks, palm sugar is used throughout South and Southeast Asia. Chinese stews and glazes often call for unrefined golden sugar. Dark brown or light brown sugar approximates the flavor of both.

In Japan, a sweet rice wine called *mirin* lends sheen and soft sweetness to marinades, stews, and glazes.

SOUR

The tartness in Asian foods comes from a wide variety of ingredients. Lime juice is the easiest and most common, with special varieties such as the tiny, orange-fleshed *calamansi* of the Philippines or the fragrant *makrut* (kaffir) lime of Thailand. Vinegars made from rice can be clear and crisp, red and sharp, or black and sweet. Coconut and palm sap are also common sources for vinegar in Southeast Asian islands. In India and Southeast Asia, tamarind provides fruity sourness in soups and sauces.

Asian cooks use ingredients such as chiles (top), cloves and cinnamon (middle), and mirin (above) to balance four key flavors.

Planning an Asian Meal

Preparing dishes from the same country is the simplest way to group recipes. A special occasion on the calendar calls for a table covered with celebratory treats. In all cases, carefully contrasting different flavors and textures is the best way to show off any Asian cuisine.

Dishes from countries in the same region—Japan and Korea, Thailand and Laos, Pakistan and India, Indonesia and Malaysia—often echo one another. A quick glance at the ingredient lists of recipes will reveal overlaps in flavor, too. Look for families of flavors and group dishes accordingly.

In general, Asian cuisines do not separate dishes into different courses. With rare exceptions, such as celebratory feasts, all dishes come to the table at once. For example, clear soups are often sipped between bites to refresh the palate, and filling noodle soups are frequently eaten as one-bowl meals.

A typical Asian meal might include two or three savory preparations. At even the simplest family meal, diners seek a balance of flavors and textures, often determined by different cooking methods as well as ingredients. Stir-fried mustard greens might accompany a spicy pork stew. Brightly flavored dishes are an ideal foil for creamy, rich dishes.

Remember that stir-fried dishes depend on cooking small amounts of food in a wok just before serving, so preparing more than one stir-fry for a large party can be a challenge. Consider instead braises or stews, which are perfect for a crowd. Serve plain rice with highly seasoned foods or when several different dishes are on the menu. Pairing one savory dish with rice that has been infused with spices or garnished with fresh herbs is a great way to make a special meal with minimal fuss.

REGIONAL MENUS

INDIAN DINNER

Spiced Lamb with Caramelized Onions

Dry-Curry Okra

Spiced Stewed Lentils and Vegetables

Raita

•

Indian Flatbread or Basmati Rice

CHERRY BLOSSOM VIEWING PICNIC

Cold Soba Noodles with Dipping Sauce

•

Vegetable Sushi Rolls

Rice Filled with Salmon and Pickled Plum

•

Sesame Cookies

Green Tea

DIM SUM BRUNCH

Steamed Pork Dumplings

Scallion Pancakes

Braised Shanghai Egg Noodles with Pork

Broccoli with Oyster Sauce

•

Egg Custard Tartlets

Pu'er Tea

REGIONAL MENUS

NIGHT-MARKET COCKTAIL PARTY

Fresh Spring Rolls with Shrimp

Chicken Satay with Peanut Sauce

Lemongrass Beef Skewers

Samosas

Lamb-Filled Flatbread

•

Assorted Drinks

CHINESE NEW YEAR FEAST

Hot-and-Sour Soup

•

Egg Noodles with Shrimp, Chicken, and Vegetables

Steamed Fish with Green Onion, Ginger, and Sizzling Oil

Five-Spice Roast Duck

Braised Pork Spareribs with Black Bean Sauce

Stir-Fried Boy Choy

Fried Rice with Pork and Shrimp

AFTERNOON MERIENDA

Empanadas

•

Fried Bananas in Lumpia Wrappers

•

Coffee, Tea, or Hot Chocolate

DIWALI VEGETARIAN FEAST

Curried Chickpeas

Spiced Potatoes, Cauliflower, and Peas

Dry-Curry Okra

Eggplant Curry

Basmati Rice

•

Cardamom-Spiced Basmati Rice Pudding

•

Spiced Chai

THAI SEAFOOD DINNER

Spicy Shrimp Soup

Spicy Fish Cakes

•

Fish with Garlic-Tamarind Sauce

Seafood in Coconut Red Curry

Jasmine Rice

•

Fresh Fruit

Light Soups and Small Plates

About Light Soups and Small Plates

In China, elegant soups help set the tone for celebratory feasts. In Southeast Asia, brightly flavored broths refresh the palate between savory bites of highly seasoned dishes. Everywhere in Asia, small plates, enjoyed alone or in a group, whet the appetite for what will follow.

In Asia, a soup and/or one or more small plates are often on the table, whether you are sitting down to the first meal of the day or you are quelling hunger pangs at midnight. They are versatile recipes, easily shifting from the role of a single dish on a menu of four or five dishes to serving as a filling snack. They can also be a meal on their own.

CLEAR BROTHS

The role a soup plays is typically defined by the richness of the broth or stock and the amount of ingredients added. The simplest examples highlight a sparkling, flavorful clear liquid garnished with minced herbs.

In Japan, Miso Soup (page 33), which traditionally arrives in attractive lidded lacquered bowls, usually includes one or two simple ingredients that hint of the season, such as chrysanthemum leaves, small radishes artfully carved to resemble cherry blossoms, or tiny *shiso* buds, along with the soybean-based miso. Like most light soups, it relies on a high-quality clear base. Japanese cooks depend on dashi, a fish-and-seaweed-based stock. In China, ginger-scented chicken stock is the foundation of such favorites as Wonton Soup (page 38).

Soups served at Chinese formal banquets often feature an array of matchstick-cut ingredients—bamboo shoots, mushrooms, onions, pork—suspended in clear broth lightly thickened with cornstarch (cornflour). Others call for swirling beaten egg into hot broth just before serving to create delicate ribbons, a technique used in Hot-and-Sour Soup (page 34) and in the familiar egg drop soup of clear broth and seasonings.

SOUR FLAVORS

In Southeast Asia, soups based on clear broths frequently include one or more acidic ingredients, such as lime juice, vinegar, or tamarind. A spoonful of soup sipped between bites of rich curry or fried fish refreshes the palate so the distinctive character of each dish is enjoyed. Filipino *sinagang*, with chopped greens floating in a sour broth, is a classic example of this type of accompanying soup. Thailand's *tom yam gung,* Spicy Shrimp Soup (page 42), includes tamarind, lemongrass, galangal, and chiles to create its complexly aromatic, pleasantly sour flavor.

Hot-and-sour soups are served in Vietnam, Cambodia, Laos, and Malaysia. Traditionally these soups were spooned over rice, but nowadays they may appear alone as a first course in a larger meal. Similarly, the English Raj adapted southern India's thin, tart, peppery *rasam* to create Mulligatawny (page 37) for a Western-style soup course. Some versions, which include lentils and other ingredients, are substantial enough to be a main dish.

A SNACKER'S PARADISE

Like soups, small plates turn up in various guises on Asian menus. But their most popular role is as snacks. Indeed, snacking is a way of life in Asia. Food vendors serve savory treats from small carts, balance baskets on their heads, or set their pots to simmer right on the sidewalk. Where days stretch hot and humid, eating smaller meals more frequently is preferred to sitting down to large repasts.

Plentiful fuel for brief, hot fires—banana trunks, coconut shells, fragrant cinnamon wood—has made grilling a favorite method for cooking meats, seafood, and vegetables. In Indonesia and Thailand, sidewalk vendors sit next to narrow grills fanning hot coals beneath skewers of chicken *satay* (page 44). Small eating establishments in Japan specialize in *yakitori* (page 48), marinated chicken on bamboo skewers cooked on charcoal braziers. They cater to an after-work crowd of friends and colleagues who get together for a simple bite with beer or sake before heading home.

Deep-frying bite-sized morsels, such as Corn Fritters (page 53) and Split Pea Fritters (page 57), gives them an appealing and addictive crispiness. In Thailand, a sweet-spicy dipping sauce or fresh cucumber relish offers a refreshing contrast to Spicy Fish Cakes (page 56), found on restaurant menus and also enjoyed as snacks. In Southeast Asia, Indians introduced their potato-filled Samosas (page 54) wherever they put down roots. Fried Spring Rolls (page 60) followed Chinese immigrants to their new homes as well.

Small plates also lend themselves to informal meals, and many are perfect finger foods, such as Japanese *kushiyaki* (page 47), grilled skewers of beef and onion. Fresh Spring Rolls with Shrimp (page 59), a typical Vietnamese dish in which cooks wrap shrimp (prawns), herbs, vegetables, and other ingredients in rice paper and lettuce leaves, is another great choice for eating out of hand. A flavorful dipping sauce accompanies these traditional rolls as well as many other small plates throughout Asia.

Miso Soup

This simple, delicate soup is seasoned primarily with *konbu* or wakame, dried seaweed, along with miso, or fermented soybean paste. Commonly used in Japanese and Korean cuisine, *konbu* is one of the main ingredients in dashi, a broth for soups and other dishes, and wakame is added to soups and salads. Subtly sweet enoki mushrooms contribute an appealing texture.

If using *konbu*, wipe it clean with a damp cloth. Place in a bowl, add hot water to cover, and let soak until soft, about 20 minutes. If using wakame, soak in hot water to cover until soft, about 10 minutes. Drain the *konbu* or wakame and cut into strips 4 inches (10 cm) long by $1/8$ inch (3 mm) wide. Set aside.

Bring a small saucepan three-fourths full of water to a gentle boil over medium heat. Add the tofu block, reduce the heat to low, and simmer for 5 minutes to firm up the tofu. Carefully drain the tofu, place on a salad plate, and top with a second plate. The sandwiched plates act as a weight to press out excess water from the tofu. Set aside for 30 minutes. Just before making the soup, pour off any water and carefully cut the tofu into $1/2$-inch (12-mm) cubes.

In a large saucepan over low heat, bring the dashi to a bare simmer. Whisk in the miso, mirin, vinegar, and sesame oil. Simmer for 5 minutes to blend the flavors. Stir in the *konbu* or wakame and the mushrooms, and then gently add the tofu cubes along with the green onions. Be careful not to allow the soup to boil or the tofu will break apart. Season to taste with salt and white pepper.

Ladle the soup into warmed bowls and serve at once.

3 oz (90 g) *konbu* or wakame

2 oz (60 g) silken tofu

$3/4$ teaspoon granulated dashi mixed with 6 cups (48 fl oz/1.5 l) hot water, or 6 cups low-sodium chicken broth

6 tablespoons *shiro miso*

1 tablespoon mirin

1 teaspoon rice vinegar

$1/2$ teaspoon Asian sesame oil

2 oz (60 g) enoki mushrooms, stems trimmed

3 green (spring) onions, white and pale green parts, thinly sliced on the diagonal

Salt and ground white pepper

MAKES 4–6 SERVINGS

Hot-and-Sour Soup

2 oz (60 g) skinless, boneless chicken breast

2 oz (60 g) beef sirloin

½ cup (2 oz/60 g) bamboo shoots

2 oz (60 g) firm tofu

5 oz (155 g) fresh shiitake mushrooms, stems removed

2 tablespoons canola oil

4 green (spring) onions, white and pale green parts, thinly sliced on the diagonal

1 tablespoon peeled and minced fresh ginger

8 cups (64 fl oz/2 l) low-sodium chicken broth

⅓ cup (3 fl oz/80 ml) black vinegar

2 tablespoons *each* Chinese rice wine and chile bean paste

1 tablespoon dark soy sauce

2 teaspoons Asian sesame oil

¼ teaspoon ground white pepper

2 large eggs, lightly beaten

1 tablespoon cornstarch (cornflour)

¼ cup (1½ oz/45 g) fresh or thawed frozen English peas

2 tablespoons finely shredded smoked ham

MAKES 6 SERVINGS

Bring a saucepan three-fourths full of water to a boil over high heat. Cut the chicken, beef, bamboo shoots, and tofu into strips 4 inches (10 cm) long by ¼ inch (6 mm) wide. Thinly slice the mushrooms. Add the chicken, beef, bamboo shoots, tofu, and mushrooms to the pan and return the water to a boil. Cook for 3 minutes, then drain and set aside.

In a large saucepan over medium-high heat, warm the canola oil. Add the green onions and ginger and sauté until fragrant, about 1 minute. Pour in the broth and add the vinegar, rice wine, chile bean paste, soy sauce, sesame oil, and white pepper. Bring to a boil and cook for 1 minute. Reduce the heat to low and simmer, uncovered, for 10 minutes to blend the flavors.

Pour the eggs into the soup in a thin, steady stream. Let stand for about 20 seconds to allow the eggs to set in fine strands, then swirl them into the soup. In a small bowl, dissolve the cornstarch in 3 tablespoons water. Slowly pour about half of the cornstarch mixture into the soup while stirring constantly. The soup will thicken slightly. Add more of the cornstarch mixture as desired, stirring constantly, for a soup with a thicker consistency.

Ladle the soup into warmed bowls and garnish with the peas and smoked ham. Serve at once.

A signature dish from western China, this spicy, tangy soup obtains its smoky sweetness from the addition of black vinegar, the best of which is made from black sticky rice. The flavorful broth makes a delicious backdrop for any meat or vegetable.

Mulligatawny Soup

Representing flavors of East and West, mulligatawny is a thin curry that Anglo-Indian communities adapted from Indian cuisine. Historically, this dish was accompanied with rice, relishes, and chutneys. It has migrated beyond India and evolved into a thick, rich soup that is a meal in itself.

Pick over the lentils, removing any stones or misshapen or discolored lentils. Rinse and place in a bowl with warm water to cover. Let soak for 30 minutes.

In a small bowl, combine the cumin, coriander, turmeric, cinnamon, and cardamom and stir to mix well. Set aside.

In a large saucepan over medium-high heat, warm the oil. Add the onion, ginger, garlic, and chile and sauté until fragrant, about 1 minute. Add the spice mixture and cook, stirring, for 1 minute longer. Pour in the broth and bring to a boil. Drain the lentils and add to the soup. Stir in the carrots, apple, and potato and return to a boil. Reduce the heat to low and simmer, uncovered, until the vegetables and lentils are just tender, 25–30 minutes.

Stir in the lemon juice and ¹/₂ teaspoon salt. Taste and adjust the seasoning. Working in batches, transfer about 3 cups (24 fl oz/750 ml) of the warm soup to a blender or food processor and process to a smooth purée. Return to the saucepan and reheat gently, stirring; the consistency should be fairly thick.

Ladle the soup into warmed bowls and garnish with the cilantro. Serve at once.

1 cup (7 oz/220 g) red lentils

1 teaspoon ground cumin

1 teaspoon ground coriander

¹/₂ teaspoon ground turmeric

¹/₄ teaspoon ground cinnamon

¹/₈ teaspoon ground cardamom

2 tablespoons canola oil

1 yellow onion, chopped

1 tablespoon peeled and grated fresh ginger

4 cloves garlic, minced

2 teaspoons seeded and minced jalapeño chiles

6 cups (48 fl oz/1.5 l) low-sodium chicken broth

2 carrots, chopped

1 large green apple, peeled, cored, and chopped

1 large boiling potato, peeled and chopped

1 tablespoon fresh lemon juice

Salt

2 tablespoons chopped fresh cilantro (fresh coriander)

MAKES 4–6 SERVINGS

Wonton Soup

For the wontons

2 oz (60 g) shrimp (prawns)

3 oz (90 g) fresh water chestnuts

3 green (spring) onions

¼ lb (125 g) ground (minced) pork

1 tablespoon peeled and grated fresh ginger

1 clove garlic, minced

1 large egg, lightly beaten

1 tablespoon *each* light soy sauce, Chinese rice wine, and Asian sesame oil

1 tablespoon cornstarch (cornflour), plus extra for dusting

½ teaspoon sugar

⅛ teaspoon ground white pepper

30 square wonton wrappers

For the soup

6 cups (48 fl oz/1.5 l) low-sodium chicken broth

2 tablespoons light soy sauce

1 tablespoon rice wine

1 teaspoon ginger juice (page 278)

½ teaspoon Asian sesame oil

Salt

1 green (spring) onion, thinly sliced on the diagonal

MAKES 4 OR 5 SERVINGS

To make the wontons, peel and devein the shrimp, then coarsely chop. Peel and finely chop the water chestnuts. Mince the green onions, including the pale green parts. In a large bowl, combine the shrimp, water chestnuts, green onions, pork, ginger, garlic, egg, soy sauce, rice wine, sesame oil, 1 tablespoon cornstarch, sugar, white pepper, and 1 tablespoon water. Using a rubber spatula, stir vigorously until the ingredients are well incorporated. Refrigerate the filling for 30 minutes.

To make the soup, in a large saucepan over medium heat, combine the broth, soy sauce, rice wine, ginger juice, sesame oil, and ½ teaspoon salt and bring to a gentle boil. Remove from the heat, cover, and set aside.

To assemble the wontons, working with 1 wrapper at a time, place it on a work surface and moisten the edges with cold water; keep the other wrappers covered with a damp kitchen towel to prevent them from drying out. Place 1 teaspoon of the filling in the center of the wrapper and fold over into a triangle. Press the edges together firmly to seal. Fold the 2 outer points across the top of the mound and pinch the corners together to seal. If they do not stick, moisten with a little water. Place the finished wontons on a baking sheet dusted with cornstarch.

Meanwhile, reheat the soup over low heat. Bring a large pot three-fourths full of water to a boil over high heat and stir in 1 tablespoon salt. Add the wontons to the boiling water, reduce the heat to medium, and simmer gently until they rise to the surface and the wrappers are tender, about 6 minutes.

Using a slotted spoon or wire skimmer, carefully lift out the wontons and divide among warmed bowls. Ladle the hot soup over the wontons and garnish with the sliced green onion. Serve at once.

The word *wonton* literally means to "swallow a cloud," an appropriate description for these delicate dumplings filled with pork and shrimp and floated in a lightly seasoned chicken broth. Any ground (minced) meat or seafood may be used in place of the pork or shrimp in the filling.

Seafood and Vegetable Soup

Korean cooks turn out hearty soups made from a variety of meats, seafood, and vegetables. They are eaten as a part of a meal with rice, kimchi, and an assortment of *banchan*, or small side dishes. For added spice, this seafood soup uses Japanese ground red *sansho* pepper, which has a tangy flavor with lingering heat. Be sure to use the freshest fish and shellfish you can find.

In a small bowl, combine the ginger juice, chile bean paste, vinegar, sugar, sesame oil, *sansho* pepper, and 1 tablespoon salt and stir to mix well. Set aside.

In a large saucepan over medium-high heat, warm the canola oil. When the oil is hot, add the green onions, garlic, and chile and sauté until fragrant, about 10 seconds. Pour in 6 cups (48 fl oz/1.5 l) water and bring to a boil. Add the *konbu*, daikon, and ginger juice mixture. Reduce the heat to low and simmer until the daikon is tender, about 10 minutes.

Meanwhile, in a deep saucepan, bring ½ cup (4 fl oz/125 ml) water to a boil over medium-high heat. Add the clams, discarding any that do not close to the touch. Cover the pan and steam just until the shells open, about 3 minutes. Transfer the clams to a bowl, discarding any that failed to open. Strain the cooking liquid through a fine-mesh sieve into the soup.

When the daikon is tender, add the fish and shrimp to the soup and cook just until they turn opaque, about 3 minutes. Add the steamed clams and cook gently until heated through, about 1 minute longer. Remove the *konbu* and discard.

Ladle the soup into warmed bowls, dividing the seafood evenly. Garnish with the parsley and serve at once.

2 tablespoons ginger juice (page 278)

1 teaspoon chile bean paste

1 teaspoon rice vinegar

1 teaspoon sugar

½ teaspoon Asian sesame oil

⅛ teaspoon ground red *sansho* pepper or cayenne pepper

Salt

2 tablespoons canola oil

2 green (spring) onions, thinly sliced on the diagonal

2 cloves garlic, minced

2 teaspoons seeded and minced jalapeño chile

3-by-5-inch (7.5-by-13-cm) sheet *konbu* or wakame, wiped clean with a damp cloth

½ lb (250 g) daikon, peeled and cut into strips 3 inches (7.5 cm) long by ⅛ inch (3 mm) wide and thick

1 lb (500 g) clams, scrubbed

10 oz (315 g) sea bass or halibut fillets, cut into pieces 3 inches (7.5 cm) long by 1 inch (2.5 cm) wide

½ lb (250 g) medium shrimp (prawns), peeled and deveined

1 tablespoon chopped fresh flat-leaf (Italian) parsley

MAKES 4–6 SERVINGS

Spicy Shrimp Soup

For the chile paste

4 cloves garlic, chopped

2 serrano chiles, seeded and chopped

3 tablespoons chopped fresh cilantro (fresh coriander) stems

1½ teaspoons peppercorns, coarsely ground

2 tablespoons canola oil

10 fresh shiitake mushrooms, stems removed and caps sliced

3 lemongrass stalks, tender midsections only

4 fresh galangal slices, each about ¼ inch (6 mm) thick

4 shallots, thinly sliced

8 cups (64 fl oz/2 l) low-sodium chicken broth

1 teaspoon grated lime zest

¼ cup (2 fl oz/60 ml) *each* fish sauce and fresh lime juice

1 tablespoon chopped palm sugar

1 lb (500 g) large shrimp (prawns), peeled and deveined

¼ cup (⅓ oz/10 g) *each* fresh Thai basil leaves and fresh cilantro (fresh coriander) leaves

MAKES 4–6 SERVINGS

To make the chile paste, in a mini food processor or mortar, combine the garlic, chiles, cilantro stems, and peppercorns and process or grind with a pestle until a coarse paste forms. Add 1–2 tablespoons water if needed to facilitate the grinding. Set the paste aside.

In a large saucepan over high heat, warm the oil. Add the mushrooms and sauté until they begin to release their juices, about 2 minutes. Smash the lemongrass stalks and galangal slices with the side of a chef's knife and add to the pan. Add the shallots and sauté until fragrant, about 2 minutes longer.

Pour in the broth, add the lime zest, and bring to a boil. Reduce the heat to medium and simmer for 5 minutes. Add the chile paste and simmer, stirring, for 3–5 minutes longer to blend the flavors. Stir in the fish sauce, lime juice, and palm sugar. If not serving the soup immediately, reduce the heat to maintain a low simmer and keep the soup warm.

Just before serving, add the shrimp to the simmering soup and cook just until they turn bright orange and opaque, about 3 minutes. Remove and discard the lemongrass and galangal.

Coarsely chop the basil and cilantro leaves. Ladle the soup into warmed bowls, dividing the shrimp evenly. Garnish with the basil and cilantro and serve at once.

Called *tom yum gung*, this hot-and-sour soup has become popular well outside Thailand's borders. It is characterized by a harmony of flavors—hot, bitter, salty, sour, and sweet—enhanced by a generous garnish of fragrant fresh herbs.

Chicken and Noodle Soup

This soup, found in Indonesia as well as Malaysia, gains spiciness from a chile paste that includes ground turmeric, a rhizome that gives the dish its distinctive yellow hue. Rather than poach chicken especially for the soup, you can use already roasted chicken and about 7 cups (56 fl oz/1.75 l) purchased low-sodium broth.

In a saucepan over high heat, bring 8 cups (64 fl oz/2 l) water to a boil. Add the chicken and 1 tablespoon salt and return to a boil. Reduce the heat to medium and simmer, uncovered, until the chicken pieces are opaque throughout, 20–25 minutes. Using tongs, transfer the chicken to a plate to cool. Reserve the broth. Meanwhile, place the rice noodles in a bowl, add warm water to cover, and let soak for 15 minutes. Drain and set aside.

Remove the seeds from 1 chile and then chop. Cut the other chile crosswise into thin slices and remove the seeds; set aside. Smash the lemongrass stalks with the side of a chef's knife and then chop. In a mini food processor or blender, combine the chopped chile, lemongrass, shallots, garlic, ginger, almonds, turmeric, and coriander and process until a coarse paste forms. Add 1–2 tablespoons water if needed to facilitate the grinding.

In a large saucepan over medium-high heat, warm the oil. Add the chile paste and sauté until fragrant, about 1 minute. Strain the reserved chicken broth through a fine-mesh sieve into the pan and bring to a boil. Reduce the heat to low and simmer, uncovered, for 15 minutes. Stir in the fish sauce and lemon juice.

While the soup is simmering, shred the chicken into thin pieces and discard the bones. Bring a saucepan three-fourths full of water to a boil, add the drained noodles, and cook until just tender, 15–20 seconds. Drain the noodles and divide evenly among warmed bowls.

Top the noodles with the shredded chicken, bean sprouts, green onions, sliced chile, and cilantro, dividing them evenly. Ladle the hot soup over the top and garnish with the egg quarters and Fried Shallots. Serve at once.

½ lb (250 g) *each* skinless, bone-in chicken breast and thighs

Salt

¾ lb (375 g) dried rice vermicelli

2 jalapeño chiles

2 lemongrass stalks, tender midsections only

4 shallots, chopped

3 cloves garlic, chopped

1 tablespoon peeled and chopped fresh ginger

5 blanched almonds

½ teaspoon ground turmeric

¼ teaspoon ground coriander

2 tablespoons canola oil

2 tablespoons *each* fish sauce and lemon juice

1 cup (1 oz/30 g) mung bean sprouts

3 green (spring) onions, thinly sliced on the diagonal

¼ cup (⅓ oz/10 g) chopped fresh cilantro (fresh coriander)

3 hard-boiled eggs, peeled and quartered

½ cup (1½ oz/45 g) Fried Shallots (page 274)

MAKES 4–6 SERVINGS

Chicken Satay with Peanut Sauce

⅓ cup (3 fl oz/80 ml)
coconut milk

¼ cup (2 fl oz/60 ml)
fish sauce

2 tablespoons chopped
palm sugar

1 tablespoon Madras curry
powder

3 cloves garlic, minced

1 tablespoon peeled and
minced fresh galangal

1 tablespoon chopped fresh
cilantro (fresh coriander)

2 lb (1 kg) skinless, boneless
chicken thighs, cut into
strips 3 inches (7.5 cm) long
by 1 inch (2.5 cm) wide

Canola oil for brushing

For the peanut sauce

2 tablespoons canola oil

2 tablespoons minced
shallots

3 cloves garlic, minced

½ cup (4 fl oz/125 ml)
coconut milk

¼ cup (2½ oz/75 g) creamy
peanut butter

2 tablespoons tamarind paste

1 teaspoon chile paste

Salt

¼ cup (1¼ oz/37 g) minced
unsalted dry-roasted peanuts

MAKES 4–6 SERVINGS

Highly seasoned meat woven onto skewers and grilled, *satay* probably originated in Indonesia, where it remains a popular snack sold by street vendors. The preparation traveled elsewhere in Southeast Asia, including Malaysia, Singapore, and Thailand. Each country has contributed its own versions, with pork, beef, lamb, or shrimp (prawns) used in place of chicken. *Satay* is typically served with peanut sauce.

In a large nonreactive bowl, combine the coconut milk, fish sauce, palm sugar, curry powder, garlic, galangal, and cilantro and stir to mix well. Add the chicken strips and stir to coat thoroughly. Cover and marinate in the refrigerator for at least 1 hour or up to overnight.

Prepare a charcoal or gas grill for direct grilling over high heat. Soak 24–32 bamboo skewers, each 8 inches (20 cm) long, in water to cover for 30 minutes.

Meanwhile, to make the sauce, in a saucepan over medium heat, warm the 2 tablespoons oil. Add the shallots and garlic and sauté until fragrant, about 1 minute. Reduce the heat to low and add the coconut milk, peanut butter, tamarind paste, chile paste, ¼ teaspoon salt, and ¼ cup (2 fl oz/60 ml) water. Cook, stirring constantly, until the sauce begins to simmer and thicken, about 2 minutes. Add the peanuts and mix well. Transfer the peanut sauce to a bowl and set aside at room temperature.

Drain the skewers and remove the chicken strips from the marinade. Discard the marinade. Thread the chicken strips lengthwise onto skewers, pressing them together tightly. Brush the grill rack with oil. Arrange the skewers on the rack so they are not touching one another and sear the chicken, turning once, until golden brown on both sides, 2–3 minutes per side. Move the skewers away from the direct flame, cover the grill, and cook until the chicken is opaque throughout, about 5 minutes longer.

Arrange the skewers on a platter and serve at once with the peanut sauce.

Beef and Green Onion Skewers

In Japan, there are many variations of *kushiyaki*, bite-sized pieces of meat and vegetables seasoned with a light soy-based marinade or simply with salt and then grilled over charcoal. This version, pairing beef and green onions, not only is easy to assemble but also cooks quickly over a hot fire.

In a large nonreactive bowl, combine the soy sauces, mirin, garlic, ginger, sugar, and 1/8 teaspoon pepper and stir to mix well. Add the beef cubes and stir to coat thoroughly. Cover and refrigerate for at least 2 hours or up to overnight.

Prepare a charcoal or gas grill for direct grilling over high heat. Soak 16 bamboo skewers, each 8 inches (20 cm) long, in water to cover for 30 minutes.

Pour the beef and its marinade into a fine-mesh sieve set over a small saucepan, tapping the sieve so that the excess marinade drains into the saucepan. Set the beef aside. Bring the marinade to a boil over medium heat and cook until thickened to a syrupy consistency, about 2 minutes. Set aside.

Drain the skewers. Thread 3 pieces of beef alternating with 3 pieces of green onion on each skewer, piercing the green onions crosswise through the middle. Brush the grill rack with oil. Arrange the skewers on the rack so they are not touching one another and sear, turning as needed, until the beef is crisp and brown on all sides, about 8 minutes total. Transfer the skewers to a warmed platter, brush with the sauce, and serve at once.

1/3 cup (3 fl oz/80 ml) tamari soy sauce

2 tablespoons dark soy sauce

2 tablespoons mirin

3 cloves garlic, minced

1 tablespoon peeled and minced fresh ginger

1 tablespoon sugar

Freshly ground pepper

1 lb (500 g) beef tenderloin, cut into 1-inch (2.5-cm) cubes

10 green (spring) onions, white and pale green parts, cut into 1-inch (2.5-cm) pieces

Canola oil for brushing

MAKES 4–6 SERVINGS

Grilled Chicken Skewers with Sweet Soy Sauce

For the marinade

1½ tablespoons peeled and grated fresh ginger

3 cloves garlic, minced

⅓ cup (3 fl oz/80 ml) tamari soy sauce

3 tablespoons mirin

2 tablespoons dark soy sauce

2 tablespoons sake

1½ tablespoons sugar

1½ lb (750 g) skinless, boneless chicken thighs, cut into 1-inch (2.5-cm) pieces

1 large yellow onion, cut into 1-inch (2.5-cm) cubes

2 large green bell peppers (capsicums), seeded and cut into 1-inch (2.5-cm) squares

Canola oil for brushing

1 lemon, cut into wedges

Ground red *sansho* pepper for garnish

MAKES 4–6 SERVINGS

To make the marinade, in a large nonreactive bowl, combine the ginger, garlic, tamari, mirin, dark soy sauce, sake, and sugar and stir to mix well. Add the chicken pieces and stir to coat thoroughly. Cover and refrigerate for at least 2 hours or up to overnight.

Prepare a charcoal or gas grill for direct grilling over high heat, or preheat the broiler (grill). Soak 12 bamboo skewers, each 8 inches (20 cm) long, in water to cover for 30 minutes.

Pour the chicken pieces and marinade into a fine-mesh sieve set over a small saucepan, tapping the sieve so that the excess marinade drains into the saucepan. Set the chicken aside. Bring the marinade to a boil over medium heat and cook until the sauce has thickened to a syrupy consistency, 5–7 minutes. Cover the pan and keep the sauce warm.

Drain the skewers. Thread 1 piece of chicken onto a skewer, followed by 1 cube of onion and 1 square of bell pepper. Repeat 2 more times, pressing the pieces together tightly. Repeat to skewer the remaining chicken and vegetable pieces.

Brush the grill rack or a broiler pan with oil. Arrange the skewers on the rack or pan so they are not touching one another and cook until the chicken is golden brown on the first side, about 3 minutes. Turn and cook until golden brown on the second side and opaque throughout, 2–3 minutes longer.

Brush the warm sauce on both sides of the chicken skewers and arrange on a platter with the lemon wedges. Sprinkle with *sansho* pepper and serve at once.

Yakitori is the Japanese version of grilled chicken on a skewer, known as *satay* in Southeast Asian cuisine. A favorite in Japan, the savory small plate is served here with *sansho* pepper and lemon wedges, garnishes that provide a contrast of spicy and sweet.

Lemongrass Beef Skewers

Here, a distinctive paste made from aromatic ingredients regularly stocked in the Cambodian kitchen is the foundation for a marinade that both tenderizes and flavors thin strips of beef before they are threaded onto skewers and grilled. Lettuce leaves serve as wrappers for the grilled meat, crunchy bean sprouts, and fragrant herbs.

In a mini food processor or mortar, combine the lemongrass, shallot, garlic, and ginger and process or grind with a pestle until a coarse paste forms. Add 1–2 tablespoons water if needed to facilitate the grinding. Transfer the paste to a large nonreactive bowl. Add the fish sauce, soy sauce, 1 tablespoon oil, palm sugar, chile paste, and sesame seeds and stir to mix well. Add the beef strips and stir to coat thoroughly. Cover and marinate in the refrigerator for at least 1 hour or up to overnight.

Prepare a charcoal or gas grill for direct grilling over high heat, or preheat the broiler (grill). Soak 16 bamboo skewers, each 8 inches (20 cm) long, in water to cover for 30 minutes.

Drain the skewers and remove the beef strips from the marinade. Discard the marinade. Thread 2 beef strips lengthwise onto each skewer, pressing them together tightly. Brush the grill rack or a broiler pan with oil. Arrange the skewers on the rack or pan so they are not touching one another and cook, turning once, until crisp and brown on both sides, 3–4 minutes per side. Transfer the skewers to a warmed platter.

To serve, pour the dipping sauce into small saucers. Arrange the lettuce, cilantro, and mint leaves and the bean sprouts on a platter. Instruct each diner to pull the meat off a skewer; place it on a lettuce leaf; top it with cilantro, mint, and bean sprouts; roll up into a cylinder; dip it into the sauce; and eat out of hand.

2 lemongrass stalks, tender midsections only, smashed with the side of a chef's knife and chopped

1 shallot, chopped

3 cloves garlic, chopped

1 tablespoon peeled and chopped fresh ginger

2 tablespoons fish sauce

1 tablespoon dark soy sauce

1 tablespoon canola oil, plus more for brushing

1 tablespoon chopped palm sugar

1 teaspoon chile paste

1 tablespoon sesame seeds

1 lb (500 g) beef tri-tip or sirloin, cut into strips 3 inches (7.5 cm) long by 1/8 inch (3 mm) thick

Nuoc Cham Dipping Sauce (page 272) for serving

16 red-leaf lettuce leaves, stems removed

1 cup (1 oz/30 g) fresh cilantro (fresh coriander) leaves

1 cup (1 oz/30 g) fresh mint leaves

1 cup (1 oz/30 g) mung bean sprouts

MAKES 4 SERVINGS

Grilled Shrimp Paste
on Sugarcane

1 can (12 oz/375 g)
sugarcane, drained

1 tablespoon canola oil, plus
extra for coating

3 tablespoons minced
shallots

3 cloves garlic, minced

1 lb (500 g) medium shrimp
(prawns), peeled and
deveined

$4^1/_2$ teaspoons cornstarch
(cornflour)

1 large egg white, lightly
beaten

1 tablespoon fish sauce

1 teaspoon sugar

$^1/_8$ teaspoon ground white
pepper

Salt

$^1/_4$ cup ($^3/_4$ oz/20 g) minced
green (spring) onions

Nuoc Cham Dipping Sauce
(page 272) for serving

12 rice-paper rounds

12 red-leaf lettuce leaves,
stems removed

12 fresh mint sprigs

12 fresh cilantro
(fresh coriander) sprigs

MAKES 4–6 SERVINGS

Rinse the sugarcane under cold running water and drain well. Using a sharp knife, split the sugarcane sections lengthwise to make a total of 12 pieces, each 4 inches (10 cm) long and $^1/_2$ inch (12 mm) wide. Set aside.

In a frying pan over medium heat, warm the 1 tablespoon oil. Add the shallots and garlic and sauté until fragrant, about 1 minute. Transfer the shallot mixture to a food processor. Add the shrimp, cornstarch, egg white, fish sauce, sugar, white pepper, and $^1/_2$ teaspoon salt and pulse just until a coarse paste forms. Do not overmix or the cooked shrimp will be tough. Transfer the shrimp mixture to a bowl and fold in the green onions. Cover and refrigerate for 20 minutes.

Prepare a charcoal or gas grill for direct grilling over high heat. Lightly oil your hands and form about 2 tablespoons of the shrimp paste into a ball. Flatten the ball and center a sugarcane piece on top. Mold the paste evenly around the cane, shaping it about 1 inch (2.5 cm) thick and 3 inches (7.5 cm) long. There should be about $^1/_2$ inch (12 mm) of sugarcane exposed on each end to use as handles. Place the shrimp-wrapped sugarcane on a lightly oiled heatproof plate. Repeat with the remaining shrimp paste and sugarcane pieces, arranging them on the oiled plate so they are not touching one another.

Pour water to a depth of 2 inches (5 cm) into a deep, wide frying pan and place a steamer rack in the pan. Bring the water to a boil over high heat. Carefully place the plate of shrimp-wrapped sugarcane on the rack, cover the pan tightly, and steam until the shrimp paste turns opaque, 5–7 minutes. Brush the grill rack with oil. Transfer the steamed shrimp-wrapped sugarcane to the grill, again placing them so they do not touch. Grill, turning as needed, until lightly browned on all sides, 2–3 minutes total. Arrange on a warmed platter.

To serve, pour the dipping sauce into small bowls. Place the rice-paper rounds on a plate. Arrange the lettuce leaves and mint and cilantro sprigs on a platter. Set a wide, shallow bowl of warm water on the table. Invite each diner to slip a rice-paper round into the warm water and let soak until softened, about 1 minute. Remove the round from the bowl, gently shake off the excess water, and place on a plate. Put a lettuce leaf on top and then a few leaves or small sprigs of mint and cilantro. Pull the shrimp paste off a sugarcane piece and lay it on the herbs. Roll the rice paper into a cylinder, dip it into the sauce, and eat out of hand.

Lengths of sugarcane serve as skewers for a shrimp purée that is steamed, briefly grilled, and then wrapped in rice paper along with aromatic herbs at the table. This classic Vietnamese snack is popular in Thailand as well. The grilled skewers can also be arranged on bowls of rice vermicelli with shredded lettuce and fresh herbs, and finished with a drizzle of the dipping sauce.

Corn Fritters

Introduced to Indonesia by the Spanish in the seventeenth century, corn was quickly assimilated into Indonesian cooking. These fritters, a contemporary preparation of the New World vegetable, use rice flour to ensure lightness and a spicy seasoning paste to impart complex flavors.

To make the dipping sauce, in a small bowl, whisk together the soy sauce, vinegar, warm water, and chile sauce. Set aside.

In a mini food processor or mortar, combine the shallots, garlic, ginger, and chile and process or grind with a pestle until a smooth paste forms. Transfer the paste to a large bowl.

Add the corn, egg, sugar, coriander, $1/2$ teaspoon salt, and $1/8$ teaspoon pepper to the bowl and stir to mix well. Just before frying the fritters, fold the rice flour into the batter just until incorporated.

Preheat the oven to 250°F (120°C). Pour oil to a depth of 2 inches (5 cm) into a deep frying pan over high heat and heat to 370°F (188°C) on a deep-frying thermometer. Scoop up 1 heaping tablespoon of the corn batter and use another spoon to slide it into the hot oil. Repeat to add 4 or 5 fritters to the oil; do not crowd the pan. Deep-fry until the edges are golden, about 2 minutes. Using tongs, carefully turn the fritters and fry until golden brown on the second side, 1–2 minutes longer. Using the tongs, transfer to paper towels to drain. Arrange the fritters on an ovenproof platter and keep warm in the oven while you cook the remaining batter. Allow the oil to return to 370°F between batches.

Serve the hot fritters with the dipping sauce alongside.

For the dipping sauce

$1/4$ cup (2 fl oz/60 ml) sweet soy sauce

2 tablespoons rice vinegar

$1 1/2$ tablespoons warm water

1 teaspoon Sriracha chile sauce

3 tablespoons chopped shallots

3 cloves garlic, chopped

1 tablespoon peeled and grated fresh ginger

1 serrano chile, seeded and chopped

$2 1/2$ cups (15 oz/470 g) fresh corn kernels (about 6 ears)

1 large egg, lightly beaten

1 tablespoon sugar

1 teaspoon ground coriander

Salt and freshly ground pepper

$1/2$ cup ($2 1/2$ oz/75 g) rice flour

Canola oil for deep-frying

MAKES 16 FRITTERS

Samosas

For the pastry

1½ cups (7½ oz/235 g) all-purpose (plain) flour, plus extra for dusting

¼ teaspoon salt

2 tablespoons vegetable shortening, at room temperature, cut into small pieces

2 tablespoons cold unsalted butter, cut into small pieces

Canola oil for coating

For the filling

2 boiling potatoes, about 1 lb (500 g) total weight, peeled

2 tablespoons canola oil

½ yellow onion, minced

1 tablespoon peeled and minced fresh ginger

1 tablespoon seeded and minced jalapeño chile

2 cloves garlic, minced

½ teaspoon ground coriander

½ teaspoon ground cumin

½ teaspoon Madras curry powder

½ cup (2½ oz/75 g) fresh or thawed frozen English peas

1 teaspoon fresh lemon juice

Salt

Canola oil for deep-frying

MAKES 12 SAMOSAS

To make the pastry, sift together the 1½ cups flour and the salt into a large bowl. Add the shortening and butter pieces and use your fingers, a pastry blender, or 2 knives to blend them into the flour mixture until it is the consistency of coarse meal. Drizzle in water, 1 tablespoon at a time, tossing, gathering, and pressing with your hands to incorporate, until the mixture comes together in a rough mass; you will need about ⅓ cup (3 fl oz/80 ml) water total. The dough should not be too wet. Turn out onto a lightly floured work surface. Knead until smooth and elastic, about 5 minutes, dusting with flour as needed. Rub the dough with canola oil, cover with plastic wrap, and refrigerate for at least 1 hour or up to overnight.

To make the filling, in a saucepan over high heat, combine the potatoes with water to cover generously. Bring to a boil and cook until just tender, about 15 minutes. Drain, let cool, and cut into ¼-inch (6-mm) dice. Set aside.

In a large frying pan over medium heat, warm the 2 tablespoons oil. Add the onion and sauté until lightly browned, 5–10 minutes. Add the ginger, chile, garlic, coriander, cumin, and curry powder and cook, stirring, until the spices are fragrant, about 1 minute. Add the potatoes, peas, lemon juice, and 1 teaspoon salt and cook until the flavors meld, 1–2 minutes longer. Remove from the heat and let cool.

On a lightly floured work surface, using your hands, roll the dough into a cylinder about 18 inches (45 cm) long, and cut into 12 equal pieces. Roll each piece into a neat ball and cover with a damp kitchen towel. Working with 1 dough ball at a time, use a rolling pin to flatten it into a disk and then roll it out into a 6-inch (15-cm) round, dusting often with flour. Cut the dough round in half. Turn the straight edge so it is facing you and moisten it with water. Holding the 2 corners, lift them to form a cone; pinch the seam to seal. Holding the cone with the open end toward you, stuff it with 1 heaping tablespoon of the filling. Moisten the edges of the open end of the cone with water and bring the edges together. Fold over ¼ inch (6 mm) of the seam and pinch to seal.

Preheat the oven to 250°F (120°C). Pour oil to a depth of 2 inches (5 cm) into a deep frying pan over high heat and heat to 370°F (188°C) on a deep-frying thermometer. Using a spatula, slide 5 or 6 samosas into the hot oil; do not crowd the pan. Deep-fry, turning often, until golden brown on all sides, 2–3 minutes total. Using tongs or a wire skimmer, transfer to paper towels to drain. Arrange the fried samosas on an ovenproof platter and keep warm in the oven while you fry the remaining samosas. Allow the oil to return to 370°F between batches. Serve the samosas warm.

These popular Indian snacks, traditionally filled with curried potatoes and peas, fry into pastries perfect for eating out of hand as an appetizer or snack. For a variation with meat, add ¼ pound (125 g) ground (minced) lamb or beef when cooking the onion with the spices. Serve the warm samosas with Cilantro Chutney (page 274) or Tamarind Chutney (page 274).

Spicy Fish Cakes

1 lb (500 g) catfish or sea bass fillets, finely diced

¼ lb (125 g) yard-long beans or green beans, trimmed and cut crosswise into paper-thin slices

1 lemongrass stalk, tender midsection only, smashed with the side of a chef's knife and chopped

1-inch (2.5-cm) piece fresh galangal, peeled and chopped

1 serrano chile, seeded and chopped

1 shallot, chopped

3 cloves garlic, chopped

2 tablespoons minced fresh cilantro (fresh coriander) stems

2 kaffir lime leaves, spines removed

1 tablespoon fish sauce, plus extra for serving

2 teaspoons fresh lime juice

1 teaspoon sugar

½ teaspoon cornstarch (cornflour)

1 large egg white, lightly beaten

Canola oil for deep-frying

MAKES 16 FISH CAKES

Put the fish in a food processor and pulse just until a coarse paste forms, about 10 seconds. Transfer to a large bowl and fold in the beans. Combine the lemongrass, galangal, chile, shallot, garlic, cilantro, and lime leaves in the food processor and process until a coarse paste forms. Add the 1 tablespoon fish sauce, lime juice, and sugar and process just until combined. Add the lemongrass mixture, cornstarch, and egg white to the bowl with the fish paste and gently fold together just until incorporated.

Preheat the oven to 250°F (120°C). Pour oil to a depth of 2 inches (5 cm) into a deep frying pan over high heat and heat to 370°F (188°C) on a deep-frying thermometer. Moisten your hands with water and divide the fish mixture into 16 balls. Shape each ball into a patty about 3 inches (7.5 cm) in diameter. Place on a lightly oiled baking sheet.

Using a spatula, slide 5 or 6 fish patties into the hot oil; do not crowd the pan. Deep-fry until golden brown on the first side, about 1 minute. Using tongs, carefully turn the fish cakes and fry until golden brown on the second side and crisp, about 1 minute longer. Using the tongs or a wire skimmer, transfer to paper towels to drain. Arrange the fried fish cakes on an ovenproof platter and keep warm in the oven while you fry the remaining fish cakes. Allow the oil to return to 370°F between batches.

Arrange the fish cakes on a warmed platter and serve with fish sauce for dipping.

Enjoyed throughout Thailand as a snack and found widely outside the country on restaurant menus, fish cakes vary from kitchen to kitchen in their seasonings. Here, a trio of Thai aromatics, lemongrass, kaffir lime, and galangal, flavors the cakes, which are deep-fried to give them a crisp, tender golden crust. Serve them with Sweet-and-Sour Red Onion and Cucumber Salad (page 129) and Nam Pla Dipping Sauce (page 272).

Split Pea Fritters

A typical street snack, these mildly spicy vegetarian fritters call for a combination of bright-colored ground turmeric, chile, and shallot characteristic of Burmese food. The crisp, golden exterior gives way to a tender interior. The tangy tamarind dipping sauce is the perfect accompaniment.

Pick over the split peas, removing any stones or misshapen or discolored peas. Place the split peas in a bowl with water to cover. Set aside to soak for at least 8 hours or up to overnight.

To make the dipping sauce, in a mini food processor or mortar, combine the chile, cilantro, garlic, and sugar and process or grind with a pestle until a smooth paste forms. Add 1–2 tablespoons water if needed to facilitate the grinding. Transfer to a bowl. Add the tamarind paste, 2 tablespoons water, and the fish sauce and stir to mix well. Transfer the sauce to a serving bowl and set aside.

Drain the split peas. In a food processor or blender, combine about three-fourths of the soaked split peas with 3 tablespoons water and process to a coarse purée. Transfer to a large bowl. Add the remaining soaked peas, shallots, garlic, ginger, chile, turmeric, baking powder, and 1 teaspoon salt and stir to mix well.

Preheat the oven to 300°F (150°C). Pour oil to a depth of 2 inches (5 cm) into a deep frying pan over high heat and heat to 370°F (188°C) on a deep-frying thermometer. Moisten your hands with water, scoop 1 heaping tablespoon of the split-pea mixture, and shape into an oval patty about 2½ inches (6 cm) long and 1½ inches (4 cm) wide. Place on a lightly oiled baking sheet. Repeat with the remaining split-pea mixture.

Using a spatula, slide 5 or 6 patties into the hot oil; do not crowd the pan. Deep-fry until golden brown on the first side, 1–2 minutes. Using tongs, turn the patties and fry until golden brown on the second side, about 1 minute. Using the tongs or a wire skimmer, transfer to a baking sheet lined with paper towels to drain. Repeat to fry the remaining fritters, allowing the oil to return to 370°F between batches. Remove the paper towels from the baking sheet, place in the oven, and bake until the fritters are firm, about 7 minutes.

Arrange the fritters on a warmed platter and serve with the dipping sauce.

1 cup (7 oz/220 g) dried yellow split peas

For the dipping sauce

1 serrano chile, seeded and chopped

1 tablespoon chopped fresh cilantro (fresh coriander) stems

1 clove garlic, chopped

1 teaspoon sugar

¼ cup (2 oz/60 g) tamarind paste

1 teaspoon fish sauce

2 shallots, minced

2 cloves garlic, minced

1 tablespoon peeled and minced fresh ginger

1 serrano chile, seeded and minced

½ teaspoon ground turmeric

½ teaspoon baking powder

Salt

Canola oil for deep-frying

MAKES 30 FRITTERS

Fresh Spring Rolls with Shrimp

Rice papers, dried, translucent sheets made from rice flour and water, are used primarily in Vietnamese cuisine as wrappers for various ingredients, such as the shrimp and fresh vegetables and herbs in this recipe. Fairly bland, the rice paper takes on a noodlelike texture when reconstituted and, just as noodles do, soaks up the flavor of sauces, here the classic Vietnamese dipping sauce called *nuoc cham*.

Bring a saucepan three-fourths full of water to a boil. Add the shrimp and 1 teaspoon salt and return to a boil. Reduce the heat to medium and simmer until the shrimp turn bright orange and opaque, about 2 minutes. Drain and let cool. Cut each shrimp in half lengthwise.

To assemble the rolls, drain the noodles. Fill a wide, shallow bowl with warm water. Working with 1 rice-paper round at a time, soak it in the warm water until softened, 5 or 6 seconds. Remove it from the bowl, gently shake off the excess water, and place it on a work surface. Place a lettuce leaf horizontally on the bottom half of the moistened rice paper. In a line across the base of the lettuce, place 1 teaspoon of the carrot, 1 teaspoon of the cucumber, several strands of the noodles, and several bean sprouts. Be careful not to overstuff the rolls. Lift the bottom edge of the rice paper and carefully roll up halfway into a tight cylinder. Place 2 shrimp halves and several mint and cilantro leaves tightly along the inside seam of the roll. Fold in the sides of the rice paper and continue to roll the rice paper and filling into a cylinder. Moisten the edge of the roll to seal.

Repeat with the remaining ingredients. Place the prepared rolls, seam side down, on a platter and cover with plastic wrap. The rolls will keep at room temperature for several hours before serving.

Cut the rolls in half on the diagonal and serve with the dipping sauce.

6 medium shrimp (prawns), peeled and deveined

Salt

2 oz (60 g) cellophane noodles, soaked in boiling water for 15 minutes

6 rice-paper rounds, each 8 inches (20 cm) in diameter

6 red-leaf or butter lettuce leaves, stems removed

1 small carrot, shredded

½ small cucumber, peeled, seeded, and shredded

½ cup (½ oz/15 g) mung bean sprouts

18 *each* fresh mint leaves and fresh cilantro (fresh coriander) leaves

Nuoc Cham Dipping Sauce (page 272) for serving

MAKES 6 SPRING ROLLS

Fried Spring Rolls

For the dipping sauce

3 tablespoons hoisin sauce

1 teaspoon Sriracha chile sauce

24 large shrimp (prawns) in the shell, about 1 lb (500 g) total weight

2 cloves garlic, minced

1 tablespoon minced fresh cilantro (fresh coriander) stems

1 teaspoon peppercorns, coarsely ground

1 tablespoon fish sauce

1 tablespoon light soy sauce

24 square wonton wrappers

12 fresh Chinese egg noodles, each about 12 inches (30 cm) long, halved and kept moist under a damp kitchen towel

Canola oil for deep-frying

MAKES 24 SPRING ROLLS

To make the dipping sauce, in a small bowl, combine the hoisin sauce, chile sauce, and 1 teaspoon warm water and stir to mix well. Set aside.

Peel and devein the shrimp, leaving the tail segments intact. Cut 4 or 5 horizontal slits on the bottom, or concave, side of each shrimp to prevent them from curling when they cook. Rinse the shrimp well, drain, and place in a bowl.

In a mini food processor or mortar, combine the garlic, cilantro, and peppercorns and process or grind with a pestle until a coarse paste forms. Add 1–2 tablespoons water if needed to facilitate the grinding. Add the garlic-cilantro paste, fish sauce, and soy sauce to the bowl with the shrimp and stir to coat thoroughly. Cover and refrigerate for at least 30 minutes or up to 1 hour.

To assemble the spring rolls, trim a ¼-inch (6-mm) triangle from a corner of each wonton wrapper. Place 1 shrimp on the wrapper with the tail extending beyond the edge of the trimmed corner and the head of the shrimp in the center of the wrapper. Starting at one edge, roll the wrapper around the shrimp, being careful to leave the tail of the shrimp exposed. Wrap a noodle around the center of the roll and tie to secure the roll. Place the wrapped shrimp on a baking sheet. Repeat with the remaining wrappers and shrimp.

Preheat the oven to 250°F (120°C). Pour oil to a depth of 2 inches (5 cm) into a wok or deep frying pan over high heat and heat to 370°F (188°C) on a deep-frying thermometer. Slide 6–8 rolls into the hot oil; do not crowd the pan. Deep-fry the rolls, turning them with tongs, until the wrappers are golden brown on all sides, 15–30 seconds total. Using the tongs or a wire skimmer, transfer the rolls to paper towels to drain. Arrange the fried spring rolls on an ovenproof platter and keep warm in the oven while you fry the remaining rolls. Allow the oil to return to 370°F between batches. Serve the hot rolls with the dipping sauce alongside.

Thai cuisine can be quite elaborate in its presentation, from beautifully carved vegetables and fruits to artfully wrapped appetizers such as these fried rolls. Each roll encloses a seasoned whole shrimp in an attractive package. The assembly may seem time-consuming at first, but will become easier and faster after you wrap a few shrimp.

Breads, Dumplings, and Pancakes

About Breads, Dumplings, and Pancakes

Bread is a staple in the cooler, more arid regions of China, India, and Pakistan. It turns up flat and shaped into buns, steamed and baked, filled and plain, flaky and chewy. Myriad filled dumplings and pancakes, part of the same tradition, appear on tables in a wider swath of the region.

Asian cooks use primarily wheat and rice flours to create their breads, dumplings, and pancakes, with different types of both grains and various milling methods contributing to a remarkably large, diverse repertoire. In some areas, particularly South Asia, flours ground from dried chickpeas (garbanzos), lentils, millet, and corn are also used, especially for making flatbreads.

BREADS, FLAT AND FILLED

In northern India, the chapati accompanies nearly every meal. Made from *atta*, a soft whole-wheat (wholemeal) flour, the small rounds are cooked on a griddle without oil. Larger ovals of leavened naan (page 67), baked inside wood-fired tandoors (clay ovens), are puffier and have a distinct smoky flavor.

Different grains, ingredients, and cooking methods define other breads eaten across the country. Some gain distinction with a simple sprinkling of cumin, or poppy or sesame seeds. The dough for *paratha* (page 68) is enriched with ghee (clarified butter) or oil and folded a few times before rolling and cooking, resulting in flaky layers for more sumptuous meals. Bite-sized *puri* fry up hollow and crisp. Regional flatbread favorites include the deep-fried *lucci* of Bengal, the fenugreek-flavored *thepla* of Gujarat, and the crisp *batti* of Rajasthan, which is broken open and dipped in ghee.

Indian Muslims brought the filled bread known as *murtabak* (page 71) with them to Malaysia, Singapore, and Indonesia. Highly skilled cooks, with a few flicks of the wrist, flip and stretch a tiny piece of dough into a large, paper-thin round in mere seconds. It is immediately folded over a filling of egg, lamb, or chicken, cooked until crisp on a flat griddle, and served hot with a bowl of curry sauce.

In the Philippines, light, tender white flour rolls such as *pan de sal* and *ensaimada* were readily adopted from the Spanish, though local ingredients such as purple yam, coconut, and palm sugar soon found their way into them. Filipinos borrowed empanadas (page 72), or turnovers, from the same colonial rulers and made them their own as well.

The northern Chinese also prepare white flour rolls, which they fashion from a soft dough and then steam to accompany meals. For special occasions, the rolls can take unusual and creative shapes such as lotus flowers, butterflies, or fanciful swirls. When filled with bits of roast pork, brushed with an egg glaze, and baked until golden brown, the simple bread dough is transformed into Barbecued Pork Buns (page 80).

THE BIG DUMPLING FAMILY

These pork buns are sometimes included among a selection of dim sum, the traditional southern Chinese repast of small bites accompanied by tea. But the most iconic elements of this midday meal are steamed filled dumplings, in which translucent wrappers usually made from wheat or tapioca starch enclose meat, seafood, or vegetables. Each dumpling has a traditional shape: a filling of minced pork, napa cabbage, and water chestnuts peeks out from the gathered crown of *shaomai* (page 75), and delicately pinched pleats and a full-bodied curve identify shrimp (prawn)–filled *har gow*.

Meat-filled dumplings, or *jiaozi*, appear in the north during the Chinese New Year. Next door in Korea, families prepare similar dumplings called *mandu*, including one that spices up the filling with kimchi (page 76). Pot stickers, called *gyoza* in Japan (page 79), have a thinner, more delicate wrapping and a filling of pork and vegetables.

Wontons are among the most popular members of the big dumpling family. Their noodle wrappers become silken sheaths when the savory mouthfuls are boiled and floated in the signature Chinese soup (page 38). But wontons can also be deep-fried until golden brown and crisp (page 77) and served piping hot with a sweet-and-sour dipping sauce.

HEARTY PANCAKES

Banh xeo (page 83), Vietnamese pancakes filled with shrimp and vegetables, also arrive at the table golden brown and crisp. Made from rice flour tinted yellow with turmeric, they take their name from the sizzling sound the batter makes when it hits the hot pan.

In specialty restaurants in Japan, diners seated at long counters cook their own meat, seafood, and vegetables for *okonomiyaki* (page 84), a hearty pancake that commonly fuels a young, late-night crowd. Koreans fill up on small, crisp *jun*, which can be made from seafood (page 86) or vegetables but always include a generous sprinkling of green (spring) onions. Abundant green onions, also called scallions, are worked into the dough for Chinese Scallion Pancakes (page 87), which are cut into wedges for dipping into an accompanying sauce.

Indian Flatbread

Naan, a leavened flatbread enjoyed throughout India, is eaten with almost any meat or vegetable dish. It is traditionally baked in a special dome-shaped clay oven called a tandoor, but cooking dough rounds on a pizza stone or baking tile in a very hot conventional oven will produce the same puffed-up, crispy breads with spots of black and golden brown. You can also grill the breads directly over a hot fire. To store leftover baked breads, let them cool, wrap tightly in aluminum foil, and freeze for up to 3 months. To serve, reheat the frozen breads in a 300°F (150°C) oven until warm and crisp, about 10 minutes.

In a small bowl, whisk together the warm milk, sugar, and yeast and let stand until the mixture becomes frothy, 10–15 minutes.

Sift together the 3¼ cups flour, the salt, and the baking powder into a large bowl. Add the yeast mixture, the yogurt, the ¼ cup oil, and the egg. Stir until the wet ingredients are incorporated, then toss, gather, and press the mixture with your hands until it comes together in a rough mass. Turn the dough out onto a lightly floured work surface and knead until smooth, 5–10 minutes, dusting with flour as needed to prevent sticking. Form the dough into a ball, place in an oiled bowl, and turn to coat with the oil. Cover with plastic wrap and place in a warm, draft-free place until doubled in size, about 1 hour.

Place a pizza stone or unglazed baking tiles on the bottom rack of the oven and preheat to 500°F (260°C). Again turn the dough out onto a lightly floured work surface and knead until smooth and elastic, about 3 minutes. Divide the dough into 6 equal pieces. Using your hands, roll each piece into a ball and cover with a damp kitchen towel. Working with 1 dough ball at a time, use the palm of your hand to flatten it into a disk and then shape it into a 7-inch (18-cm) round, pressing out any air bubbles. Pick up the dough and toss it back and forth between your hands, using your fingers to stretch it into a round about 10 inches (25 cm) in diameter. Rub both sides of the round with oil.

Working quickly, place the oiled dough round on the stone in the oven and close the oven. Bake until puffed up, about 3 minutes. Again working quickly, open the oven, turn the bread with tongs, close the oven, and bake until the second side is crisp and browned in spots, about 3 minutes longer. Wrap in aluminum foil to keep warm while you bake the remaining breads. Serve at once.

½ cup (4 fl oz/125 ml) warm milk (110°F/43°C)

1 tablespoon sugar

1 package (2½ teaspoons) active dry yeast

3¼ cups (17 oz/530 g) all-purpose (plain) flour, plus extra for dusting

1½ teaspoons salt

1 teaspoon baking powder

½ cup (4 oz/125 g) plain whole-milk yogurt

¼ cup (2 fl oz/60 ml) canola oil, plus extra for greasing

1 large egg, lightly beaten

MAKES 6 FLATBREADS

Flaky Whole-Wheat Flatbread

1½ cups (7½ oz/235 g) whole-wheat (wholemeal) flour

1½ cups (7½ oz/235 g) all-purpose (plain) flour, plus extra for dusting

1 teaspoon salt

¼ cup (2 oz/60 g) ghee or ¼ cup (2 fl oz/60 ml) canola oil, plus extra for greasing and frying

1¼ cups (10 fl oz/310 ml) cold water

MAKES 12 FLATBREADS

Sift together the 1½ cups whole-wheat flour, the 1½ cups all-purpose flour, and the salt into a large bowl. Add the ¼ cup ghee and use your fingers to rub it into the flour mixture until it is the consistency of coarse meal. Slowly drizzle in the cold water, tossing, gathering, and pressing with your hands to incorporate, until the mixture comes together in a rough mass. Turn out onto a lightly floured work surface. Knead until smooth and elastic, 5–10 minutes, dusting with flour as needed to prevent sticking. Rub the dough with ghee, cover with plastic wrap, and let rest at room temperature for 30 minutes.

On a lightly floured work surface, using your hands, roll the dough into a cylinder about 18 inches (45 cm) long, and cut into 12 equal pieces. Roll each piece into a neat ball and cover with a damp kitchen towel. Working with 1 dough ball at a time, use a rolling pin to flatten it into a disk and then roll it out into a 6-inch (15-cm) round, dusting often with flour. Brush the dough with ghee and fold the round in half. Brush more ghee over the top and fold the half-circle in half again to form a triangle. Roll out the triangle into a larger triangle with sides about 8 inches (20 cm) long.

Preheat the oven to 250°F (120°C). Heat a large, heavy frying pan over high heat until hot. Brush the pan with ghee, place a bread in it, and reduce the heat to medium-high. Fry until the first side is golden brown in spots, about 2 minutes. Turn and cook until golden brown on the second side, about 3 minutes longer. Keep warm in the oven while you fry the remaining breads. Serve at once.

A popular griddle bread served throughout the day, *paratha* is made with a combination of all-purpose and whole-wheat flours shortened with ghee, or clarified butter, and then folded into layers with more ghee. In India, the triangular breads are fried on a concave cast-iron plate called a *tava* until the layers rise, the bread is lightly browned, and the edges are crisp. This recipe uses a large cast-iron or other heavy-bottomed frying pan to achieve the same result.

Lamb-Filled Flatbread

Street vendors throughout Indonesia serve these meat-filled breads that originated in India. Flaky and tender, *murtabak* is similar in texture to strudel pastry, and is filled with morsels of egg and spicy lamb. Be patient when stretching this dough by hand; the thinner the dough, the more chewy and crisp the flatbread will be.

To make the dough, sift together the 3 cups flour and the salt into a large bowl. Add the 2 tablespoons ghee and use your fingers to rub it into the flour mixture until the mixture is the consistency of coarse meal. Slowly drizzle in the warm water, tossing, gathering, and pressing with your hands to incorporate, until the mixture comes together in a rough mass. Turn out onto a lightly floured work surface. Knead until smooth and elastic, 5–10 minutes, dusting with flour as needed to prevent sticking. Divide the dough into 6 equal pieces. Using your hands, roll each piece into a neat ball. Rub the balls of dough with ghee, cover with a damp kitchen towel, and let rest at room temperature for 30 minutes.

To make the filling, in large frying pan over medium-high heat, warm the oil. Add the onion and sauté until softened, about 5 minutes. Add the garlic, ginger, chile, coriander, cumin, and turmeric and sauté until fragrant, about 1 minute. Crumble the lamb into the pan and sauté, using a wooden spoon to break up the meat, until no longer pink, about 3 minutes. Add the cilantro, 1/2 teaspoon salt, and 1/8 teaspoon pepper and stir to mix well. Let the filling cool to room temperature.

Brush a clean work surface with ghee. Working with 1 dough ball at a time, use a rolling pin to flatten it into a disk and then roll it out into an oval about 1/8 inch (3 mm) thick. Using your fingers, spread the dough gently into a thinner oval about 6 by 10 inches (15 by 25 cm); it should be paper-thin, smooth, and elastic.

Preheat the oven to 250°F (120°C). Spoon about 1 teaspoon of the beaten egg onto each dough round and spread all over the surface with the back of the spoon. Sprinkle one-sixth of the filling on one-half of the dough and fold the other half over to cover. Fold in the edges of the dough and pinch to seal and enclose the filling. Heat a large nonstick frying pan over medium heat and brush with ghee. Working in batches, add the filled dough to the pan and cook until crisp and golden brown on the first side, about 5 minutes. Carefully turn and cook until the second side is crisp and golden brown, about 5 minutes longer. Keep warm in the oven while you assemble and fry the remaining breads.

Cut each flatbread into 4 pieces, arrange on a warmed platter, and serve at once.

For the dough

3 cups (15 oz/470 g) all-purpose (plain) flour, plus extra for dusting

1 teaspoon salt

2 tablespoons ghee or canola oil, plus extra for greasing and frying

3/4 cup (6 fl oz/180 ml) warm water

For the filling

2 tablespoons canola oil

1/2 yellow onion, minced

3 cloves garlic, minced

1 tablespoon peeled and minced fresh ginger

1 tablespoon seeded and minced jalapeño chile

1/2 teaspoon ground coriander

1/2 teaspoon ground cumin

1/2 teaspoon ground turmeric

1/2 lb (250 g) ground (minced) lamb

1 tablespoon minced fresh cilantro (fresh coriander)

Salt and freshly ground pepper

1 large egg, lightly beaten

MAKES 6 FLATBREADS

Empanadas

For the pastry

1½ cups (7½ oz/235 g) all-purpose (plain) flour

1 teaspoon sugar

1½ teaspoons salt

4 tablespoons (2 oz/60 g) *each* cold vegetable shortening and cold unsalted butter

1 large egg, lightly beaten

¼ cup (2 fl oz/60 ml) ice water

For the filling

1 boiling potato, about ¼ lb (125 g)

2 tablespoons canola oil

½ yellow onion, minced

2 cloves garlic, minced

1 carrot, cut into ⅛-inch (3-mm) dice

6 oz (185 g) ground (minced) beef

3 tablespoons light soy sauce

2 tablespoons rice wine

1 tablespoon rice vinegar

Freshly ground pepper

¼ cup (1½ oz/45 g) fresh or thawed frozen English peas

¼ cup (1½ oz/45 g) small raisins or dried currants

1 large egg, lightly beaten

MAKES ABOUT 25 EMPANADAS

To make the pastry, sift together the 1½ cups flour, the sugar, and the salt into a large bowl. Cut the shortening and butter into small pieces. Add to the flour mixture and use your fingers, a pastry blender, or 2 knives to rub them into the flour mixture until the mixture is the consistency of coarse meal. In a small bowl, beat together the egg and ice water. Add the egg mixture to the dry ingredients and stir with a fork just until the mixture comes together into a rough mass. Turn the dough out onto a lightly floured work surface and pat into a disk. Cover with plastic wrap and refrigerate for at least 1 hour or up to 24 hours.

To make the filling, peel the potato and cut into ⅛-inch (3-mm) dice. In a large frying pan over medium-high heat, warm the oil. Add the onion and sauté until softened, about 5 minutes. Add the garlic, carrot, and potato and sauté until the carrot is softened, about 5 minutes. Raise the heat to high. Crumble the beef into the pan and sauté, using a wooden spoon to break up the meat, until no longer pink, about 5 minutes. Stir in the soy sauce, rice wine, vinegar, and ⅛ teaspoon pepper. Reduce the heat to medium, cover, and cook until the potatoes are tender, about 15 minutes. Add the peas and raisins and simmer, uncovered, until most of the liquid has evaporated, 5–7 minutes. Remove from the heat and let the filling cool to room temperature.

On a lightly floured work surface, roll out the dough ⅛ inch (3 mm) thick. Using a 4-inch (10-cm) cookie cutter, cut out circles of dough. Quickly and briefly knead the dough scraps together just until smooth, pat out the dough, and cut out additional circles. Transfer the dough circles to a baking sheet lined with parchment (baking) paper and refrigerate for 20 minutes. Spoon 1 tablespoon of the filling into the center of each dough circle and brush the edges with beaten egg. Fold the dough in half over the filling to form a half-moon and crimp the edges with a fork, preferably one with rounded tines. Arrange the empanadas 1 inch (2.5 cm) apart on a baking sheet lined with clean parchment (baking) paper. Refrigerate for 15 minutes.

Preheat the oven to 375°F (190°C). Brush the tops of the empanadas with the remaining beaten egg and bake until golden brown, 25–30 minutes. Serve warm or at room temperature.

Spain's colonization of the Philippines in the sixteenth century brought many dramatic influences to the Asian country's culture and cuisine. One of the best-known and tastiest examples is the Filipino half-moon–shaped empanada. The savory pastries, filled with ground beef, pork, and/or chicken; onions, potatoes, peas, and raisins; and a seasoning of soy sauce and rice wine contain a meeting of East and West in every bite.

Steamed Pork Dumplings

A popular Cantonese dim sum dish, these flavorful bite-sized pork dumplings are attractively wrapped in wheat-flour wrappers and steamed in a traditional bamboo basket or in a conventional steamer. Be sure to drain the cabbage thoroughly as directed before mixing it with the pork, water chestnuts, and other ingredients, to ensure that the filling holds together and the dumpling does not become soggy.

In a bowl, combine the minced cabbage and 1 teaspoon salt and toss to mix well. Let stand for 20 minutes to allow the salt to draw the water out of the cabbage.

In a large bowl, combine the pork, water chestnuts, green onions, ginger, garlic, soy sauce, rice wine, sesame oil, sugar, 1½ tablespoons cornstarch, and white pepper. Drain the cabbage and use your hands to squeeze out any remaining water. Add to the bowl with the pork mixture. Using a rubber spatula, stir vigorously until the ingredients are well incorporated. Refrigerate the filling for 30 minutes.

To assemble the dumplings, working with 1 wonton wrapper at a time, place it in the palm of one hand; keep the other wrappers covered with a slightly damp kitchen towel to prevent them from drying out. Put 1 heaping tablespoon of the filling in the center of the wrapper. Lightly brush the edges of the wrapper with water. Cup the wrapper in your hand, and using the thumb and index finger of your other hand, slowly form a pleated basket, squeezing the pleats gently to seal them. Place the finished dumplings on a baking sheet dusted with cornstarch, pressing gently to flatten the bottoms so they sit upright. Flatten down any filling that is threatening to spill out the top of the dumplings, and press a piece of diced carrot and a pea in the center of each dumpling to secure the filling.

In a large saucepan or a wok, bring 2 inches (5 cm) of water to a boil over high heat. Line a bamboo steamer basket or a plate with a single layer of cabbage leaves and top with half of the dumplings, leaving some space between them. Place the basket in the pan or place the plate on a steamer rack in the pan; the water should not touch the steamer. Cover tightly, reduce the heat to maintain a gentle simmer, and steam until the dumplings are firm to the touch and the visible filling is opaque, about 10 minutes. Transfer the dumplings to a warmed platter and keep warm while you steam the remaining dumplings. Serve at once with the dipping sauce.

2 cups (7 oz/220 g) minced napa cabbage, plus 6 whole leaves

Salt

½ lb (250 g) ground (minced) pork

½ cup (3 oz/90 g) fresh water chestnuts, peeled and minced

3 green (spring) onions, white and pale green parts, minced

1 tablespoon peeled and minced fresh ginger

2 cloves garlic, minced

2 tablespoons light soy sauce

1 tablespoon Chinese rice wine

1 teaspoon Asian sesame oil

¼ teaspoon sugar

1½ tablespoons cornstarch (cornflour), plus extra for dusting

⅛ teaspoon ground white pepper

20 round wonton wrappers

¼ cup (1½ oz/45 g) *each* thawed frozen English peas and diced carrots

Soy-Ginger Dipping Sauce (page 273) for serving

MAKES 20 DUMPLINGS

Kimchi Dumplings

For the filling

10 oz (315 g) firm tofu

1 jar (15 oz/470 g) kimchi, drained and minced

3 green (spring) onions, white and pale green parts, minced

1 tablespoon peeled and grated fresh ginger

2 cloves garlic, minced

1 teaspoon Asian sesame oil

1 large egg, lightly beaten

1 teaspoon cornstarch (cornflour)

Salt and freshly ground pepper

30 round wonton wrappers

Cornstarch (cornflour) for dusting

Chile-Soy Dipping Sauce (page 272) for serving

MAKES 30 DUMPLINGS

To make the filling, wrap the tofu in a double layer of cheesecloth (muslin) or a clean kitchen towel and squeeze out as much water as possible. The tofu will crumble. Place the tofu in a large bowl and crumble into uniform pieces about the size of small peas. Place the kimchi in a fine-mesh sieve and press out any excess liquid. Add the kimchi to the bowl with the tofu along with the green onions, ginger, garlic, sesame oil, egg, cornstarch, $1/2$ teaspoon salt, and $1/4$ teaspoon pepper. Using a rubber spatula, stir vigorously until the ingredients are well incorporated. Refrigerate the filling for 30 minutes.

To assemble the dumplings, working with 1 wonton wrapper at a time, place it in the palm of your hand; keep the other wrappers covered with a slightly damp kitchen towel to prevent them from drying out. Put 1 heaping tablespoon of the filling in the center of the wrapper. Lightly brush the edges with water and fold the wrapper in half over the filling to form a half-moon. Pinch the edges to seal. Place the dumplings on a baking sheet dusted with cornstarch.

In a large saucepan or a wok, bring 2 inches (5 cm) of water to a boil over high heat. Line a bamboo steamer basket or a plate with wet cheesecloth (muslin) and top with 8–10 dumplings, leaving some space between them. Place the basket in the pan or place the plate on a steamer rack in the pan; the water should not touch the steamer. Cover tightly, reduce the heat to maintain a gentle simmer, and steam until the dumplings are firm to the touch, about 10 minutes. Transfer the dumplings to a warmed platter and keep warm while you steam the remaining dumplings. Serve at once with the dipping sauce.

What defines these unique Korean dumplings is the filling of sweet-and-sour kimchi—fermented cabbage, daikon, or another vegetable— an ancient condiment that is still a ubiquitous staple. Kimchi made from cabbage is preferred for these dumplings. It ranges from mild to very spicy. Choose the degree of spiciness that suits your preference. The dumplings can be steamed as here, or fried or boiled.

Fried Wontons

These classic pork-and-shrimp dumplings are highly versatile. They are steamed for a light appetizer or are served in a seasoned broth for wonton soup (page 38). When deep-fried as in this traditional recipe for a starter or snack, the wonton wrapper turns golden brown, with crisp edges that provide some crunch in contrast to the succulent filling.

To make the filling, place the mushrooms in a heatproof bowl with boiling water to cover, keeping them submerged with a lid or plate. Let soak for 30 minutes, then drain and trim off the tough stems and discard. Mince the caps. In a large bowl, combine the mushrooms, pork, shrimp, water chestnuts, green onions, ginger, garlic, egg, soy sauce, rice wine, sesame oil, cornstarch, sugar, and white pepper. Using a rubber spatula, stir vigorously until the ingredients are well incorporated. Refrigerate the filling for 30 minutes.

To assemble the wontons, working with 1 wrapper at a time, place it on a work surface and moisten the edges with cold water; keep the other wrappers covered with a slightly damp kitchen towel to prevent them from drying out. Place 1 teaspoon of the filling in the center of the wrapper and fold over into a triangle. Press the edges together firmly to seal. Fold the 2 outer points across the top of the mound and pinch the corners together to seal. If they do not stick, moisten with a little water. Place on a baking sheet dusted with cornstarch.

Preheat the oven to 250°F (120°C). Pour canola oil to a depth of 3–4 inches (7.5–10 cm) into a wok or deep frying pan over high heat and heat to 370°F (188°C) on a deep-frying thermometer. Using a spatula, slide 6 or 7 wontons into the hot oil; do not crowd the pan. Deep-fry, using tongs or a wire skimmer to move the wontons around in the hot oil, until evenly crisp and golden brown, 20–30 seconds. Using the tongs or wire skimmer or a slotted spatula, transfer to paper towels to drain. Arrange the fried wontons on an ovenproof platter and keep warm in the oven while you cook the remaining wontons. Allow the oil to return to 370°F between batches. Serve at once with the dipping sauce.

For the filling

5 or 6 dried shiitake mushrooms, rinsed

Boiling water as needed

¼ lb (125 g) ground (minced) pork

2 oz (60 g) shrimp (prawns), peeled, deveined, and chopped

½ cup (3 oz/90 g) fresh water chestnuts, peeled and minced

2 green (spring) onions, white and pale green parts, minced

1 tablespoon peeled and grated fresh ginger

1 clove garlic, minced

1 large egg, lightly beaten

1 tablespoon *each* light soy sauce, Chinese rice wine, and Asian sesame oil

1 tablespoon cornstarch (cornflour)

½ teaspoon sugar

⅛ teaspoon ground white pepper

30 square wonton wrappers

Cornstarch (cornflour) for dusting

Canola oil for deep-frying

Sweet-and-Sour Dipping Sauce (page 272) for serving

MAKES 30 WONTONS

Pork and Vegetable Pot Stickers

Known in Japan as *gyoza*, these panfried dumplings, filled with pork and vegetables, have become universal favorites, found everywhere from restaurant menus to the frozen-food section at the supermarket to international airports. Using purchased wonton wrappers makes preparing homemade pot stickers a simple matter of cooking the filling and pinching it into the wrappers to make the familiar half-moons. Frying them first in a little oil and then adding water to the pan produces moist, tender dumplings with crisp, golden bottoms.

To make the filling, place the mushrooms in a heatproof bowl with boiling water to cover, keeping them submerged with a lid or plate. Let soak for 30 minutes, then drain and trim off the tough stems and discard. Mince the caps and set aside. Meanwhile, in a large bowl, combine the cabbage and 1 teaspoon salt and toss to mix well. Let stand at room temperature for 20 minutes to allow the salt to draw the water out of the cabbage.

In another large bowl, combine the pork, green onions, ginger, garlic, soy sauce, mirin, sesame oil, cornstarch, and white pepper. Drain the cabbage and use your hands to squeeze out any remaining water. Add to the bowl with the pork mixture. Add the mushrooms. Using a rubber spatula, stir vigorously until the ingredients are well incorporated. Refrigerate the filling for 30 minutes.

To assemble the pot stickers, working with 1 wonton wrapper at a time, place it in the palm of your hand; keep the other wrappers covered with a slightly damp kitchen towel to prevent them from drying out. Put a heaping tablespoon of the filling in the center of the wrapper. Lightly brush the edges of the wrapper with water and fold the dough in half over the filling to form a half-moon. Use the thumb and index finger of your other hand to make 4 or 5 pleats along the round edge of the dumpling, pressing the pleats gently to seal. Gently flatten the bottom of the dumpling so that it sits upright when placed on a flat surface. Place the finished pot stickers on a baking sheet dusted with cornstarch.

In a large nonstick frying pan over medium heat, warm 1 tablespoon of the canola oil. When the oil is hot, add 8–10 pot stickers; do not overcrowd the pan. Cook until the bottoms of the pot stickers are golden brown, 1–2 minutes. Add ¼ cup (2 fl oz/60 ml) water to the pan, cover tightly, and steam until all the water has evaporated, and the pot stickers are tender but still firm, 5–7 minutes.

Wrap in aluminum foil to keep warm while you cook the remaining pot stickers. Transfer to a warmed platter and serve at once with the dipping sauce.

For the filling

8 dried shiitake mushrooms, rinsed

Boiling water as needed

3 cups (10 oz/315 g) minced napa cabbage

Salt

½ lb (250 g) ground (minced) pork

3 green (spring) onions, white and pale green parts, minced

1 tablespoon peeled and minced fresh ginger

2 cloves garlic, minced

1 tablespoon light soy sauce

1 tablespoon mirin

1 teaspoon Asian sesame oil

1 tablespoon cornstarch (cornflour)

⅛ teaspoon ground white pepper

30 round wonton wrappers

Cornstarch (cornflour) for dusting

4 tablespoons (2 fl oz/60 ml) canola oil, or as needed

Tamari-Sesame Dipping Sauce (page 272) for serving

MAKES 30 POT STICKERS

Barbecued Pork Buns

For the dough

1¼ cups (10 fl oz/310 ml) warm milk (110°F/43°C)

⅓ cup (3 oz/90 g) sugar

1 package (2½ teaspoons) active dry yeast

1 large egg, lightly beaten

4–4½ cups (20–22½ oz/ 625–700 g) all-purpose (plain) flour

1½ teaspoons salt

½ cup (4 oz/125 g) unsalted butter, at room temperature, in small pieces

6 tablespoons (3 oz/90 g) vegetable shortening, at room temperature, in small pieces

Canola oil for greasing

For the filling

1 tablespoon *each* light soy sauce and oyster sauce

1 teaspoon *each* tomato ketchup, dark soy sauce, and Asian sesame oil

1 tablespoon sugar

½ teaspoon cornstarch (cornflour)

⅛ teaspoon ground white pepper

½ lb (250 g) barbecued pork, cut into ¼-inch (6-mm) dice

1 large egg white, beaten with 1 teaspoon sugar

MAKES 8 BUNS

To make the dough, in a small bowl, whisk together the milk, sugar, yeast, and egg and let stand until frothy, about 10 minutes. Sift 4 cups (20 oz/625 g) of the flour and the salt into the bowl of a stand mixer fitted with the paddle. With the mixer on low speed, add the yeast mixture in a steady stream and beat just until the flour is moistened, 1–2 minutes. Slowly add the butter and shortening, beating just until each piece is incorporated before adding the next. On medium speed, beat the dough until it pulls away from the sides of the bowl, about 2 minutes. Replace the paddle with the dough hook and knead the dough on medium speed until smooth but still sticky, about 5 minutes. Add more flour, 1 tablespoon at a time, if needed for the dough to pull away from the sides of the bowl. Turn the dough out onto a lightly floured work surface and knead by hand until no longer sticky, about 1 minute. Transfer to a large, well-oiled bowl and turn to coat with the oil. Cover and place in a warm, draft-free place until doubled in size, about 1 hour.

To make the filling, in a large saucepan over medium heat, combine the light soy sauce, oyster sauce, ketchup, dark soy sauce, sesame oil, sugar, cornstarch, white pepper, and 2 tablespoons water. Cook, stirring constantly, until the sauce begins to bubble and thicken, about 3 minutes. Add the pork to the sauce and stir to mix well. Remove from the heat and let the filling cool to room temperature.

Again turn the dough out onto a lightly floured work surface and knead until smooth and elastic, about 5 minutes. Using your hands, roll the dough into a cylinder about 16 inches (40 cm) long, and cut into 8 equal pieces. Roll each piece into a ball and cover with a damp kitchen towel. Flatten each ball into a 5-inch (13-cm) disk with the center slightly thicker than the edges. Brush the edges with water and place 1 heaping tablespoon of the filling in the center. Pull the dough up and around the filling, pinching and twisting the edges together to enclose the filling. Turn and use your palms to form into a smooth bun about 3 inches (7.5 cm) in diameter and 2 inches (5 cm) thick. Place the buns 3 inches apart on a baking sheet lined with parchment (baking) paper. Cover with a kitchen towel and let rise in a warm, draft-free place until slightly puffy, about 1 hour.

Preheat the oven to 325°F (165°C). Brush each bun with the egg wash and bake until puffy and golden brown, 25–30 minutes. Let rest for 15 minutes. Serve warm or at room temperature.

These lightly sweet baked buns are filled with barbecued pork, or *char siu*, a rich Chinese version of roasted pork. Make your own barbecued pork (page 228) or purchase freshly roasted pork from a Chinese delicatessen, butcher, or grocery.

Shrimp and Vegetable Crepes

These savory crepes are made from dried mung beans softened in hot water and blended to a smooth purée with coconut milk. The addition of turmeric to the batter deepens the yellow hue of the crepes and gives them a touch of earthy, peppery flavor and a subtle scent of mustard. Crisp and slightly chewy, they are a popular snack made by street vendors in southern Vietnam, who fill each crepe with a mixture like this one of shrimp, mushrooms, and bean sprouts and serve it with fresh herbs, crisp lettuce leaves, and a flavorful sauce.

Place the mung beans in a heatproof bowl with boiling water to cover and let soak for 30 minutes. Drain the beans and place in a blender with the coconut milk, 1 ½ teaspoons of the sugar, and ½ teaspoon salt and blend to a smooth purée. Add the rice flour and turmeric and blend until smooth. Refrigerate the batter for at least 30 minutes or up to 2 hours.

In a bowl, whisk together the fish sauce, garlic, remaining ½ teaspoon sugar, and ⅛ teaspoon pepper until the sugar dissolves. Add the shrimp, toss to coat thoroughly, and let marinate at room temperature for 30 minutes. In a large frying pan over high heat, warm 2 tablespoons of the oil. Add the onion and sauté until golden brown, about 5 minutes. Add the mushrooms and sauté until they begin to wilt, about 5 minutes longer. Transfer the mushroom mixture to a bowl. Return the same frying pan to high heat. Add the shrimp with its marinade and 1 tablespoon of the oil. Cook, stirring, until the shrimp turns opaque, about 5 minutes. Return the mushroom mixture to the pan, add the bean sprouts, and sauté until heated through, about 1 minute.

In a small nonstick pan over medium heat, warm 1 tablespoon of the oil. When the oil is hot, pour ¼ cup (2 fl oz/60 ml) of the batter into the hot pan. Quickly swirl the batter to cover the bottom of the pan evenly. Cook until crisp and brown at the edges and set in the middle, 5–7 minutes. Using a wide spatula, slide the crepe, crisp side down, onto a warm plate. Spread one-sixth of the warm shrimp mixture onto one-half of the crepe. Carefully fold the other half of the crepe over the shrimp. Transfer to a plate. Repeat with the remaining batter and shrimp, adding 1 tablespoon oil to the pan for each crepe and making 6 crepes in all.

Arrange the lettuce and herbs on a platter or individual plates. Cut the crepes in half and instruct diners to wrap each half with lettuce, garnish with the fresh herbs, and drizzle with the dipping sauce.

½ cup (3½ oz/105 g) dried yellow mung beans

Boiling water as needed

1½ cups (12 fl oz/375 ml) coconut milk

2 teaspoons sugar

Salt and freshly ground pepper

½ cup (2½ oz/75 g) rice flour

½ teaspoon ground turmeric

2 tablespoons fish sauce

2 cloves garlic, minced

1 lb (500 g) medium shrimp (prawns), peeled, deveined, and chopped

9 tablespoons (5 fl oz/160 ml) canola oil, or as needed

1 small yellow onion, thinly sliced

8 fresh white mushrooms, stems removed and caps thinly sliced

2 cups (2 oz/60 g) mung bean sprouts

1 head red-leaf lettuce, separated into leaves, stems removed

½ cup (½ oz/15 g) *each* small fresh mint sprigs, cilantro (fresh coriander) sprigs, and Thai basil sprigs

Nuoc Cham Dipping Sauce (page 272) for serving

MAKES 6 CREPES

Pancakes with Vegetables and Pork

2 tablespoons dark soy sauce

2 tablespoons Worcestershire sauce

2 tablespoons tomato ketchup

1 teaspoon sugar

½ teaspoon cornstarch (cornflour)

1½ cups (7½ oz/235 g) all-purpose (plain) flour

½ teaspoon baking powder

½ teaspoon salt

5 large eggs

5 tablespoons (3 fl oz/80 ml) canola oil

1 yellow onion, thinly sliced

¼ lb (125 g) pork tenderloin, cut into strips 3 inches (7.5 cm) long by ⅛ inch (3 mm) wide

2 cups (6 oz/185 g) thinly sliced napa cabbage

MAKES 4 PANCAKES

In a small saucepan over medium heat, combine the soy sauce, Worcestershire sauce, ketchup, sugar, cornstarch, and ½ cup (4 fl oz/125 ml) water. Bring to a simmer and cook, whisking, until the sauce thickens, 1–2 minutes. Remove from the heat and set aside.

Sift together the flour, baking powder, and salt into a large bowl. In another bowl, beat together the eggs and ¼ cup (2 fl oz/60 ml) water. Pour the egg mixture into the dry ingredients and stir with a fork until well combined.

In a nonstick frying pan over medium heat, warm 1 tablespoon of the oil. Add the onion and sauté until tender and lightly browned, about 5 minutes. Add the pork and sauté just until the meat is no longer pink, about 2 minutes. Stir in the cabbage and ½ teaspoon salt and sauté just until the cabbage wilts, about 3 minutes. Transfer the cabbage mixture to a bowl.

Preheat the oven to 200°F (95°C). Return the same frying pan to medium heat and add 1 tablespoon of the oil. When the oil is very hot but not smoking, pour ½ cup (4 fl oz/125 ml) of the batter into the pan and quickly scatter one-fourth of the cabbage mixture on top of the batter. Fry until the crisp and brown at the edges and still slightly loose in the middle, about 5 minutes. Using a wide spatula, turn the pancake and cook until brown on the second side, about 5 minutes longer. Transfer to a baking sheet and keep warm in the oven while you repeat with the remaining batter and cabbage mixture, adding 1 tablespoon oil to the pan for each pancake and making 4 pancakes in all.

Place the pancakes on a warmed platter. Serve warm with the sauce.

A cross between an omelet and a pancake in consistency, these cakes are made by allowing a rich egg-based batter to cook up around the filling before the pancakes are turned and fried until golden and crisp. The batter and choice of toppings vary from region to region in Japan, but a thick, sweet, and salty sauce like the one here is a common accompaniment.

Noodles and Rice

About Noodles and Rice

Noodles and rice span the culinary spectrum, from humble breakfast bowls to bountiful platters presented at festivals. They are simmered, stir-fried, or steamed and served hot or cold. Their presence on the daily table defines the flavor, texture, and contours of Asian cuisines.

Every country in Asia boasts a distinctive cuisine, as expressed in its cooking styles, unique ingredients, and preferred flavors. But two foods are daily offerings on these singular national tables: noodles and rice. Not surprisingly, cooks in kitchens from Mumbai to Manila, Kyoto to Kuala Lumpur prepare these pantry staples differently to suit local tastes and traditions. Noodles vary in what they are made from—wheat, rice, mung bean, sweet potato, buckwheat. They also vary in the many ways they are served.

ONE-DISH MEALS

Noodle soups are a classic one-dish meal. In China in 300 BCE, when noodles were still enjoyed only by the nobility, poets wrote verses on the pleasures of a steaming bowl of the prized food.

Today, in many countries, noodle soups are frequently eaten at breakfast. Early in the morning, students with backpacks and men and women in business suits sit side by side slurping noodles. In Burma, fish-based *mohinga* (page 94) is the bowl of choice, and in Vietnam, beef-laced *pho* (page 99) starts the day. Noodle soups can be bold and complex, like Malaysia's coconut-and-curry-rich *laksa lemak* (page 98), or more subdued if no less filling, like Japan's chicken-and-vegetable *nabeyaki* udon (page 97), with each bowlful topped with an egg or even tempura.

Quick to make and eat, a plate of stir-fried noodles is a lunchtime standard throughout much of Asia. The noodles can be served with nothing but a fried egg, or they can feature roast duck and pork, mushrooms, or seafood. Wheat, egg, rice, and mung bean noodles all find their way into the pan. Resettled Chinese communities were the originators of such dishes as *pancit bihon* (rice vermicelli with chicken, Chinese sausage, and vegetables) in the Philippines (page 109), *mee goreng* (egg noodles with shrimp/prawns, chicken, and vegetables) in Singapore (page 103), and *pad Thai* (rice noodles with shrimp and mung beans) in Thailand (page 100). In the Koreas, *chapchae* (page 104) combines potato starch or mung bean noodles with beef, shiitake mushrooms, and greens such as spinach.

WARM-WEATHER DISHES

In hot months, chilled noodles provide a refreshing option. Japanese enjoy *hiyashi ramen* (wheat noodles with various toppings) or minimalist *zaru soba* (page 93), plain buckwheat noodles with a dipping sauce and simple garnishes. Vietnamese dig into rice-noodle salads flavored with fresh herbs, and Koreans cool down with *naengmyun*, noodles and crisp pear slices in an icy broth. Diners in Sichuan favor *dan dan mian* (page 107), wheat noodles topped with a spicy mixture of sesame paste, pork, soy sauce, ginger, and chili oil.

The best-known cold rice dishes of Asia are Japan's myriad sushi preparations, with the home-style *onigiri* (page 110) being a particular favorite for school lunch boxes. Traditionally formed into triangles by hand, *onigiri* marries short-grain rice and a savory filling such as tuna, salmon, or preserved plum. Modern cooks can select from a variety of creatively shaped molds for making *onigiri*.

RICE DISHES

Visitors to Asia will quickly discover that rice is most commonly served hot and plain as the foundation for a meal or as the base for other foods, such as the *donburi* (rice-bowl dishes) of Japan. But Asian cooks have numerous ways of dressing it up, too. In Southeast Asia, it is enriched with coconut milk and flavored with lemongrass (page 112), infused with the delicate nutty, grassy scent of pandanus, or tossed with handfuls of chopped, fresh dill, mint, and cilantro (coriander). Koreans may cook rice with a handful of peas, black or red beans, barley, sorghum, or other grains to add nutrients, color, and texture.

In India, cooks make *pullao* by sautéing the rice in ghee (clarified butter) and flavoring it with spices such as cumin, cinnamon, cloves, and cardamom, a technique adopted from Arab and Persian cooks. *Biryani* (page 116), also from the Persians, is made with basmati rice and richly marinated meats and appears at wedding feasts in India and Pakistan.

Leftover plain rice is never discarded. Instead, it is often transformed into fried rice, a catchall dish that can incorporate any number of meats and vegetables, though a few combinations have become classics. China's Yangzhou fried rice (page 113), with pork, shrimp, peas, and eggs, appears as the final course at banquets. In Indonesia and Malaysia, *nasi goreng* (page 115), which includes shrimp, chicken, and vegetables, helps start the day or fuels workers at lunchtime. Leftover rice also becomes *jook* or *congee*, a thick soup commonly eaten for breakfast or enjoyed as a late-night snack in southern China.

Chilled Soba Noodles with Dipping Sauce

Japanese soba noodles get their unique nutty flavor and tan hue from a combination of buckwheat and whole wheat (wholemeal) flours. Roughly as thick as spaghetti and toothsome in texture, the noodles are used in a variety of hot and cold dishes. This recipe is one of the most basic soba dishes, *zaru soba*, where the noodles are boiled, refreshed in cold water, and garnished with green onions, crumbled seaweed, and sesame seeds. Wasabi and a soy dipping sauce are the traditional accompaniments.

Bring a large saucepan three-fourths full of water to a boil over high heat. Stir in 1 teaspoon salt. Add the noodles and cook until tender, 2–3 minutes. Drain into a colander, rinse under cold running water, and drain again. Set aside.

To make the dipping sauce, in a small saucepan over low heat, combine the dashi, mirin, soy sauce, and sugar and bring to a simmer. Cook, stirring to dissolve the sugar, for 2 minutes. Add the bonito flakes and remove from the heat. Let the bonito flakes steep for 2 minutes and then strain the sauce through a fine-mesh sieve into a bowl. Discard the bonito flakes. Set the dipping sauce aside and let cool to room temperature.

Heat a small, dry frying pan over medium heat. Add the sesame seeds and toast, stirring occasionally, until golden brown, 4–5 minutes. Immediately transfer to a small plate and set aside.

Using your fingers, separate the noodles into individual strands and divide into 4 equal portions. Arrange a portion in a neat coil on each of 4 individual plates. Top with the green onions, crumbled seaweed, and sesame seeds. Serve at room temperature with the dipping sauce, daikon, and wasabi on the side.

Salt

½ lb (250 g) buckwheat soba noodles

For the dipping sauce

Scant ⅛ teaspoon granulated dashi mixed with ¾ cup (6 fl oz/180 ml) hot water

3 tablespoons mirin

2 tablespoons light soy sauce

1 teaspoon sugar

3 tablespoons bonito flakes

½ teaspoon sesame seeds

2 green (spring) onions, green parts only, thinly sliced on the diagonal

1 sheet toasted nori seaweed, crumbled

½ cup (4 oz/125 g) shredded daikon, gently squeezed dry

2 teaspoons prepared wasabi paste

MAKES 4 SERVINGS

Fish and Noodle Soup

2½ lb (1.25 kg) whole catfish

4 lemongrass stalks, tender midsections only

3 slices peeled fresh ginger, plus 2 tablespoons peeled and chopped fresh ginger

1 teaspoon ground turmeric

Salt and freshly ground pepper

3 tablespoons minced shallots

3 cloves garlic, chopped

1 tablespoon seeded and chopped jalapeño chile

1 teaspoon shrimp paste

10 oz (315 g) dried rice vermicelli

2 tablespoons canola oil

3 tablespoons fish sauce

1 tablespoon rice vinegar

2 tablespoons toasted rice powder (see note)

1 teaspoon sugar

½ cup (1½ oz/30 g) Fried Shallots (page 274)

3 hard-boiled eggs, peeled and cut into wedges

8 fresh cilantro (fresh coriander) sprigs

2 limes, cut into wedges

2 tablespoons chopped unsalted dry-roasted peanuts

MAKES 4–6 SERVINGS

Considered by many to be the national dish of Burma, this fish soup with rice vermicelli topped with an abundance of extras is available in most regions of the country, with street hawkers and roadside stalls selling piping-hot bowls to passers-by, most often for breakfast. Toasted rice powder is the local secret for both seasoning the soup with a mild roasted flavor and thickening the broth. Available commercially at most Asian markets, the pale tan powder can also be made by toasting white rice in a dry frying pan over medium-high heat, stirring often, until golden brown, then grinding the toasted rice into a fine powder in a spice grinder or coffee mill reserved for spices.

In a stockpot over medium heat, combine the catfish and 7 cups (56 fl oz/1.75 l) water. Add 3 of the lemongrass stalks, the ginger slices, ½ teaspoon of the turmeric, and 1 teaspoon salt and bring to a gentle boil. Reduce the heat to low and simmer for 20 minutes. Using tongs, transfer the catfish to a plate, remove the skin, and pull the flesh into bite-sized pieces. Discard the skin and bones. Set the fish aside. Strain the fish stock through a fine-mesh sieve into a large bowl.

Smash the remaining lemongrass stalk with the side of a chef's knife, then chop it and place in a mortar or mini food processor. Add the shallots, chopped ginger, garlic, chile, shrimp paste, remaining ½ teaspoon turmeric, ¼ teaspoon pepper, and 3 tablespoons water and process or grind with a pestle until a mostly smooth paste with some texture forms.

Place the noodles in a bowl and add water to cover. Let stand for 15 minutes. Drain the noodles and set aside.

Meanwhile, in a large saucepan over medium heat, warm the oil. Add the chile paste and cook, stirring often, until most of the water has evaporated and the paste is fragrant, about 2 minutes. Pour the fish stock into the pan. Stir in the fish sauce, vinegar, rice powder, and sugar and simmer for 10 minutes to blend the flavors.

Bring a saucepan three-fourths full of water to a boil. Add the noodles and cook until just tender, 1–2 minutes. Drain.

Arrange the Fried Shallots, eggs, cilantro sprigs, lime wedges, and peanuts on a platter or individual plates. Divide the noodles among warmed bowls. Arrange the fish pieces on top of the noodles, dividing them evenly, and ladle the hot broth over the top. Serve at once with the platter of accompaniments.

Udon with Chicken and Vegetables

¹/₈ teaspoon granulated dashi mixed with 1 cup (8 fl oz/ 250 ml) hot water

1 tablespoon mirin

1 tablespoon dark soy sauce

1 teaspoon sugar

¹/₂ teaspoon cornstarch (cornflour)

¹/₈ teaspoon ground white pepper

³/₄ lb (375 g) skinless, boneless chicken breasts, cut into 1-inch (2.5-cm) pieces

For the broth

³/₄ teaspoon granulated dashi mixed with 6 cups (48 fl oz/1.5 l) hot water

3 tablespoons dark soy sauce

2 tablespoons light soy sauce

2 tablespoons rice vinegar

Like Japanese soba noodles, udon noodles are often served chilled in the summer and hot in the winter, and toppings are chosen to reflect the seasons. In this recipe, they are served hot in a mildly flavored broth and are topped with chicken and spinach. Just before serving, an egg is cracked over the noodles and is cooked gently by the hot broth ladled on top. If you prefer, you can poach the eggs individually and carefully transfer them to the bowls. The udon may also be topped with vegetable tempura (page 177).

In a saucepan over high heat, combine the dashi, mirin, soy sauce, sugar, cornstarch, and white pepper and bring to a boil. Add the chicken pieces, reduce the heat to medium, and simmer, uncovered, until the chicken is opaque throughout, 10–12 minutes. Remove from the heat.

To make the broth, in a large saucepan over medium-high heat, combine the dashi, soy sauces, vinegar, sugar, and white pepper and bring to a boil. Reduce the heat to medium-low and simmer the broth for 5 minutes. Set aside and keep warm.

Bring a saucepan three-fourths full of water to a boil over high heat. Stir in 1 teaspoon salt. Add the noodles and cook until just tender, 2–3 minutes. Drain the noodles and divide among warmed bowls. Top each serving with one-fourth each of the warm chicken mixture and spinach. Crack an egg into each bowl and gently pour the hot broth over the top. Garnish with the green onions and a dusting of chili powder. Serve at once.

1 tablespoon sugar

¹/₈ teaspoon ground white pepper

Salt

1 lb (500 g) udon noodles or thick rice noodles

3 cups (3 oz/90 g) loosely packed spinach leaves, stemmed, cut into 2-inch (5-cm) strips, immersed in boiling water for 1 minute, drained, and squeezed dry

4 large eggs

4 green (spring) onions, white and pale green parts, thinly sliced on the diagonal

1 teaspoon chili powder

MAKES 4 SERVINGS

Coconut Curry Soup with Noodles and Seafood

2 tablespoons canola oil

Malaysian Chile Paste
(page 273)

3 cups (24 fl oz/750 ml)
coconut milk

¼ cup (2 fl oz/60 ml) fish
sauce

2 tablespoons *each* fresh lime
juice and chopped palm sugar

1 tablespoon tamarind paste

Salt

1 lb (500 g) fresh egg
noodles

½ lb (250 g) large shrimp
(prawns), peeled and
deveined

½ lb (250 g) cleaned squid
bodies, cut into rings ½ inch
(12 mm) wide

1 lb (500 g) mussels,
scrubbed and debearded

2 green (spring) onions

Omelet Garnish (page 273)

1 cup (1 oz/30 g) mung bean
sprouts

¼ cup (⅓ oz/10 g) *each*
fresh cilantro (fresh
coriander) and fresh Thai
basil sprigs

1 red Fresno or serrano chile,
seeded and thinly sliced

1 lime, cut into wedges

MAKES 4–6 SERVINGS

In a large saucepan over medium-high heat, warm the oil. Add the chile paste and sauté until fragrant, about 2 minutes. Add the coconut milk, fish sauce, lime juice, palm sugar, tamarind paste, and 2 cups (16 fl oz/500 ml) water and bring to a gentle boil. Cook for 2 minutes, then reduce the heat to low and simmer the soup until the flavors are blended, about 10 minutes longer.

Meanwhile, bring a large saucepan three-fourths full of water to a boil over high heat. Stir in 1 teaspoon salt. Add the noodles and cook until just tender, 2–3 minutes. Drain the noodles into a colander and divide them among warmed bowls. In the same pan, bring 4 cups (32 fl oz/1 l) water to a boil. Reduce the heat to low, add the shrimp, and cook until they just turn opaque, about 1 minute. Using a slotted spoon, transfer the shrimp to a large bowl. Add the squid to the same simmering water and cook until they turn opaque, about 1 minute. Transfer to the bowl with the shrimp. Add the mussels to the simmering water, discarding any that do not close to the touch. Cook just until the shells open, 2–3 minutes. Transfer the cooked mussels to the bowl of seafood, discarding any that failed to open. Discard the cooking liquid.

Just before serving, ready all of the garnishes: Thinly slice the green onions, including the pale green parts, on the diagonal. Place on the work surface along with the omelet, mung bean sprouts, cilantro and basil sprigs, chile slices, and lime wedges. Add all of the seafood to the simmering soup and cook just to heat through, about 3 minutes. Use tongs to top each bowl of noodles with a variety of seafood, and then ladle the hot soup over the seafood. Generously top each bowl with the garnishes. Serve at once.

This popular spicy noodle soup with seafood originates with the Peranakans, people of Chinese and Malay descent who reside primarily in Malaysia and Singapore. The rich coconut-curry broth is given body with fresh egg noodles, while the briny sweetness of the shellfish blends perfectly with the broth's citrus-spice notes. Like the many meal-worthy soups of the region, this one is served with a variety of flavorful and substantive toppings. To save time on the day you plan to serve the soup, make the chile paste a day in advance, cover, and refrigerate until ready to use.

Beef and Rice Noodle Soup

Dubbed the national soup of Vietnam, *pho* typically combines a clear beef broth, paper-thin slices of raw beef sirloin, shredded tender brisket, and sometimes beef tendon. The key to this simple soup is the preparation of the rich, deeply flavored broth, made by simmering roasted beef bones and onions and aromatic spices like clove and cinnamon. Ask your butcher to slice the sirloin paper-thin, or you can freeze it for 30 minutes to firm it up and thinly slice it yourself.

Pour the beef broth into a large stockpot and bring to a simmer over medium heat. Add the brisket and 1 tablespoon salt, cover partially, and cook until the brisket is very tender, about 2 hours. Adjust the heat as needed to maintain a simmer.

When the brisket is tender, using tongs or a slotted spoon, transfer the meat to a bowl, let cool, cover, and refrigerate until ready to serve. Stir the fish sauce, 1 tablespoon of the vinegar, the sugar, and the white pepper into the broth and simmer, uncovered, for 1 hour longer. Strain the broth through a large fine-mesh sieve into a clean pot or bowl. Discard the solids. Let the broth cool to room temperature, then refrigerate for at least 3 hours or up to overnight. Scrape the solidified fat from the surface of the broth and discard. Place the broth over medium heat and bring to a simmer. Shred the brisket and add to the broth. Taste and adjust the seasoning.

Place the noodles in a bowl and add water to cover. Let stand for 15 minutes. Drain the noodles and set aside.

Just before serving, bring a saucepan three-fourths full of water to a boil over high heat. Arrange the bean sprouts, chile slices, lime wedges, and basil sprigs on a platter. In a small bowl, stir together the yellow onion, green onions, cilantro, chile sauce, and remaining 1 tablespoon vinegar and set aside. Add the noodles to the boiling water and cook until just tender, 1–2 minutes. Drain and divide among warmed bowls. Top each serving with the raw beef slices, dividing them evenly, and about 1 tablespoon of the onion mixture. Ladle the hot broth into each bowl, using tongs if necessary to distribute the pieces of brisket. Serve at once with the platter of accompaniments and dipping sauce.

Roasted Beef Broth
(page 273)

1½ lb (750 g) beef brisket or chuck, trimmed and cut into 4-inch (10-cm) pieces

Salt

¼ cup (2 fl oz/60 ml) fish sauce

2 tablespoons rice vinegar

1 teaspoon sugar

½ teaspoon ground white pepper

14 oz (440 g) dried rice vermicelli

2 cups (2 oz/60 g) mung bean sprouts

2 jalapeño chiles, thinly sliced on the diagonal

2 limes, cut into wedges

8 fresh Thai basil sprigs

1 yellow onion, thinly sliced

3 green (spring) onions, thinly sliced on the diagonal

2 tablespoons chopped fresh cilantro (fresh coriander)

1 tablespoon Sriracha chile sauce

½ lb (250 g) beef sirloin, sliced paper-thin (see note)

Nuoc Cham Dipping Sauce
(page 272) for serving

MAKES 4–6 SERVINGS

Pad Thai

For the chile paste

2 red Fresno or serrano chiles, seeded and chopped

2 shallots, chopped

3 cloves garlic, chopped

½ lb (250 g) dried flat rice noodles, ¼ inch (6 mm) wide

2 tablespoons canola oil

¼ cup (2 fl oz/60 ml) fish sauce

3 tablespoons tamarind paste

2 tablespoons dark soy sauce

2 tablespoons chopped palm sugar

2 tablespoons fresh lime juice

½ lb (250 g) shrimp (prawns), peeled, deveined, and chopped

1¼ cups (1½ oz/45 g) mung bean sprouts

½ cup (4 fl oz/125 ml) low-sodium chicken broth

Omelet Garnish (page 273)

2 tablespoons chopped unsalted dry-roasted peanuts

1 tablespoon chopped fresh cilantro (fresh coriander)

MAKES 4–6 SERVINGS

To make the chile paste, in a mortar or mini food processor, combine the chiles, shallots, garlic, and 1 tablespoon water and process or grind with a pestle until a thick paste forms.

Place the noodles in a bowl and add water to cover. Let stand for 15 minutes. Drain the noodles and set aside.

In a large wok or frying pan over high heat, warm the oil. When the oil is hot, add the chile paste and sauté until fragrant, about 10 seconds. Stir in the fish sauce, tamarind paste, soy sauce, palm sugar, and lime juice. Add the shrimp and sauté just until they turn opaque, about 1 minute.

Add the noodles to the pan along with 1 cup (1 oz/30 g) of the bean sprouts and the broth. Bring to a boil, reduce the heat to low, cover, and cook, stirring the mixture 2 or 3 times, until most of the sauce has been absorbed, 5–7 minutes.

Transfer the noodles to a warmed platter. Top with the Omelet Garnish, remaining bean sprouts, peanuts, and cilantro. Serve at once.

Outside Thailand, *pad thai* is one of the best-known Thai dishes. Combining sweet, salty, and sour flavors, it is made with linguine-sized rice noodles cooked in a tangy sauce of fresh chile paste, fish sauce, palm sugar, and tamarind paste until the noodles absorb most of the sauce. Strips of cooked egg, bean sprouts, and chopped peanuts are among the traditional garnishes. For a variation, substitute strips of roasted chicken or pan-seared tofu cubes for the shrimp.

Egg Noodles with Shrimp, Chicken, and Vegetables

The cooking of Singapore is derived from the traditional cuisines of China, Malaysia, and India. Immigrants from these countries brought their styles of cooking to their new home kitchens and to the roadside food stalls known as "hawker centres." Hawker food is usually a one-dish meal or a snack that can be eaten throughout the day. This panfried egg noodle dish, a true representation of this Singaporean fast food, is essentially Chinese in origin with the accents of typical Malay seasoning: sweet soy sauce, fish sauce, and lime juice. *Choi sum*, Chinese flowering cabbage, is a sturdy green readily available at Chinese produce markets. If you are unable to find it, substitute Swiss chard or bok choy.

Bring a large saucepan three-fourths full of water to a boil over high heat. Stir in 1 teaspoon salt. Add the noodles and cook until just tender, about 2 minutes. Drain into a colander, rinse under cold running water, and drain again. Set aside.

Fill the same saucepan three-fourths full of water and bring to a boil. Add 1 teaspoon salt and the chicken and return to a boil. Reduce the heat to medium and simmer, uncovered, until the chicken is opaque throughout, 10–15 minutes. Using tongs, transfer the chicken to a plate to cool. Shred the chicken; set aside.

In a bowl, stir together the soy sauce, fish sauce, lime juice, ¼ teaspoon pepper, and ¼ cup (2 fl oz/60 ml) water to make a stir-fry sauce. Set the sauce aside.

In a large wok or frying pan over high heat, warm the oil. When the oil is hot, add the chicken and shrimp and cook just until the shrimp turns opaque, about 30 seconds. Stir in half of the green onions, the ginger, and the garlic and stir-fry until fragrant, about 1 minute. Stir in the eggs and let set for 2 minutes, then toss well to distribute. Add the *choi sum* and the sauce and bring to a boil. Separate the strands of the noodles and add to the pan. Toss and stir until most of the sauce has been absorbed and the noodles have plumped, 3–4 minutes.

Transfer the noodles to a warmed platter. Garnish with the bean sprouts, Fried Shallots, remaining green onions, and lime wedges. Serve at once.

Salt

½ lb (250 g) thin fresh egg noodles

¼ lb (125 g) skinless, boneless chicken thighs

3 tablespoons sweet soy sauce

1½ tablespoons fish sauce

1 tablespoon fresh lime juice

Freshly ground pepper

2 tablespoons canola oil

3 oz (90 g) medium shrimp (prawns), peeled, deveined, and chopped

2 green (spring) onions, white and pale green parts, thinly sliced on the diagonal

1 tablespoon peeled and minced fresh ginger

2 cloves garlic, minced

2 large eggs, lightly beaten

4 cups (4 oz/125 g) loosely packed *choi sum* or Swiss chard leaves, stemmed and cut into strips 2 inches (5 cm) wide

1 cup (1 oz/30 g) mung bean sprouts

½ cup (1½ oz/45 g) Fried Shallots (page 274)

1 lime, cut into wedges

MAKES 4–6 SERVINGS

Sweet Potato Starch Noodles with Vegetables and Beef

6 oz (185 g) dried sweet potato starch noodles, soaked in warm water for 15 minutes and drained

1 tablespoon tamari soy sauce, plus ¼ cup (2 fl oz/ 60 ml)

4 teaspoons Asian sesame oil

1¼ teaspoons sugar

½ lb (250 g) beef tenderloin, thinly sliced across the grain and cut into strips 1 inch (2.5 cm) long by ⅛ inch (3 mm) wide

3 tablespoons canola oil

1 large yellow onion, thinly sliced

1 small green bell pepper (capsicum), seeded and cut into strips ⅛ inch (3 mm) wide

1 large carrot, cut into matchsticks about 3 inches (7.5 cm) long

3 cloves garlic, minced

8 fresh shiitake mushrooms, stems removed and caps thinly sliced

2 cups (2 oz/60 g) loosely packed spinach leaves, stemmed and cut into strips 1 inch (2.5 cm) wide

1 tablespoon sesame seeds, toasted

MAKES 4–6 SERVINGS

Bring a saucepan three-fourths full of water to a boil. Add the noodles and cook until just tender, about 2 minutes. Drain in a colander, rinse under cold running water, and drain again. Set aside.

In a large nonreactive bowl, stir together the 1 tablespoon soy sauce, 1 teaspoon of the sesame oil, and ¼ teaspoon of the sugar. Add the tenderloin strips and toss to coat. Let marinate at room temperature for 15 minutes. In a small bowl, stir together the remaining ¼ cup soy sauce, the remaining 3 teaspoons sesame oil, and the remaining 1 teaspoon sugar. Set the sauce aside.

In a large wok or frying pan over high heat, warm 2 tablespoons of the canola oil. When the oil is hot, add the onion, bell pepper, carrot, and garlic and stir-fry until the vegetables are tender, 3–4 minutes. Add the mushrooms and stir-fry until the mushrooms begin to brown, 2–3 minutes. Transfer the vegetables to a bowl.

Wipe the pan clean, return to high heat, and add the remaining 1 tablespoon canola oil. When the oil is hot, add the beef and its marinade and stir-fry until it just begins to turn opaque, about 30 seconds. Using your fingers, separate the strands of noodles and add to the pan. Add the spinach and return the onion mixture to the pan. Pour in the sauce and stir-fry until most of the sauce has been absorbed and the noodles have plumped and are translucent, 3–4 minutes.

Transfer the noodles to a platter, garnish with the sesame seeds, and serve.

This Korean specialty is traditionally reserved for celebratory occasions. It uses sweet potato starch noodles, long, thin, translucent noodles with a chewy texture. If they are unavailable, substitute cellophane noodles, which have a similar texture. Cutting the beef and vegetables into thin, uniform strips not only helps them cook quickly and evenly, but also looks attractive on the plate.

Braised Shanghai Egg Noodles with Pork

¹/₄ teaspoon baking soda (bicarbonate of soda)

Salt

¹/₂ lb (250 g) pork loin, cut into thin strips 4 inches (10 cm) long by ¹/₈ inch (3 mm) wide

8 dried shiitake mushrooms, rinsed

Boiling water

¹/₃ cup (3 fl oz/80 ml) low-sodium chicken broth

3 tablespoons dark soy sauce

2 tablespoons *each* light soy sauce and black vinegar

1 teaspoon sugar

¹/₄ teaspoon ground white pepper

³/₄ lb (375 g) fresh thick, round egg noodles or udon

¹/₄ head napa cabbage

¹/₂ cup (4 oz/125 g) pickled cabbage (see note)

3 tablespoons canola oil

1 yellow onion, thinly sliced

1 red bell pepper (capsicum), seeded and cut into strips 4 inches (10 cm) long by ¹/₈ inch (3 mm) wide

1 tablespoon peeled and minced fresh ginger

2 cloves garlic, minced

MAKES 4–6 SERVINGS

In a nonreactive bowl, stir together the baking soda, ¹/₄ teaspoon salt, and 1 tablespoon water. Add the pork and toss to coat. Let stand at room temperature for 30 minutes. Rinse the mushrooms, place in a heatproof bowl, and add boiling water to cover, keeping them submerged with a lid or plate. Let soak for 15 minutes, then drain and trim off the tough stems and discard. Thinly slice the caps and set aside.

In a small bowl, stir together the broth, soy sauces, vinegar, sugar, and white pepper to make a stir-fry sauce. Set the sauce aside.

Bring a saucepan three-fourths full of water to a boil. Add 1 teaspoon salt and the noodles and cook until the noodles are tender with a little bite, about 2 minutes. Drain in a colander, rinse under cold running water, and drain again. Set aside.

Cut the napa cabbage into ribbons about ¹/₈ inch (3 mm) wide. Rinse and drain the pickled cabbage, then cut into strips ¹/₈ inch wide. Set aside.

In a large wok or frying pan over high heat, warm 2 tablespoons of the oil. Add the onion and bell pepper and sauté until just tender, about 2 minutes. Add the mushrooms and sauté until brown on the edges, about 2 minutes longer. Transfer the mushroom mixture to a bowl. Return the pan to high heat and add the remaining 1 tablespoon oil. Add the pork, ginger, and garlic and stir-fry just until the meat turns opaque, about 2 minutes. Return the mushroom mixture to the pan, add the fresh and pickled cabbage, and stir-fry for 1 minute.

Stir in the sauce and bring to a boil. Using your fingers, separate the strands of noodles, and add to the pan. Stir-fry the noodles with the pork, vegetables, and sauce until well combined. Reduce the heat to low, cover, and cook until most of the sauce has been absorbed and the noodles have plumped, about 15 minutes. Transfer to a warmed serving bowl or individual bowls and serve at once.

This braised noodle dish has two signature ingredients from eastern China: Shanghai noodles, which are thick, round egg noodles with a slightly chewy texture, and sour, crunchy pickled cabbage. Tender pork loin and earthy shiitakes are stir-fried before a salty-sweet sauce goes into the pan to flavor the cooked noodles. Look for pickled napa cabbage in the produce section of Asian markets. You can also use other pickled vegetables such as mustard greens.

Noodles with Pork and Sesame Sauce

In this classic dish from Sichuan Province, egg noodles are combined with a spicy pork and sesame sauce. It is called *dan dan mian* and is named after the bamboo shoulder pole (*dan dan*) used by street vendors to carry the makings for the dish. Rich and creamy toasted sesame paste gives this dish its distinct Sichuan flavor. The Sichuan preserved vegetable, which is mustard green root pickled with salt, chiles, and garlic and then fermented, is sold in cans and crocks in Chinese markets. For a spicier dish, add more soybean paste or more chili oil.

Bring a large saucepan three-fourths full of water to a boil over high heat. Stir in 1 teaspoon salt. Add the noodles and cook until just tender, 2–3 minutes for fresh noodles, 3–5 minutes for dried noodles. Ladle 1 cup (8 fl oz/250 ml) of the cooking water into a bowl and reserve. Drain the noodles and place in a large bowl. Pour the cooking water over the noodles and toss to coat well. Set aside.

In a small bowl, stir together the broth, soy sauces, sesame paste, soybean paste, vinegar, chili oil, and sugar. Set the broth mixture aside.

In a large frying pan over high heat, warm the canola oil. Add the pork, green onions, ginger, and garlic and sauté, using a wooden spoon to break up the meat, until the meat just turns opaque, about 2 minutes. Pour in the broth mixture and simmer the meat sauce for 10 minutes to blend the flavors.

Meanwhile, to make the topping, rinse the preserved vegetable and then drain and mince. In a small frying pan over medium heat, warm the oil. Add the green onions and sauté until fragrant, about 30 seconds. Stir in the peanuts and preserved vegetable and cook until crisp, about 1 minute. Remove from the heat.

Separate the strands of the noodles and divide among warmed bowls. Spoon the hot meat sauce over the noodles and sprinkle with the topping. Serve at once.

Salt

1 lb (500 g) fresh or ¾ lb (375 g) dried thin round Chinese egg noodles

1½ cups (12 fl oz/375 ml) low-sodium chicken broth

3 tablespoons light soy sauce

2 tablespoons dark soy sauce

3 tablespoons toasted sesame paste

1 tablespoon soybean paste

1 tablespoon rice vinegar

1 tablespoon chili oil

1 teaspoon sugar

2 tablespoons canola oil

½ lb (250 g) ground (minced) pork

2 green (spring) onions, white parts only, minced

2 tablespoons peeled and minced fresh ginger

4 cloves garlic, minced

For the topping

2 tablespoons Sichuan preserved vegetable

1 tablespoon canola oil

2 green (spring) onions, white and pale green parts, minced

¼ cup (1½ oz/45 g) minced unsalted dry-roasted peanuts

MAKES 4–6 SERVINGS

Stir-fried Rice Vermicelli

Stir-fried noodles are second in popularity to rice in the Philippines. Eaten as part of a meal or as a snack, this classic noodle stir-fry has seemingly endless variations. Here, a small amount of mildly sweet cured pork sausage, a specialty of southern China, where it is known as *lop cheong*, creates a chewy, smoky foundation for fine pieces of chicken and shrimp. Look for it in Chinese and other Asian markets. The vegetables are shredded or thinly sliced to match the delicate structure of the noodles. Substitute Chinese barbecued pork (page 228) or shredded roast chicken if the Chinese sausage is unavailable.

Bring a saucepan three-fourths full of water to a boil. Add 1 teaspoon salt and the chicken and return to a boil. Reduce the heat to medium and simmer, uncovered, until the chicken is opaque throughout, 10–15 minutes. Using tongs, transfer the chicken to a plate to cool. Shred the chicken and set aside.

Meanwhile, place the sausages in a small saucepan with water to cover. Bring to a boil, then reduce the heat to low and simmer the sausages for 5 minutes to render the fat. Drain and let cool. Cut the sausages on the diagonal into slices 1/8 inch (3 mm) thick and set aside.

In a small bowl, stir together the broth, fish sauce, soy sauces, and sugar to make a stir-fry sauce. Set the sauce aside.

Heat a large wok or frying pan over high heat until very hot. Add the sausage slices to the hot pan and stir-fry until crisp and brown on the edges, about 1 minute. Add the shrimp and stir-fry until the shrimp just turn opaque, about 30 seconds. Transfer the sausage slices and shrimp to a bowl. Return the pan to high heat and add 1 tablespoon of the oil. When the oil is hot, add the ginger, garlic, onion, and carrot and stir-fry until just tender, about 2 minutes. Transfer the vegetables to the bowl with the sausage and shrimp.

Wipe the pan clean, return it to high heat, and add the remaining 1 tablespoon oil. When the oil is hot, add the noodles and stir-fry until they begin to dry, 2–3 minutes. Return the vegetables, sausages, and shrimp to the pan, add the cabbage and chicken, and stir-fry until the cabbage begins to wilt and the chicken is heated through, about 5 minutes. Pour in the sauce and stir-fry until most of the sauce has been absorbed, and the noodles have plumped and are translucent, 3–4 minutes.

Transfer the noodles to a warmed platter or bowl and garnish with the green onions. Serve at once, passing the lemon wedges at the table.

Salt

1/4 lb (125 g) skinless, boneless chicken thighs

1/4 lb (125 g) Chinese sausages (see note)

3/4 cup (6 fl oz/180 ml) low-sodium chicken broth

3 tablespoons fish sauce

2 tablespoons dark soy sauce

1 tablespoon soy sauce

1 teaspoon sugar

1/4 lb (125 g) medium shrimp (prawns), peeled, deveined, and chopped

2 tablespoons canola oil

1 tablespoon peeled and minced fresh ginger

2 cloves garlic, minced

1 small yellow onion, thinly sliced

1 large carrot, cut into matchsticks about 3 inches (7.5 cm) long

12 oz (375 g) dried rice vermicelli, soaked in warm water for 15 minutes and drained

2 cups (6 oz/185 g) shredded napa cabbage

2 green (spring) onions, thinly sliced on the diagonal

1 lemon, cut into wedges

MAKES 4–6 SERVINGS

Rice Filled with Salmon and Pickled Plum

1½ cups (10½ oz/330 g) short-grain rice

Salt

1 sheet toasted nori seaweed (optional)

1 teaspoon canola oil

3 oz (90 g) salmon fillet

3 pickled plums

¼ cup (½ oz/15 g) packed bonito flakes

1 tablespoon dark soy sauce

1 tablespoon sesame seeds (optional)

MAKES 12 RICE TRIANGLES OR BALLS

Onigiri is a snack of cooked short-grain rice formed into triangular or oval shapes and often wrapped in toasted seaweed. Traditionally, the rice shapes are filled with salty or sour ingredients, such as the Japanese pickled plum known as *umeboshi*, cooked salmon, or soy sauce mixed with *katsuobushi*, or bonito flakes. One of the most popular snacks in Japan, *onigiri* is not a form of sushi, but a way of making rice portable and easy to eat, and most convenience stores in Japan stock the snack in many popular fillings.

Place the rice in a large fine-mesh sieve and rinse under cold running water until the water runs clear. In a large saucepan over medium-high heat, combine the rice, 3 cups (24 fl oz/750 ml) water, and 1 teaspoon salt and bring to a boil. Reduce the heat to low, cover, and simmer until the rice is tender and all the water has been absorbed, about 20 minutes. Remove from the heat and let the rice rest, covered, for 10 minutes. Transfer the rice to a bowl.

Meanwhile, if making rice triangles, cut the toasted nori into strips 1 inch (2.5 cm) wide. Set aside.

In a frying pan over medium-high heat, warm the oil. Add the salmon and sprinkle with 1 teaspoon salt. Cook, turning once, until opaque throughout, about 4 minutes total. Transfer to a plate and let cool. Using a fork or your fingers, separate the salmon into flakes, discarding any skin or errant bones.

Put the flaked salmon in a small bowl. Remove the pits from the pickled plums and discard. Mince the plums and put them in another small bowl. In a third small bowl, stir together the bonito flakes and soy sauce.

If using the sesame seeds, heat a small, dry frying pan over medium heat. Add the sesame seeds and toast, stirring occasionally, until golden brown, 4–5 minutes. Immediately transfer to a small plate and set aside. In a medium bowl, stir together 1 cup (8 fl oz/250 ml) warm water and 1 teaspoon salt.

To make filled rice triangles, dampen your hands with the salted water and spoon ½ cup (2½ oz/75 g) unpacked rice into the palm of your hand. Keep the rice in the bowl covered with a damp towel to prevent it from drying out. (Do not refrigerate the rice.) Flatten the rice in your palm into a disk and use your thumb to create a small depression in the center. Place about 1 teaspoon of the salmon in the depression and shape the rice into a triangle ½ inch (12 mm) thick with

3-inch (7.5-cm) sides. Pass the rice triangle back and forth between your cupped hands, pressing just hard enough to make the rice hold together.

Shape the remaining rice to make a total of 12 triangles, filling 4 triangles with the salmon, 4 with the plums, and 4 with the bonito flakes. Wrap a nori strip around the edges of the triangles and moisten the ends with water to seal. Use your fingers to fill any gaps gently with rice.

To make filled rice balls, dampen your hands with the salted water and spoon $1/2$ cup unpacked rice into the palm of your hand. Flatten the rice in your palm into a disk and use your thumb to create a small depression in the center. Place about 1 teaspoon of filling in the depression. Shape the rice into a ball, passing it back and forth between your cupped hands and pressing the rice just hard enough so it holds together. Sprinkle the tops of the balls with the toasted sesame seeds, if using, dividing them evenly.

Arrange the triangles or balls of rice on a platter or individual plates and serve at room temperature.

Lemongrass and Coconut Jasmine Rice

2 cups (14 oz/440 g) jasmine rice

1 tablespoon canola oil

1 large shallot, minced

1 teaspoon peeled and minced fresh ginger

1 cup (8 fl oz/250 ml) coconut milk

Salt

3 lemongrass stalks, tender midsections only

MAKES 4–6 SERVINGS

Place the rice in a fine-mesh sieve and rinse well under cold running water until the water runs clear. Set aside.

In a large saucepan over medium-high heat, warm the oil. Add the shallot and ginger and sauté until fragrant, about 30 seconds. Add the rice to the pan and stir to mix well.

Add 1 1/4 cups (10 fl oz/310 ml) water, the coconut milk, and 1 teaspoon salt and bring to a boil. Reduce the heat to low. Smash the lemongrass with the side of a chef's knife and stir into the rice. Cover and simmer for 20 minutes.

Remove the pan from the heat and continue to let the rice steam, covered, until tender, about 10 minutes longer. Discard the lemongrass stalks and fluff the rice with a fork. Transfer the rice to a warmed bowl and serve hot.

This simple rice preparation, made with softly nutty, fragrant jasmine rice, combines the refreshing scent of lemongrass with a hint of ginger and the sweet creaminess of coconut milk.

Fried Rice with Pork and Shrimp

3 tablespoons canola oil

¼ lb (125 g) medium shrimp (prawns), peeled, deveined, and chopped

¼ lb (125 g) Roast Pork (page 228), diced

4 green (spring) onions, white and pale green parts, thinly sliced on the diagonal

1 tablespoon peeled and minced fresh ginger

2 cloves garlic, minced

1 tablespoon rice wine

Among the many recipes for Chinese fried rice, this is one of the best-known versions of Yangzhou fried rice, named for the city where it originated. The dish is distinguished by the generous proportions of shrimp, eggs, and barbecued pork.

In a large wok over high heat, warm 2 tablespoons of the oil. Add the shrimp and pork and sauté until the shrimp just turns opaque, about 1 minute. Add the green onions, ginger, and garlic and stir-fry for several seconds. Pour in the rice wine, quickly toss, and transfer to a bowl.

In a bowl, combine the broth, soy sauce, sugar, and white pepper. Wipe the wok clean, return to high heat, and add the remaining 1 tablespoon oil. Add the rice and stir-fry until heated through, 3 minutes. Make a deep well in the center, pour in the eggs, and let cook just until set, about 1 minute. Return the shrimp and pork to the pan along with the peas and toss. Pour in the broth mixture and stir-fry until absorbed, about 2 minutes. Transfer to a warmed bowl and serve hot.

3 tablespoons reduced-sodium chicken broth

1 tablespoon light soy sauce

¼ teaspoon sugar

¼ teaspoon ground white pepper

3 cups (15 oz/470 g) cold cooked long-grain rice (page 274)

2 large eggs, lightly beaten

½ cup (2½ oz/75 g) fresh or thawed frozen English peas

MAKES 4–6 SERVINGS

Fried Rice with Chicken, Shrimp, and Vegetables

Originating in Malaysia and Indonesia, *nasi goreng* is essentially a template for the most familiar style of fried rice, and is treated to infinite variations and accompaniments. It is eaten at any time of day—it is a popular breakfast—and is often made from rice and other leftovers from the previous day's dinner. To prevent the rice from sticking when it is stir-fried, steam it ahead of time, spread it out on a baking sheet, and let it cool completely. Serve the fried rice with chicken *satay* (page 44) or fried chicken (page 213).

To make the chile paste, in a mortar or mini food processor, combine the chiles, shallots, galangal, garlic, shrimp paste, and 2 tablespoons water and process or grind with a pestle until a smooth paste forms. Set aside.

Bring a saucepan three-fourths full of water to a boil. Add 1 teaspoon salt and the chicken and return to a boil. Reduce the heat to medium and simmer, uncovered, until the chicken is opaque throughout, 10–15 minutes. Using tongs, transfer the chicken to a plate to cool. Shred the chicken and set aside.

In a large wok or frying pan over high heat, warm 2 tablespoons of the oil. Add the chile paste and sauté until fragrant, about 10 seconds. Stir in the cabbage and carrots and sauté until the cabbage begins to wilt, about 3 minutes. Add the shrimp and chicken and sauté until the shrimp just turns opaque, about 1 minute. Transfer the cabbage mixture to a bowl.

In a small bowl, combine the soy sauce, fish sauce, and lime juice. Wipe the pan clean, return to high heat, and add the remaining 1 tablespoon oil. When the oil is hot, add the eggs and scramble until just set. Add the rice and stir-fry for 1 minute, using a spatula to break up any large chunks of rice. Stir in the peas, return the shrimp mixture to the pan, and stir-fry until the rice is heated through, about 5 minutes. Pour in the soy sauce mixture and toss and stir until the rice absorbs the sauce, about 3 minutes longer. Transfer the rice to warmed individual bowls and garnish with the Fried Shallots. Serve at once.

For the chile paste

2 red Fresno chiles, seeded and chopped

3 shallots, chopped

1 tablespoon peeled and chopped fresh galangal

3 cloves garlic, chopped

1 teaspoon shrimp paste

Salt

¼ lb (125 g) skinless, boneless chicken breast

3 tablespoons canola oil

½ small head napa cabbage, trimmed, cored, and cut into ½-inch (12-mm) dice

2 carrots, cut into ¼-inch (6-mm) dice

¼ lb (125 g) medium shrimp (prawns), peeled, deveined, and chopped

2 tablespoons sweet soy sauce

1½ tablespoons fish sauce

1 tablespoon fresh lime juice

3 large eggs, lightly beaten

2½ cups (12½ oz/390 g) cold cooked long-grain rice (page 274)

⅓ cup (1½ oz/45 g) fresh or thawed frozen English peas

¼ cup (1 oz/30 g) Fried Shallots (page 274)

MAKES 4–6 SERVINGS

Chicken and Basmati Rice

1½ teaspoons ground cumin

1 teaspoon *each* ground coriander and ground turmeric

½ teaspoon ground cinnamon

¼ teaspoon *each* ground cardamom and nutmeg

⅛ teaspoon cayenne pepper

4 star anise

3 bay leaves

2 large yellow onions, plus 1 small yellow onion

4 tablespoons (2 oz/60 g) ghee

5 cloves garlic, chopped

2 tablespoons peeled and chopped fresh ginger

1 jalapeño chile, seeded and chopped

1 lb (500 g) skinless, boneless chicken thighs

Salt

½ cup (4 oz/125 g) plain whole-milk yogurt

3 tablespoons lemon juice

1½ cups (10½ oz/330 g) basmati rice

¼ cup (1½ oz/45 g) cashews

2 hard-boiled eggs

¼ cup (⅓ oz/10 g) chopped fresh cilantro (fresh coriander)

¼ cup (1½ oz/45 g) raisins

MAKES 6 SERVINGS

In a small bowl, stir together the cumin, coriander, turmeric, cinnamon, cardamom, nutmeg, cayenne, star anise, and bay leaves. Set the spice mixture aside.

Thinly slice the large onions. Chop the small onion and set aside.

In a Dutch oven or large, ovenproof frying pan over medium heat, warm 2 tablespoons of the ghee. Add the sliced onions to the pan, and cook, stirring often, until golden brown, 15–20 minutes. Transfer to a bowl and set aside.

Meanwhile, in a mortar or mini food processor, combine the chopped onion, garlic, ginger, and chile and process or grind with a pestle until a thick paste forms.

Cut the chicken into ½-inch (12-mm) dice. Place the pot over high heat and add 1 tablespoon of the ghee. Sprinkle the diced chicken with ¼ teaspoon salt and arrange in the pot in a single layer. Sear, turning as needed, until golden brown on all sides, about 5 minutes total. Transfer to a bowl and set aside.

Return the pot to medium heat and warm the remaining 1 tablespoon ghee. Add the onion-garlic paste and sauté until golden brown, about 5 minutes. Add the spice mixture and sauté until fragrant, about 1 minute. Add the caramelized onions, reserving about ⅓ cup (2 oz/60 g) for garnish. Stir in the yogurt, the lemon juice, and ¼ cup (2 fl oz/60 ml) water. Reduce the heat to low, add the seared chicken, and simmer for 2 minutes.

Preheat the oven to 350°F (180°C). Add the rice to the simmering liquid in the pot and stir until well coated. Pour in 2 cups (16 fl oz/500 ml) water, raise the heat to medium, and bring to a boil. Cover the pot and transfer to the oven. Bake for 30 minutes. Remove from the oven and let rest, covered, for 10 minutes.

Spread the cashews in a single layer on a baking sheet. Toast in the oven, stirring occasionally, until the nuts are golden and fragrant, about 10 minutes. Remove from the oven and transfer to a plate to cool. Chop the nuts.

Fluff the rice with a fork and transfer the chicken and rice to a warmed platter. Cut the eggs into wedges. Garnish with the reserved caramelized onions, cashews, egg wedges, cilantro, and raisins. Serve at once.

Introduced throughout the Middle East and South Asia by Muslim travelers and merchants and very popular in India, Pakistan, and Bangladesh, *biryani* is an elaborate rice dish made with basmati rice, meat, vegetables, and yogurt and is served with a variety of garnishes. A mixture of sweet and earthy spices imparts rich color and flavor to the dish. Diced beef, lamb, or shrimp (prawns) may be substituted for the chicken, or a vegetarian version can be prepared by replacing the chicken with diced vegetables such as carrots, green beans, cauliflower, and peas.

Salads, Vegetables, and Tofu

About Salads, Vegetables, and Tofu

Seasonal greens and other vegetables are a hallmark of the Asian table. No meal is complete without a colorful stir-fry, crisp salad, or full-bodied curry made from freshly harvested produce. Vegetables also co-star with legumes and tofu in time-honored meat-free cuisines.

At the central market in Kota Bharu in Malaysia, with its octagonal floors overlooking a sun-filled atrium, women sit on raised platforms selling large bunches of *kangkong* (water spinach), tapering bamboo shoots, ribbonlike pods of *petai* beans, tiny white eggplants (aubergines), jungle ferns, and pale, green, bumpy-skinned bitter melon. Similar scenes occur throughout Asia, at small neighborhood stalls in the most remote regions and at sprawling central markets in every country's capital.

BRIGHT-FLAVORED SALADS

Many of the vegetables and fruits that fill markets in tropical Southeast Asia are used raw in cooling, refreshing salads. Composed on platters for diners to mix themselves or served lightly tossed, they combine crisp textures, vivid colors, fragrant herbs, and hints of sourness and spiciness.

Two popular versions that cross borders are Pomelo Salad (page 124), which marries the ancestor of the grapefruit with coconut, and Green Papaya Salad (page 123), which uses thin shreds of the still-green fruit, combining them with shredded carrot, fresh chile, and a pungent dressing that blends fish sauce, lime juice, and chile sauce.

Dark greens like watercress, water spinach, and the nutritious leaves of taro, sweet potato, bitter melon, and a host of other locally grown plants appear in wilted salads topped with tomato wedges, hard-boiled egg slices, or toasted nuts.

Koreans favor simple salads offered among the side dishes at meals, such as mung bean sprouts blanched briefly to preserve their crunchy texture and tossed with a sesame oil–rice vinegar dressing (page 128).

Perhaps the most distinctive salads are the carefully composed *thoke* of Burma. Served to just-arrived guests or at the end of a meal to refresh the palate and aid digestion, the arrangement of finely chopped ingredients might include fried garlic, dried shrimp (prawns), roasted peanuts, toasted sesame seeds, lime zest, and pickled ginger or fermented tea leaves, known as *lephet* (page 133). Guests choose their favorite flavors and mix their own servings. Eaten in small bites, these bright-tasting mixtures encourage long conversation into the night.

A WEALTH OF VEGETABLES

Bright flavors also characterize the wide array of dishes eaten by the many Hindus, Sikhs, and Jains who follow strict vegetarian diets. Along with such familiar vegetables as potatoes, cauliflower, eggplants, okra, bitter melon, pumpkin, and green beans, South Asians, vegetarian and nonvegetarian alike, enjoy a multitude of local produce like drumstick, banana stem, and angled squash. Dried beans, lentils, and peas provide valuable protein in soups, curries, and pilafs. A popular dish found across the subcontinent is *channa masala* (page 145), a hearty mixture of chickpeas (garbanzos), tomatoes, and spices, including cumin, corriander, and turmeric.

In China, vegetables such as eggplant (page 154), pea sprouts, bok choy (page 150), spinach, watercress, long beans, and cabbage are stir-fried to help preserve their nutrients and texture. Japanese cooks prepare rustic braises with daikon and *kabocha* squash (page 141) in wintertime and lightly cooked vegetables topped with sesame seeds and miso (page 151) in the summer months.

VERSATILE TOFU

Many of these vegetables are often paired with tofu, which has been central to the cuisines of East and Southeast Asia for nearly two thousand years. Itinerant Chinese monks were the first to spread simple recipes using tofu, and local cooks quickly adopted the versatile ingredient, adding it to a variety of soups, braises, and stir-fries.

Making tofu is similar to making fresh cheese: a natural coagulant is stirred into warm soy milk, creating curds that are then drained and formed into blocks. The longer tofu is pressed, the drier and firmer it becomes.

Japanese-style silken tofu retains much of its moisture and has a custardlike texture. In Japan, cooks float tiny cubes of it in miso soup, deep-fry larger pieces to make golden brown *agedashi dofu*, and top chilled slices with green (spring) onions, bonito flakes, and a drizzle of soy. The firmer texture of Chinese-style tofu holds up better to stir-frying and more readily absorbs flavors, whether delicate broths or the intense spices of *mapo doufu* (page 160), a specialty of Sichuan Province.

In Vietnam, tofu is stir-fried with generous amounts of two popular local ingredients, lemongrass and ginger (page 156), and in the Koreas, it is stuffed with a richly seasoned meat mixture, panfried, and served with a chile-soy dipping sauce.

Green Papaya Salad

This refreshing salad is a mainstay on the tables of Laos and its neighbors. Tangy and at once sweet and savory, it complements grilled or deep-fried meat, poultry, or seafood and is usually served with sticky rice (page 274). Green papayas, which are the unripe fruit, have firm, dark green skin and light green flesh, and are available in most Asian markets. The more familiar jicama, which has a similar sweet flavor and crunchy texture, can be substituted.

Using a vegetable peeler, peel the papaya. Cut the papaya in half lengthwise and then scoop out and discard the seeds. Using the largest holes on a grater-shredder or a mandoline, and holding each papaya half lengthwise, shred the flesh into long, thin strips. Peel the carrot and shred into long, thin strips.

In a large bowl, combine the papaya, carrot, sliced shallots, chile, and cilantro and toss gently to mix well.

In a mini food processor or mortar, combine the chopped shallot, garlic, and sugar and process or grind with a pestle until a smooth paste forms. Add 1–2 teaspoons water if needed to facilitate the grinding. Transfer the garlic paste to a bowl and whisk in the vinegar, fish sauce, lime juice, and chile sauce. Gradually drizzle in the oil while continuing to whisk.

Pour the dressing over the papaya mixture and toss to coat thoroughly. Refrigerate for at least 2 hours or up to overnight before serving.

1 large green papaya,
about 1½ lb (750 g)

1 carrot

4 shallots, thinly sliced, plus
1 tablespoon chopped

1 red Fresno chile, cut into
thin rings and seeded

2 tablespoons chopped fresh
cilantro (fresh coriander)

2 cloves garlic, chopped

1 teaspoon sugar

¼ cup (2 fl oz/60 ml) *each*
rice vinegar and fish sauce

2 tablespoons *each* **fresh lime**
juice and Sriracha chile sauce

3 tablespoons canola oil

MAKES 4–6 SERVINGS

Pomelo Salad

For the dressing

4 cloves garlic, minced

2 tablespoons minced fresh cilantro (fresh coriander) stems

Freshly ground pepper

3 tablespoons fish sauce

2 tablespoons fresh lime juice

1 tablespoon rice vinegar

4½ teaspoons chopped palm sugar

1 tablespoon canola oil

2 tablespoons unsweetened shredded coconut

2 pomelos or 4 grapefruits, about 3 lb (1.5 kg) total weight

2 shallots, thinly sliced

1 serrano chile, seeded and thinly sliced on the diagonal

½ cup (½ oz/15 g) packed fresh mint leaves, thinly sliced

1 tablespoon chopped unsalted dry-roasted peanuts

1 small head red-leaf or Bibb lettuce, separated into leaves, stems removed

MAKES 4–6 SERVINGS

To make the dressing, in a mini food processor or mortar, combine the garlic, cilantro, ½ teaspoon pepper, and 1 tablespoon water and process or grind with a pestle until a smooth paste forms. Transfer the garlic paste to a bowl and whisk in the fish sauce, lime juice, vinegar, palm sugar, and oil. Set the dressing aside.

Put the coconut in a small, dry frying pan over medium heat. Cook, stirring often, until lightly toasted, about 5 minutes. Immediately pour onto a plate to cool.

Using a sharp knife and working on a cutting board, cut a slice off both ends of each pomelo to reveal the flesh. Stand the pomelo on a cut side on the cutting board. Cut downward to remove all of the peel and white pith, following the contour of the fruit. Holding the fruit over a large bowl, cut on either side of each segment to free it from the membrane, letting it fall into the bowl.

When all of the fruit is segmented, pour off any juice that has accumulated at the bottom of the bowl and discard or reserve for another use. Add the shallots, chile, mint, peanuts, and toasted coconut and toss gently to mix well. Pour the dressing over the pomelo mixture and toss to coat thoroughly. Line a platter with the lettuce leaves, spoon the pomelo salad on top, and serve.

Larger than grapefruit, pomelo is a citrus fruit that is pale green to yellow when ripe. The fruit has a thick, spongy rind surrounding flesh that is light pink or pale yellow. Pomelo tastes like a sweet, mild grapefruit, with little or none of a grapefruit's bitterness. When removing the segments from the pomelos, be sure to avoid the bitter membranes that encase them.

Spicy Minced Chicken Salad

Originating in Laos and popular in Thailand, this salad, called *larb gai*, centers on minced meat flavored with herbs, fish sauce, chile sauce, and lime. A versatile dish, it is also made with pork or beef and even with seafood, and is a perfect way to use leftover cuts of meat and to incorporate additional fresh vegetables. The salad can be accompanied with steamed sticky rice (page 274).

Freeze the cubed chicken for 15 minutes to firm it up and facilitate the mincing.

Meanwhile, to make the dressing, in a mini food processor or mortar, combine the chopped shallot, garlic, chile, sugar, and $1/8$ teaspoon pepper and process or grind with a pestle until a smooth paste forms. Add 1–2 teaspoons water if needed to facilitate the grinding. Transfer the garlic paste to a bowl and whisk in the fish sauce, lime juice, vinegar, and chile sauce. Gradually drizzle in the 3 tablespoons oil while continuing to whisk. Set the dressing aside.

Remove the chicken from the freezer and place in a food processor. Process just until uniformly and finely minced, about 10 seconds. Do not overprocess or the meat will become mushy.

In a large nonstick frying pan over medium-high heat, warm the 2 tablespoons oil. Add the minced chicken and sauté, using a wooden spoon to break up the meat, until opaque throughout, 4–5 minutes. Scrape into a fine-mesh sieve and drain thoroughly, then transfer to a large bowl. Add the sliced shallots, serrano chile, cilantro, and mint and toss gently to mix.

Pour the dressing over the chicken mixture and toss to coat thoroughly. Line individual plates or a platter with the lettuce leaves. Divide the chicken salad among the leaves and garnish with the peanuts. Serve at room temperature.

1 lb (500 g) skinless, boneless chicken thighs, cut into 2-inch (5-cm) cubes

For the dressing

1 tablespoon chopped shallot

2 cloves garlic, chopped

1 tablespoon seeded and minced jalapeño chile

1 teaspoon sugar

Freshly ground pepper

$1/4$ cup (2 fl oz/60 ml) fish sauce

$1/4$ cup (2 fl oz/60 ml) fresh lime juice

1 tablespoon rice vinegar

1 teaspoon Sriracha chile sauce

3 tablespoons canola oil

2 tablespoons canola oil

3 shallots, thinly sliced

1 red or green serrano chile, cut into thin rings and seeded

2 tablespoons chopped fresh cilantro (fresh coriander)

2 tablespoons chopped fresh mint

6–8 red-leaf lettuce leaves, stems removed

$1/4$ cup ($1\frac{1}{2}$ oz/45 g) chopped unsalted dry-roasted peanuts

MAKES 4–6 SERVINGS

Seasoned Bean Sprout Salad

1½ lb (750 g) mung bean sprouts

2 tablespoons rice vinegar

1 tablespoon canola oil

2 teaspoons Asian sesame oil

2 green (spring) onions, white and pale green parts, minced

3 cloves garlic, minced

1 tablespoon sesame seeds, toasted

½ teaspoon chili powder

Salt

MAKES 4–6 SERVINGS

Place the bean sprouts in a saucepan and add water just to cover. Bring to a boil over high heat and cook for 1 minute. Remove the pan from the heat, cover, and let stand for 2 minutes. Drain the sprouts into a colander and rinse under cold running water. Drain again well, then gently squeeze the excess water from the sprouts. Transfer the sprouts to a clean kitchen towel, wring out gently, and pat dry. Put the dry sprouts in a large bowl.

In a small bowl, whisk together the vinegar, canola oil, and sesame oil until well blended. Add the green onions, garlic, sesame seeds, chili powder, and 1½ teaspoons salt and stir to mix well. Taste and adjust the seasoning. Pour the dressing over the bean sprouts and toss to coat thoroughly. Let stand at room temperature for 30 minutes before serving, or cover and refrigerate for at least 1 hour or up to overnight. Serve at room temperature or chilled.

Traditional Korean meals are noted for the number of side dishes offered along with the usual steamed short-grain rice and soup. These small dishes range from pickled vegetables to this bean sprout salad, and they vary with the meal, but the servings are always ample. The salad may be made a day in advance. Mung bean sprouts release water as they marinate, so be sure to drain any excess liquid before serving the salad.

Sweet-and-Sour Red Onion and Cucumber Salad

A perfect accompaniment to grilled meats such as chicken *satay* (page 44), this cucumber salad is a simple recipe that can be made in advance. Salting the sliced cucumbers removes excess water so that the salad remains crunchy and absorbs the dressing. The result is a mixture of refreshing contrasts.

Peel the cucumbers and cut each in half lengthwise. Using the tip of a spoon, remove the seeds. Cut each half crosswise into slices ¼ inch (6 mm) thick. Place the cucumbers in a colander, sprinkle with 1 teaspoon salt, and toss to mix well. Set aside at room temperature and let drain for 1 hour.

In a small saucepan, combine the vinegar, sugar, and 1 teaspoon salt. Bring to a simmer over medium heat and cook, stirring to dissolve the sugar, for 2 minutes. Set aside and let cool to room temperature.

Pat the cucumbers dry with paper towels. In a large bowl, combine the cucumbers, shallots, chile, and cilantro and toss to mix well. Pour the dressing over the cucumber mixture and toss to coat thoroughly. Cover and refrigerate for at least 2 hours or up to overnight. Serve chilled.

2 lb (1 kg) cucumbers

Salt

½ cup (4 fl oz/125 ml) rice vinegar

2 tablespoons sugar

4 shallots, thinly sliced

1 red Fresno chile, cut into thin rings and seeded

2 tablespoons chopped fresh cilantro (fresh coriander)

MAKES 4–6 SERVINGS

Grilled Beef Salad with Lime Dressing

3 cloves garlic, minced

1 tablespoon peeled and minced fresh galangal

1 cup (8 fl oz/250 ml) coconut milk

¼ cup (2 fl oz/60 ml) fish sauce

2 tablespoons chopped palm sugar

1 tablespoon minced fresh cilantro (fresh coriander)

1 lb (500 g) beef sirloin steak, 1½–2 inches (4–5 cm) thick

Canola oil for brushing

Lime Dressing (page 273)

2 lemongrass stalks, tender midsections only, smashed with the side of a chef's knife and thinly sliced on the diagonal

2 shallots, thinly sliced

¼ cup (⅓ oz/10 g) thinly sliced fresh Thai basil leaves

¼ cup (⅓ oz/10 g) thinly sliced fresh mint leaves

¼ cup (⅓ oz/10 g) thinly sliced fresh cilantro (fresh coriander) leaves

1 red Fresno chile, cut into thin rings and seeded

1 tablespoon chopped unsalted dry-roasted peanuts

MAKES 4–6 SERVINGS

In a large nonreactive dish, combine the garlic, galangal, coconut milk, fish sauce, palm sugar, and minced cilantro and stir to mix well. Add the beef and turn to coat thoroughly. Cover and refrigerate for at least 3 hours or up to 24 hours.

Preheat the oven to 400°F (200°C). Prepare a charcoal or gas grill for direct grilling over high heat, or preheat a stove-top grill pan over high heat.

Remove the steak from the marinade and pat dry with paper towels. Discard the marinade. Brush the grill rack or grill pan with oil. Place the steak on the rack or pan and sear, turning once, until crisp and brown on both sides, 4–5 minutes per side. Using tongs, transfer the steak to a rimmed baking sheet, place in the oven, and cook for 5 minutes longer for medium-rare or 10 minutes for medium. Transfer to a carving board with a moat and let rest for 5 minutes. Carve the steak across the grain into slices ⅛ inch (3 mm) thick.

Pour the juices released during carving into the dressing and stir well. Add the beef, lemongrass, shallots, basil, mint, cilantro, and chile to the bowl. Toss to coat all the ingredients and mix well.

Mound the beef salad on a platter, garnish with the peanuts, and serve at once.

A sweet-and-spicy lime dressing complements the grilled meat and refreshing herbs in this substantial salad. The beef can be marinated a day in advance for a fuller flavor and a more tender texture. Serve the beef salad with slices of fresh mango or pineapple for added color and sweetness.

Tea Leaf Salad

Unique to Burmese cuisine, *lephet* is an unusual salad of fermented green tea leaves that is notable for tasting faintly astringent and being a stimulant. The salad is valued for its social ritual and elaborate presentation. The ingredients, typically including dried shrimp, fried garlic, toasted sesame seeds, chiles, and a lime-based dressing, are arranged on a platter. Diners then select their preferences and compose their own salads. Here, the ingredients are combined. Fermented Burmese tea leaves are hard to find, so this version uses high-quality Chinese Dragonwell or Ti Kuan Yin green tea leaves, found in Asian markets. The leaves are steamed to reconstitute them and release their full flavor, which mimics the fermentation process.

Place the dried shrimp in a small bowl with warm water to cover. Set aside and let the shrimp soak for 15 minutes to soften.

Meanwhile, in a small frying pan over medium heat, warm the 1 teaspoon canola oil. Add the garlic and sauté until lightly browned, about 2 minutes. Set aside.

Put the coconut in a small, dry frying pan over medium heat and heat, stirring often, until lightly toasted, about 5 minutes. Remove from the heat and immediately pour onto a plate to cool.

In a saucepan fitted with a steamer basket, bring 2 inches (5 cm) of water to a boil. Place the tea leaves in a fine-mesh sieve and rinse under cold running water, then spread the leaves on a heatproof plate small enough to fit inside the saucepan. Place the plate in the steamer basket. Cover and steam until the leaves expand, about 30 minutes. Carefully remove the plate of tea leaves and set aside to cool. Gently squeeze out the excess water.

While the tea leaves are steaming, drain the shrimp and heat a small, dry frying pan over medium heat. Add the shrimp and toast until they turn a shade darker, 2–3 minutes. Transfer to a mini food processor and pulse to chop the shrimp until almost a powder, about 10 seconds.

In a bowl, whisk together the fish sauce, lime juice, ginger juice, and sugar until the sugar dissolves. Drizzle in the 3 tablespoons canola oil and the sesame oil while continuing to whisk. Season with salt and set the dressing aside.

In a large bowl, combine the tea leaves, shrimp, fried garlic, toasted coconut, chiles, peanuts, and sesame seeds and toss gently. Pour the dressing over the salad and toss to coat. Mound on a platter and serve at room temperature.

3 tablespoons dried shrimp (prawns)

1 teaspoon canola oil, plus 3 tablespoons

5 cloves garlic, thinly sliced

3 tablespoons unsweetened flaked coconut

1/2 cup (1 oz/30 g) semifermented tea leaves such as Dragonwell or Ti Kuan Yin (see note)

3 tablespoons fish sauce

3 tablespoons fresh lime juice

1 tablespoon ginger juice (page 278)

1/4 teaspoon sugar

1 teaspoon Asian sesame oil

Salt

2 serrano chiles, cut into thin rings and seeded

3 tablespoons coarsely chopped unsalted dry-roasted peanuts

2 tablespoons sesame seeds, toasted

MAKES 4 SERVINGS

Mixed Vegetables and Tofu with Peanut Sauce

Salt

14 oz (440 g) firm tofu

4 baby red potatoes

1 small head green cabbage, about ½ lb (250 g)

2½ cups (2½ oz/75 g) mung bean sprouts

¼ lb (125 g) yard-long beans

3 carrots

For the peanut sauce

2 cloves garlic, chopped

1 tablespoon chopped shallot

1 tablespoon canola oil

1 teaspoon *each* tomato paste and Sriracha chile sauce

¼ cup (2½ oz/75 g) creamy unsalted peanut butter

1 tablespoon *each* sweet soy sauce and tamarind paste

1 teaspoon sugar

2 tablespoons finely minced unsalted dry-roasted peanuts

3 hard-boiled eggs

1 English (hothouse) cucumber, peeled and cut on the diagonal into slices ¼ inch (6 mm) thick

1 cup (3 oz/90 g) Fried Shallots (page 274)

MAKES 4–6 SERVINGS

Bring 2 large saucepans of water to a boil and stir 1 tablespoon salt into each. Reduce the heat under 1 pan to maintain a gentle simmer and add the tofu block. Blanch for 5 minutes. Using a slotted spoon, carefully transfer the tofu to a plate; reserve the blanching water. Weight the tofu with a second plate to press out the excess water. Set aside for 30 minutes.

Add the potatoes to the boiling water in the second saucepan and cook until just tender, 15–20 minutes. Return the water in the first saucepan to a boil over medium-high heat, then reduce the heat to maintain a gentle simmer. Cut the cabbage into 6–8 wedges, removing most of the core from each wedge but leaving the leaves intact. Add the cabbage to the simmering water and cook for 5 minutes. Using the slotted spoon, transfer the cabbage to a colander, rinse under cold running water, drain thoroughly, and pat dry. Repeat to drain and dry the potatoes, reserving one pan of water.

Return the saucepan of water to a boil over high heat. Add the bean sprouts and cook for 5 minutes, then using the slotted spoon, transfer the sprouts into a colander and rinse under cold running water. Drain well, then transfer the sprouts to a clean kitchen towel, wring out gently, and pat dry. Return the water to a boil. Cut the beans into 4-inch (10-cm) lengths, and cut the carrots into slices ¼ inch (6 mm) thick. Add to the boiling water and cook until just tender, about 5 minutes. Drain, rinse under cold running water, and pat dry. Set all the vegetables aside.

To make the sauce, in a mini food processor or mortar, combine the garlic and shallot and process or grind with a pestle until a thick paste forms. Add 2–3 teaspoons water if needed to facilitate the grinding. In a small saucepan over medium heat, warm the oil. Add the garlic paste and sauté until fragrant, about 10 seconds. Add the tomato paste and the chile sauce and sauté until the oil turns red, just a few seconds. Pour in ¾ cup (6 fl oz/180 ml) water and add the peanut butter, soy sauce, tamarind paste, and sugar, and stir until smooth and thickened, 3–4 minutes. Remove from the heat and stir in the peanuts. Set aside.

To assemble the salad, pour off any water from the tofu and cut into 1-inch (2.5-cm) cubes. Cut the potatoes in half. Cut the eggs into quarters. Arrange the tofu and vegetables, including the cucumber, in small mounds on a serving platter. Garnish with the eggs and Fried Shallots. Serve at room temperature with the peanut sauce on the side.

This Indonesian signature dish, called *gado-gado*, is enjoyed throughout Malaysia and in Singapore as well as in Indonesia. Showcasing a delicate balance of sweet and sour, it varies according to the region of origin. The Javanese version here accompanies an array of vegetables with a creamy peanut sauce. The vegetables and sauce may be prepared in advance and refrigerated overnight, then brought to room temperature before serving.

Stir-fried Zucchini and Shiitake Mushrooms

In this fast and simple recipe, stir-frying maintains the fresh flavor, color, and texture of the zucchini and mushrooms by rapidly cooking the small, uniform pieces in a bit of oil over high heat as they are stirred constantly. It is a quick process, so be sure to have everything you need, including ingredients, tools, and a warmed serving plate, close at hand before you begin to cook. Finishing the dish is a sesame-soy sauce typical of Korean stir-fries. Napa cabbage and red bell pepper (capsicum), cut into uniform slices, may be substituted for the zucchini and mushrooms.

Remove and discard the stems from the shiitake mushrooms. Cut the caps into slices ¼ inch (6 mm) thick. Trim the stems from the zucchini and cut each in half lengthwise. Cut each zucchini half crosswise into slices ¼ inch (6 mm) thick. Set the vegetables aside.

Heat a dry frying pan over medium heat. Add the sesame seeds and toast, stirring occasionally, until golden brown, 4–5 minutes. Immediately transfer to a small plate and set aside. In a small bowl, stir together the soy sauce, vinegar, sesame oil, and sugar to make a stir-fry sauce.

In a large frying pan or wok over high heat, warm 2 tablespoons of the canola oil. Add the mushrooms and stir-fry until they release their juices, 4–5 minutes. Transfer to a large bowl. Return the pan to high heat and warm the remaining 1 tablespoon canola oil. Add the zucchini and stir-fry until golden brown and just tender, 7–8 minutes. Add the green onions and garlic and stir-fry until fragrant, about 1 minute.

Return the mushrooms to the pan and pour in the sauce. Stir-fry until the vegetables are heated through and most of the sauce has evaporated, about 2 minutes. Transfer the vegetables to a warmed bowl, garnish with the toasted sesame seeds, and serve at once.

½ lb (250 g) fresh shiitake mushrooms

1½ lb (750 g) zucchini (courgettes)

1 teaspoon sesame seeds

2 tablespoons light soy sauce

1 tablespoon rice vinegar

2 teaspoons Asian sesame oil

½ teaspoon sugar

3 tablespoons canola oil

2 green (spring) onions, white and pale green parts, minced

2 cloves garlic, minced

MAKES 4–6 SERVINGS

Braised Vegetables with Pork

2 tomatoes

2 Asian (slender) eggplants (aubergines)

½ lb (250 g) okra

½ lb (250 g) zucchini (courgettes)

¼ cup (2 fl oz/60 ml) fish sauce

1 tablespoon soy sauce

1 teaspoon sugar

Freshly ground pepper

4 tablespoons (2 fl oz/60 ml) canola oil

6 oz (185 g) pork butt, cut into 1-inch (2.5-cm) cubes

2 shallots, thinly sliced

3 cloves garlic, minced

1 tablespoon peeled and grated fresh ginger

MAKES 4–6 SERVINGS

Cut the core from each tomato. Cut each tomato in half crosswise. Holding each half over a small bowl, gently squeeze it to release the seeds. Coarsely chop the tomatoes and set aside. Trim the stems from the eggplants, cut them in half lengthwise, and then cut each half crosswise into 1½-inch (4-cm) pieces. Trim the stems and tips from the okra and cut each in half crosswise on the diagonal. Trim the zucchini, cut each in half lengthwise, and then cut each half crosswise into 2-inch (5-cm) pieces. Set the vegetables aside.

In a small bowl, stir together the fish sauce, soy sauce, sugar, and ⅛ teaspoon pepper to make a braising sauce. Set the sauce aside.

In a Dutch oven or large frying pan over high heat, warm 2 tablespoons of the oil. When the oil is hot, add the pork and stir-fry just until it turns opaque, about 3 minutes. Transfer the pork to a large bowl.

Add the remaining 2 tablespoons oil to the pan and warm over medium heat. Add the shallots, garlic, and ginger and sauté until fragrant, about 10 seconds. Add the tomatoes and reduce the heat to medium-low. Stir in the sauce and bring to a simmer. Add the eggplant, okra, and zucchini and stir gently to mix well. Return the pork and any accumulated juices in the bowl to the pan and stir gently. Cover and simmer until all the vegetables are tender, 15–20 minutes. Transfer to a warmed bowl and serve at once.

A Filipino dish resembling the braised vegetable stew ratatouille, *pinakbet* is a popular Ilocano dish from the northern region of the Philippines closest to China. The vegetables typically include eggplant, tomato, okra, and squash. *Pinakbet* means "to dry up" or "to shrivel," and as the name suggests, the vegetables are stir-fried and then braised until they are tender and most of the moisture has cooked away. This variation of the dish has stir-fried cubes of pork for added flavor.

Soy-Braised Kabocha Squash

Kabocha is a winter squash introduced to Japan by the Portuguese in the sixteenth century. Shaped like a squat pumpkin, it has a striated green rind and orange flesh similar in texture and flavor to pumpkin combined with sweet potato. In Japanese cuisine, *kabocha* is a common ingredient in side dishes, the best known being tempura and this braise with soy sauce.

Pour oil to a depth of 2 inches (5 cm) into a deep frying pan over high heat and heat to 350°F (180°C) on a deep-frying thermometer. Meanwhile, cut the squash in half lengthwise and scoop out and discard the seeds. Peel the squash and cut lengthwise into wedges 1 inch (2.5 cm) wide by 4 inches (10 cm) long. When the oil is hot, working in batches, add the squash and fry until the edges begin to brown, 1–2 minutes. Turn and fry on the second side until light golden brown, 1–2 minutes longer. Transfer to paper towels to drain.

In a Dutch oven or large frying pan over medium-low heat, combine the dashi, mirin, soy sauce, ginger juice, and sugar and bring to a simmer, stirring to dissolve the sugar. Add the squash, return to a simmer, and cook, gently turning the squash several times, until tender when pierced with a fork, 10–15 minutes longer. Transfer the squash to warmed bowl, spoon about 1/2 cup (4 fl oz/125 ml) of the braising liquid over the top, and serve at once.

Canola oil for frying

2 lb (1 kg) *kabocha* squash

1/4 teaspoon granulated dashi mixed with 2 cups (16 fl oz/500 ml) hot water

3 tablespoons mirin

1/4 cup (2 fl oz/60 ml) tamari soy sauce

1 tablespoon ginger juice (page 278)

2 tablespoons sugar

MAKES 4–6 SERVINGS

Spinach with Soy Sauce, Dashi, and Bonito Flakes

Called *ohitashi*, blanched spinach dressed with a soy and dashi sauce makes a simple and beautiful dish that is often served as an appetizer but is also good alongside a bowl of noodles. Bonito flakes both flavor the dashi, the everyday Japanese broth, and are used as a garnish. The flakes are shavings of dried, smoked bonito, a type of tuna.

In a large saucepan fitted with a steamer basket, bring 2 inches (5 cm) of water to a boil. Have ready a large bowl of ice water. Place the spinach leaves in the steamer basket and steam until just wilted, about 2 minutes. Using tongs, immediately plunge the spinach into the ice water to stop the cooking. Drain well, and then squeeze out the remaining water. Pull the leaves apart, spread out on paper towels, and pat dry. Divide the spinach into 4 equal portions and shape each portion into a tightly packed cylinder about 2 inches (5 cm) in diameter. Cut each cylinder in half and arrange the halves, cut side up, in a small, shallow bowl.

In a small saucepan, combine the dashi, soy sauce, mirin, sugar, and cornstarch and bring to a simmer over medium-low heat, stirring to dissolve the sugar and cornstarch. Cook until the sauce thickens slightly, about 1 minute. Let cool to room temperature. Spoon the sauce over the spinach, dividing it evenly. Garnish with the bonito flakes. Serve at room temperature.

1 lb (500 g) spinach leaves, stemmed

Pinch of granulated dashi mixed with 1/4 cup (2 fl oz/60 ml) hot water

2 tablespoons dark soy sauce

1 tablespoon mirin

1/2 teaspoon sugar

1/8 teaspoon cornstarch (cornflour)

2 tablespoons bonito flakes

MAKES 4 SERVINGS

Dry-Curry Okra

1 small yellow onion, chopped

2 tablespoons peeled and chopped fresh ginger

2 cloves garlic, chopped

1$\frac{1}{2}$ lb (750 g) okra (see note)

3 tablespoons canola oil

1 teaspoon ground cumin

$\frac{1}{2}$ teaspoon ground coriander

$\frac{1}{8}$ teaspoon cayenne pepper

Salt

1 tablespoon fresh lemon juice

MAKES 4 SERVINGS

In a mini food processor or mortar, combine the onion, ginger, and garlic and process or grind with a pestle until a smooth paste forms. Add 2–3 tablespoons water if needed to facilitate the grinding.

Trim the stems and tips from the okra and cut crosswise on the diagonal into $\frac{1}{2}$-inch (12-mm) pieces. Set aside.

In a large, nonstick frying pan over medium-high heat, warm the oil. When the oil is hot, add the onion paste and sauté until fragrant, about 1 minute. Stir in the cumin, coriander, cayenne, and $\frac{1}{2}$ teaspoon salt and sauté until the mixture is fragrant, just a few seconds.

Add the okra to the pan and spread in a single layer. Cook until lightly browned, 4–5 minutes. Stir the okra and again spread into a single layer, and cook until lightly browned, about 5 minutes longer.

Add $\frac{1}{4}$ cup (2 fl oz/60 ml) water and the lemon juice to the pan, reduce the heat to medium, and cook, stirring often, until the okra is tender-crisp, 8–10 minutes. Taste and adjust the seasoning. Transfer to a warmed platter and serve at once.

The Indian diet is rich in vegetables, with okra one of the most popular choices. The elongated, fuzzy, ribbed pods are commonly used in curries, either cooked dry or braised with other vegetables in a small amount of liquid. When purchasing okra, choose pods that are firm to the touch and are mostly free of blemishes.

Vegetable Sushi Rolls

With the help of a bamboo mat, *maki-zushi* is rolled into a cylinder of steamed rice wrapped with a sheet of toasted nori seaweed. Fillings for the sushi range from raw fish to thinly sliced raw vegetables to pickled vegetables. Ideally, sushi should be served right away, but these vegetable-filled rolls can be made several hours in advance, enclosed in plastic wrap, and set aside in a cool place, but not refrigerated, before they are served.

Place the rice in a saucepan and add 1⅓ cups (11 fl oz/340 ml) water. Bring to a boil over medium-high heat, stir the rice, reduce the heat to low, cover, and cook until all the water has been absorbed, about 20 minutes. Remove from the heat, uncover, and place a kitchen towel over the pan. Re-cover the pan and let stand for 15 minutes.

Combine the ¼ cup vinegar, the 3 tablespoons sugar, and 1 tablespoon salt in a small saucepan over low heat and cook, stirring to dissolve the sugar and salt, for 2 minutes. Let cool to room temperature. Transfer the rice to a wide, shallow nonreactive bowl and use a spatula to spread to the edges of the bowl. Slowly pour in the vinegar mixture while slicing the spatula through the rice; do not stir. Cover the rice with a damp kitchen towel; do not refrigerate.

Place the mushrooms in a saucepan and add the dashi, 2 tablespoons soy sauce, mirin, and 1 teaspoon sugar. Bring to a simmer over low heat and cook, stirring occasionally to blend the flavors, about 10 minutes. Drain the mushrooms.

In a small bowl, stir the 1 tablespoon vinegar into 1 cup (8 fl oz/250 ml) water. Set a bamboo rolling mat on the work surface with a long side facing you. Place a sheet of nori on the mat. Dampen your fingers in the vinegar water, scoop up about ½ cup (2½ oz/75 g) of the sushi rice, and spread in a band 7 inches (18 cm) long and about 2 inches (5 cm) wide across the middle of the nori. Press a groove about ½ inch (12 mm) wide and ¼ inch (6 mm) deep centered along the length of the band of rice. Smear a thin trace of the wasabi along the groove. Lay the cucumber strips in the groove. Starting at the edge closest to you, use the mat to roll up the sushi into a tight cylinder about 1 inch (2.5 cm) in diameter. Lightly moisten the outer edge of the nori to seal the roll. Repeat to make a second roll with the daikon. Then make a third roll the same way with the mushroom strips. Use a sharp knife to cut each roll of sushi into 8 pieces. Serve at once with the pickled ginger and soy sauce.

1 cup (7 oz/220 g) short-grain rice, rinsed under cold running water

¼ cup (2 fl oz/60 ml) rice vinegar, plus 1 tablespoon

3 tablespoons sugar, plus 1 teaspoon

Salt

4 dried shiitake mushrooms, rinsed, stemmed, soaked in boiling water for 30 minutes, drained, and cut into thin slivers

Pinch of granulated dashi mixed with ¼ cup (2 fl oz/60 ml) hot water

2 tablespoons light soy sauce, plus extra for serving

1 tablespoon mirin

3 sheets toasted nori seaweed, each trimmed into a 7-inch (18-cm) square

1 teaspoon prepared wasabi paste

2 strips cucumber, each 5 inches long by ¼ inch (6 mm) wide

2 strips pickled daikon, each 5 inches long by ¼ inch (6 mm) wide

Pickled ginger for serving

MAKES 24 PIECES

Spiced Potatoes, Cauliflower, and Peas

Salt

1 large boiling potato,
about ½ lb (250 g)

1 small head cauliflower,
about 1¼ lb (625 g)

1 small yellow onion,
chopped

2-inch (5-cm) piece fresh
ginger, peeled and chopped

3 cloves garlic

1 serrano chile, seeded
and chopped

1 tablespoon tomato paste

1 teaspoon fresh lemon juice

½ teaspoon sugar

¼ cup (2 oz/60 g) ghee
or ¼ cup (2 fl oz/60 ml)
canola oil

1½ teaspoons ground cumin

1 teaspoon ground coriander

1 teaspoon ground turmeric

¼ teaspoon ground cinnamon

⅛ teaspoon cayenne pepper

1 cup (5 oz/155 g) English
peas or thawed frozen peas

1 tablespoon minced fresh
cilantro (fresh coriander)

MAKES 4–6 SERVINGS

This is a typical festive Punjabi-style dry curry. The popular combination of potatoes, cauliflower, and peas takes on a striking yellowish hue from the turmeric. Served as a side or main dish, this mild curry is generally eaten with breads, such as Indian Flatbread (page 67), and Raita (page 275), a refreshing cucumber-yogurt sauce.

Bring a large saucepan three-fourths full of water to a boil and stir in 1 tablespoon salt. While the water is heating, peel the potato and cut into 1-inch (2.5-cm) cubes. Trim and core the cauliflower and separate into 1-inch (2.5-cm) florets.

Add the potato cubes to the boiling water and cook until they are partly tender but still give some resistance when pierced with a knife, 6–7 minutes. Drain into a colander, rinse under cold running water, and set aside.

In a mini food processor or mortar, combine the onion, ginger, garlic, and chile and process or grind with a pestle until a smooth paste forms. Set aside. In a small bowl, whisk together the tomato paste, lemon juice, sugar, and 1 cup (8 fl oz/ 250 ml) water and set aside.

In a Dutch oven or large frying pan over medium-high heat, warm the ghee. Add the onion paste and sauté until it just begins to brown, 4–5 minutes. Add the cumin, coriander, turmeric, cinnamon, cayenne, and 1½ teaspoons salt and stir to mix. Add the cauliflower and sauté until well coated, about 2 minutes.

Reduce the heat to medium-low and stir in the tomato paste mixture, potatoes, and peas. Cover and simmer, stirring occasionally, until the vegetables are tender and the liquid has evaporated, about 10 minutes. Be careful to stir gently so the vegetables do not fall apart. Transfer to a warmed bowl, garnish with the minced cilantro, and serve at once.

Stir-fried Bok Choy

¼ cup (2 fl oz/60 ml)
low-sodium chicken broth

1 tablespoon *each* Chinese
rice wine, oyster sauce, and
ginger juice (page 278)

1 teaspoon Asian sesame oil

½ teaspoon *each* sugar and
cornstarch (cornflour)

1 lb (500 g) bok choy

8 shiitake mushrooms

4 tablespoons canola oil

4 cloves garlic

MAKES 4–6 SERVINGS

In a small bowl, whisk together the broth, rice wine, oyster sauce, ginger juice, sesame oil, sugar, and cornstarch to make a stir-fry sauce. Trim the stem ends from the bok choy, then cut each bunch lengthwise into quarters. Remove the stems from the mushrooms and discard. Cut the caps in half.

In a wok over high heat, warm 1 tablespoon of the oil. Add 2 of the garlic cloves and stir-fry until golden brown, about 20 seconds. Discard the garlic. Quickly add half of the bok choy to the hot pan and stir-fry until just wilted, 3–4 minutes. Transfer to a colander. Add 1 tablespoon oil to the pan and stir-fry the remaining garlic and bok choy in the same manner. Set the bok choy aside in the colander to drain. In the same pan over high heat, warm the remaining 2 tablespoons oil. Add the mushrooms and sauté until they release their juices, 4–5 minutes. Return the bok choy to the pan, add the sauce, and stir-fry until the sauce has thickened slightly, 1–2 minutes longer. Serve at once.

Crisply cooked vegetables are characteristic of the Chinese table. Bok choy, with its tender leaves and sturdy stems, lends itself to stir-frying. This pairing of bok choy with meaty fresh shiitake mushrooms is flavored with a trio of seasonings from the Asian pantry: rice wine, oyster sauce, and ginger. Look for bunches of bok choy that are not too large.

Green Beans with Sesame-Miso Dressing

The dressing for this simple salad of bright green beans includes nutty sesame oil and *shiro miso*, a paste of fermented soybeans that helps give the dressing a creamy texture and savory-sweet taste. The dressing is an ideal complement to other blanched vegetables, such as asparagus and broccoli.

Bring a saucepan three-fourths full of water to a boil over high heat and stir in 1 tablespoon salt. Have ready a bowl of ice water. Trim the stem ends from the green beans. Add the beans to the boiling water and cook until just tender, 3–4 minutes. Drain the beans in a colander and then immediately plunge into the ice water to stop the cooking. Drain well, pat dry, and place in a large bowl.

In a small bowl, whisk together the dashi and ¼ cup (2 fl oz/60 ml) hot water. Whisk in the sesame paste, soy sauce, ginger juice, miso, sugar, and sesame oil until the sugar dissolves. Pour over the beans and toss to mix and coat well.

Transfer the beans to a bowl and crumple the nori over the top. Serve the beans at room temperature, or cover and refrigerate for at least 1 hour or up to 24 hours and serve the beans chilled.

Salt

1 lb (500 g) green beans

Pinch of granulated dashi

2 tablespoons *each* toasted sesame paste and light soy sauce

1 tablespoon *each* ginger juice (page 278), *shiro miso*, and sugar

1 teaspoon Asian sesame oil

½ sheet toasted nori

MAKES 4–6 SERVINGS

Eggplant Curry

Roasting the eggplant gives this curry a smoky undertone and a creamy texture. Although small round Indian or slender Asian eggplants may be used, a large globe eggplant is preferred for its tender flesh. The chopped and roasted eggplant can be refrigerated overnight and the curry finished the following day. Serve the curry with Steamed Rice (page 274) or Indian Flatbread (page 67).

Preheat the oven to 400°F (200°C).

Trim the stem from the eggplant and cut in half lengthwise. Using the tip of a sharp knife, score the flesh lengthwise in several places about 1 inch (2.5 mm) apart and ¼ inch (6 mm) deep. Rub the cut sides with 2 tablespoons of the oil.

Pour ¼ cup (2 fl oz/60 ml) water into a large, rimmed baking sheet. Place the eggplant halves, cut side down, in the prepared pan. Roast until tender when pierced with a fork, about 25 minutes. Transfer to a plate and let cool. Using a large spoon, scoop out the flesh onto a cutting board. Discard the skin. Chop the eggplant flesh.

In a large frying pan over medium-high heat, warm the remaining 2 tablespoons oil. Add the onion, ginger, and garlic and sauté until the onion is beginning to brown, 4–5 minutes. Stir in the cumin, coriander, turmeric, cayenne, and 1 teaspoon salt and sauté until the spices are fragrant, about 1 minute.

Add the eggplant and tomatoes, reduce the heat to low, and simmer, stirring occasionally, until the curry has thickened, about 10 minutes. Stir in the peas and simmer for 5 minutes longer.

Taste and adjust the seasoning. Transfer the curry to a warmed bowl, garnish with the cilantro, and serve at once.

1 large globe eggplant (aubergine), about 2 lb (1 kg)

4 tablespoons (2 fl oz/60 ml) canola oil

1 small yellow onion, minced

1 tablespoon peeled and grated fresh ginger

2 cloves garlic, minced

1 teaspoon ground cumin

½ teaspoon ground coriander

½ teaspoon ground turmeric

⅛ teaspoon cayenne pepper

Salt

1 cup (6 oz/185 g) chopped tomatoes

½ cup (2½ oz/75 g) fresh or thawed frozen English peas

1 tablespoon chopped fresh cilantro (fresh coriander)

MAKE 4–6 SERVINGS

Spicy Sichuan Eggplant

1½ lb (750 g) Asian (slender) eggplants (aubergines)

Salt

For the sauce

¼ cup (2 fl oz/60 ml) low-sodium chicken broth

1 tablespoon chile bean paste

1 tablespoon black vinegar

1 tablespoon dark soy sauce

1 tablespoon light soy sauce

1 teaspoon tomato paste

1 teaspoon Asian sesame oil

½ teaspoon sugar

½ teaspoon cornstarch (cornflour)

4 tablespoons (2 fl oz/60 ml) canola oil

¼ cup (1½ oz/45 g) minced celery

2 green (spring) onions, white and pale green parts, minced

1 tablespoon peeled and minced fresh ginger

2 cloves garlic, minced

¼ lb (125 g) ground (minced) pork

MAKES 4–6 SERVINGS

Trim the stems from the eggplants and cut crosswise on an extreme diagonal into slices about 1 inch (2.5 cm) thick, to expose as much flesh as possible. Place in a large bowl with cold water to cover and stir in 1 tablespoon salt. Place a lid or plate on the eggplant slices to keep them submerged. Soak for 30 minutes, then drain well and pat dry with paper towels.

Meanwhile, make the sauce: In a bowl, whisk together the broth, bean paste, vinegar, soy sauces, tomato paste, sesame oil, sugar, and cornstarch until the sugar and cornstarch dissolve. Set the sauce aside.

In a large nonstick frying pan over medium-high heat, warm 2 tablespoons of the canola oil. When the oil is hot, add the eggplant slices to the pan in a single layer and sear until crisp and light golden brown on the first side, 3–4 minutes. Turn the eggplant slices and sear until golden on the second side, about 3 minutes longer. Transfer the eggplant to a bowl.

Place the frying pan over high heat and add the remaining 2 tablespoons canola oil. When the oil is hot, add the celery, half of the green onions, the ginger, and the garlic and stir-fry until fragrant, about 1 minute. Crumble the pork into the pan and stir-fry, using a spatula to break up the meat, just until the meat turns opaque, 2–3 minutes. Add the sauce and return the eggplant to the pan. Reduce the heat to low, cover, and cook until the eggplant is tender and the sauce has thickened, about 10 minutes.

Transfer the eggplant to a warmed bowl, garnish with the remaining green onions, and serve at once.

Eggplant is a favorite vegetable in western China. This recipe sears the eggplant to give it a roasted flavor and then stir-fries it in a spicy chile bean paste typical of Sichuan cuisine. The two common varieties of eggplant found outside Asia are the Chinese and the Japanese. The former has lavender skin; the latter is deep purple. Both are mild and tender and contain few seeds, making them suitable for this recipe.

Spiced Stewed Lentils and Vegetables

Salmon-colored *masoor* dal, also known as split red lentils, are the base for this satisfying vegetarian stew. Like other legumes, lentils are high in protein and fiber, and have the added advantage of cooking quickly without presoaking. The mild, earthy lentils are best when combined with assertive spices and seasonings. The flavor of this stew is heightened with the optional addition of curry leaves sautéed in ghee near the end of cooking. The fried leaves impart an unmistakable herbaceous fragrance. Look for fresh curry leaves in Asian markets.

Pick over the lentils, removing any stones or misshapen or discolored lentils. Rinse the lentils under cold running water and drain. Transfer to a saucepan, add the turmeric and 5 cups (40 fl oz/1.25 l) water, and bring to a boil over medium-high heat. Reduce the heat to medium-low and simmer, uncovered, until the lentils are tender, 25–30 minutes.

Meanwhile, in a small, dry frying pan over medium heat, toast the coriander, cumin, and fenugreek seeds, shaking the pan constantly to toast the seeds evenly and prevent them from burning, until fragrant, about 2 minutes. Transfer immediately to a plate to cool. When the seeds are cool, transfer to a spice grinder or a coffee mill reserved for spices and grind to a fine powder. Set aside.

Mince 4 of the garlic cloves. In a large frying pan over medium-high heat, warm the oil. Add the onion, ginger, and minced garlic and sauté until the onion begins to brown, 5–7 minutes. Stir in the spice powder and sauté for a few seconds. Add the tomatoes, bring to a simmer, and cook for 5 minutes. Drain the lentils and add to the pan. Add the tamarind paste, 3 cups (24 fl oz/750 ml) water, and 1½ teaspoons salt and stir to mix. Reduce the heat to medium and bring to a gentle boil. Add the potato, carrot, and eggplant and return to a simmer. Cook, stirring occasionally, until the potatoes and carrots are tender when pierced with a fork, 25–30 minutes.

Just before serving, mince the remaining garlic clove. In a small frying pan, warm the ghee over medium-high heat. When the ghee is hot, add the mustard seeds and sauté until they begin to pop, about 1 minute. Quickly add the garlic and the curry leaves, if using, and sauté until the garlic begins to brown and the leaves wilt, about 10 seconds. Remove from the heat and stir the mustard seed mixture into the stew. Taste and adjust the seasoning. Transfer the stewed lentils to a warmed bowl and serve at once.

½ cup (3½ oz/105 g) red lentils

½ teaspoon ground turmeric

1 tablespoon coriander seeds

1 tablespoon cumin seeds

1 teaspoon fenugreek seeds

5 cloves garlic

2 tablespoons canola oil

1 small yellow onion, minced

3 tablespoons peeled and minced fresh ginger

1½ cups (9 oz/280 g) finely chopped tomatoes

1 tablespoon tamarind paste

Salt

1 large boiling potato, peeled and cut into ½-inch (12-mm) cubes

1 carrot, cut into ½-inch (12-mm) cubes

1 Asian (slender) eggplant (aubergine), cut into ½-inch (12-mm) cubes

1 tablespoon ghee or canola oil

1 teaspoon black mustard seeds

8 fresh curry leaves (optional)

MAKES 4–6 SERVINGS

Stir-fried Tofu with Ginger and Lemongrass

For the marinade

2 lemongrass stalks, tender midsections only, smashed with the side of a chef's knife and thinly sliced on the diagonal

1 serrano chile, seeded and minced

2 tablespoons light soy sauce

1 tablespoon fish sauce

1 tablespoon fresh lime juice

1 teaspoon Sriracha chile sauce

1 tablespoon sugar

1 teaspoon ground turmeric

2 tablespoons canola oil

14 oz (440 g) firm tofu, drained and cut into 1-inch (2.5-cm) cubes

4 tablespoons (2 fl oz/60 ml) canola oil

4 large shallots, thinly sliced

2 tablespoons peeled and grated fresh ginger

3 cloves garlic, minced

1 tablespoon chopped unsalted dry-roasted peanuts

¼ cup (⅓ oz/10 g) thinly sliced fresh Thai basil leaves

MAKES 4–6 SERVINGS

This aromatic tofu dish displays the signature flavors of Vietnamese cooking: turmeric, lemongrass, shallots, and ginger, along with a garnish of Thai basil and peanuts. Stir-frying the tofu in a nonstick pan helps the cubes hold their shape. Cubes of chicken breast can be substituted for the tofu and should be marinated for at least 3 hours before searing. For added flavor, serve this dish with Nuoc Cham Dipping Sauce (page 272).

To make the marinade, in a large, nonreactive bowl, whisk together the lemongrass, chile, soy sauce, fish sauce, lime juice, chile sauce, sugar, turmeric, and oil. Add the tofu and toss gently to mix well. Let stand at room temperature for at least 30 minutes or up to 2 hours.

In a large nonstick frying pan over medium-high heat, warm 2 tablespoons of the oil. When the oil is hot, add the shallots, ginger, and garlic and stir-fry until fragrant and lightly browned, about 2 minutes. Stir in ¼ cup (2 fl oz/60 ml) water, reduce the heat to medium-low, and simmer until the liquid has evaporated, about 1 minute. Transfer the shallot mixture to a bowl.

Drain the tofu in a colander set over a bowl, reserving the marinade. In the same pan, heat the remaining 2 tablespoons oil over medium-high heat. When the oil is hot, add the tofu in a single layer and stir-fry until golden brown and crisp around the edges, 5–8 minutes.

Reduce the heat to medium-low, return the shallot mixture to the pan along with the reserved marinade, and stir gently to mix well. Simmer until the sauce thickens, about 1 minute. Transfer the tofu and sauce to a warmed bowl and garnish with the peanuts and basil. Serve at once.

Panfried Stuffed Tofu

In Asian cooking, tofu is eaten in myriad ways: raw, stewed, stir-fried, in soup, cooked in sauce, or stuffed. This Korean recipe for firm tofu filled with seasoned ground beef is an excellent example of how tofu takes on the flavor of the ingredients with which it is cooked. Tofu holds considerable moisture and tends to fall apart easily. Blanching the tofu and then pressing it removes excess moisture and makes the tofu more resilient, ensuring it will brown easily when panfried.

To make the dipping sauce, in a bowl, whisk together the soy sauce, vinegar, chile bean paste, sugar, sesame oil, green onion, ginger, and garlic, and 1 tablespoon warm water until the sugar dissolves. Set aside.

Bring a saucepan three-fourths full of water to a boil over medium-high heat. Stir in 1 tablespoon salt and add the tofu block, taking care not to let it break. Return to a boil, reduce the heat to low, and cook for 5 minutes. Using a slotted spoon or wire skimmer, transfer the tofu to a plate. Weight with a second plate to press out the excess water. Set aside for 30 minutes.

Meanwhile, in a large bowl, combine the beef, green onion, ginger, garlic, soy sauce, sesame oil, sugar, cornstarch, and ⅛ teaspoon pepper. Stir or use your hands to mix well. Set aside.

Pour off any water from the tofu. Cut the block in half lengthwise, and then cut each half into quarters to make 8 rectangles, each about 3 inches (7.5 cm) long, 2 inches (5 cm) wide, and 1 inch (2.5 cm) thick. Using a small melon baller or the tip of a teaspoon, carefully scoop out a pocket ¼ inch (6 mm) deep from each rectangle. Sprinkle each pocket with a pinch of salt. Stuff 1 heaping teaspoon of the beef mixture into each pocket, rounding the top of the filling slightly.

In a large nonstick frying pan over medium-high heat, warm the canola oil. When the oil is hot, arrange the stuffed tofu rectangles, filling side down, in the pan and gently press with a spatula so the tofu touches the pan. Sear until the tofu is crisp and golden brown, 5–6 minutes. Carefully turn the rectangles and sear until golden on the opposite side, 4–5 minutes longer.

Transfer to a warmed platter, garnish with the parsley, and serve at once with the dipping sauce.

For the dipping sauce

¼ cup (2 fl oz/60 ml) light soy sauce

2 tablespoons rice vinegar

2 teaspoons chile bean paste

1 teaspoon sugar

1 teaspoon Asian sesame oil

1 green (spring) onion, white and pale green parts, thinly sliced on the diagonal

1 teaspoon peeled and grated fresh ginger

1 clove garlic, minced

Salt

1 lb (500 g) firm tofu

3 oz (90 g) ground (minced) beef

1 tablespoon minced green (spring) onion, white part only

1 tablespoon peeled and grated fresh ginger

2 cloves garlic, minced

2 teaspoons light soy sauce

½ teaspoon Asian sesame oil

½ teaspoon *each* sugar and cornstarch (cornflour)

Freshly ground pepper

2 tablespoons canola oil

1 tablespoon minced fresh flat-leaf (Italian) parsley

MAKES 4 SERVINGS

Spicy Braised Tofu with Ground Pork

For the marinade

3 tablespoons dark soy sauce

2 teaspoons Chinese rice wine

1 teaspoon Asian sesame oil

¼ lb (125 g) ground (minced) pork

Salt

14 oz (440 g) soft tofu

½ cup (4 fl oz/125 ml) low-sodium chicken broth

1 tablespoon chile bean paste

1 tablespoon light soy sauce

1 teaspoon Asian sesame oil

1 teaspoon sugar

½ teaspoon cornstarch (cornflour)

⅛ teaspoon ground white pepper

2 tablespoons canola oil

3 tablespoons minced green (spring) onions, white and pale green parts

1 tablespoon peeled and grated fresh ginger

3 cloves garlic, minced

MAKES 4–6 SERVINGS

To make the marinade, in a large, nonreactive bowl, stir together the dark soy sauce, rice wine, and sesame oil. Add the pork and stir to mix well. Set aside.

Bring a small saucepan three-fourths full of water to a gentle boil over medium heat. Add 1 tablespoon salt and bring to a simmer over medium-low heat. Add the tofu, reduce the heat to low, and simmer for 5 minutes to firm up the tofu. Using a slotted spoon or a wire skimmer, transfer the tofu to a plate. Weight with a second plate to press out the excess water. Set aside for 30 minutes. Just before stir-frying, pour off any water and cut the tofu into ½-inch (12-mm) cubes.

In a small bowl, whisk together the broth, chile bean paste, light soy sauce, sesame oil, sugar, cornstarch, and white pepper to make a braising sauce. Set aside.

In a large work or frying pan over medium-high heat, warm the canola oil. When the oil is hot, add the pork and its marinade and stir-fry until it just turns opaque, about 2 minutes. Add 2 tablespoons of the green onions, the ginger, and the garlic and stir-fry until fragrant, about 1 minute. Stir in the sauce and simmer until the sauce begins to thicken, 2–3 minutes. Add the tofu, reduce the heat to low, and simmer, uncovered, stirring occasionally and being careful to stir gently so the tofu does not fall apart, until most of the sauce is absorbed, about 10 minutes.

Transfer to a warmed serving bowl, garnish with the remaining 1 tablespoon green onions, and serve at once.

In Sichuan Province, this popular dish is known as *mapo doufu*, literally "pockmarked old-woman tofu," reportedly named for the venerable lady who created it. Tofu, or bean curd, is quite bland, but here it is bathed in a robust sauce laced with ground pork and enlivened with spicy chile bean paste. For a variation, you can substitute minced beef or seafood.

Fish and Shellfish

About Fish and Shellfish

Asia has long, curving coastlines, and thousands of islands dot the oceans from Japan to India to Indonesia. Lakes, rivers, and flooded rice paddies and a labyrinthine network of canals cover inland areas. Local cooks have long depended on the bounty pulled from these waters.

Freshness is fundamental. Whether peeking into buckets holding the day's catch at a traditional open-air wet market or pushing a cart through a sleek, modern supermarket, many Asian cooks want to see their fish swimming before they purchase them. In Cantonese restaurants, celebrated for their seafood cookery, diners approach a wall of aquariums and point to the exact fish they want, and moments later it is at their table, lightly bathed in a fragrant sauce.

Savvy Asian cooks also know that preserved fish and shellfish are a crucial source of valuable protein. Fish, shrimp (prawns), squid, and seaweed that have been dried under the sun or layered with salt in large crocks appear at the table in various forms. Basic sauces, stocks, and seasonings, such as Japanese dashi (stock) and Thai *nam pla* (fish sauce), are based on ingredients from the sea. Even tiny brine shrimp are dried and then packed to make bricks of Indonesian *belacan*, an essential flavoring in the country's many curries and *sambals* (condiments).

FROM THE SEA

No gourmand's visit to Tokyo is complete without an early morning stop at Tsukiji Market, where mountains of fresh fish are sold every day, including richly flavored tuna and salmon, flaky halibut and snapper, silvery mackerel, and tiny blue-green anchovies. Japanese seafood cooking highlights simple methods. Salted Grilled Mackerel (page 188), served with *ponzu* sauce, and Miso-Marinated Black Cod (page 189) are everyday recipes that depend on high-quality fish rather than a long list of ingredients.

Eating fish raw is perhaps the best way to showcase its freshness. When sushi-grade fish is available at your fishmonger, prepare Sashimi on Sushi Rice (page 169) for the epitome of Japanese cuisine. People elsewhere in the region, including Cambodia, Vietnam, and the Koreas, also eat fish raw, perhaps sliced thinly and lightly sprinkled with scallion oil or pounded smooth for wrapping in lettuce leaves with fresh herbs. In the Philippines, *kinilaw* (page 166), similar to the well-known ceviche of Spain, draws on the bounty of fish and shellfish that surrounds the country's seven thousand islands.

In India, pompano and butterfish are prized for special occasions, and in the south, meals typically include fish rubbed with lime juice and turmeric and grilled. Frying and roasting in the high heat of a tandoor (page 191) are two other common methods for cooking seafood. In China, serving a whole fish at a banquet symbolizes prosperity. Steamed sea bass or striped bass drizzled with sizzling oil and finished with finely shredded ginger and green (spring) onion (page 192) are nearly always on special-occasion menus in southern China. Tender squid and large cuttlefish appear stuffed with pork, grilled and sliced like sausage, or tossed with lime dressing for a filling salad. In the Korean kitchen, squid is stir-fried with an array of colorful vegetables (page 179) and a pungent chile bean paste.

A FRESHWATER BOUNTY

Locals who live far from the sea depend on fish from lakes, rivers, and rice paddies for their tables. Tilapia, perch, carp, and snakehead are all widely enjoyed. Catfish, which can grow to legendary lengths, stars in Southeast Asian art, songs, stories, and, of course, recipes such as Vietnamese Fish Braised in Caramel Sauce (page 193) and Hanoi-Style Braised Fish with Rice Noodles (page 195). In China's Hangzhou region, the local grass carp is poached and then drizzled with a sweet-sour vinegar sauce in the classic dish known as West Lake Fish in Vinegar Sauce (page 200), which is equally delicious prepared with bass or trout. In Hanoi, diners eat flaky catfish from the region's large lakes with turmeric, green onions, and generous amounts of fresh dill (page 195).

SHELLFISH AT THE TABLE

Shellfish, both fresh- and saltwater, vie with fish for space on dinner tables. Crabs, clams, mussels, and various shrimp, large and small, thrive among the roots of mangrove trees throughout Southeast Asia. Singaporeans prepare a gingery black bean–chile sauce (page 183) for the local, meaty mud crabs, and Thai cooks simmer mussels in a highly aromatic mix of lime juice, lemongrass, chile, and galangal (page 180).

Shrimp takes well to spicy flavors, as in Malaysia's Stir-fried Shrimp Sambal (page 170), or Cantonese-style Salt-and-Pepper Shrimp (page 173). Communities near the Bay of Bengal and along the southern coasts in India and throughout Sri Lanka count spicy shrimp curries, often made with coconut milk, in their seafood repertoires (page 174). In Japan, these versatile crustaceans are coated with a delicate batter and deep-fried for tempura (page 177).

Filipino Ceviche

1½ lb (750 g) sashimi-grade tuna

½ English (hothouse) cucumber

1 red Fresno or serrano chile

¼ cup (2 fl oz/60 ml) *each* fresh lemon juice and fresh lime juice

1 teaspoon *each* light soy sauce and canola oil

2 shallots, thinly sliced

1 tablespoon peeled and grated ginger

1 clove garlic, minced

⅛ teaspoon sugar

Salt and ground pepper

¼ cup (⅓ oz/10 g) fresh cilantro (fresh coriander) leaves

MAKES 4–6 SERVINGS

Place a serving platter in the refrigerator to chill.

Cut the tuna across the grain into slices about 2 inches (5 cm) long by ¹⁄₁₆ inch (2 mm) thick. Transfer to a plate, cover, and refrigerate until ready to serve.

Peel the cucumber and cut in half lengthwise, then cut each half crosswise on the diagonal into slices ¹⁄₁₆ inch (2 mm) thick. You should have about 1 cup (6 oz/ 185 g). Transfer to a bowl, cover, and refrigerate until ready to serve.

Seed the chile and then slice it. In a small bowl, whisk together the chile, lemon juice, lime juice, soy sauce, oil, shallots, ginger, garlic, sugar, ½ teaspoon salt, and ⅛ teaspoon pepper. Let stand at room temperature for 10 minutes to allow the flavors to blend.

Just before serving, place the tuna and cucumber slices in a large bowl and pour in the marinade. Fold gently to mix well. Taste and adjust the seasoning. Stir in the cilantro leaves and serve at once.

According to Filipino lore, the practice of combining seafood with a souring agent such as citrus or vinegar originated in the Philippines when it was a Spanish colony. Here, the fish is fresh tuna, which is marinated in both lemon and lime juices, causing an immediate reaction that pickles, or "cooks," the fish without heat. Most Filipino ceviche is made from meaty ocean fish like tuna, mackerel, and marlin, but the method can be applied to any seafood. Be sure to use the freshest seafood available.

Sashimi on Sushi Rice

For *chirashi-zushi*, or "scattered sushi," a variety of sliced raw fish and other ingredients are artfully displayed on sushi rice in a bowl. Only the freshest fish is used for this dish. Be sure to ask for sashimi- or sushi-grade fish, which means the fish has been properly handled and kept on ice. A good fish market will be able to advise you on which varieties are good enough to eat raw.

Place the rice in a large fine-mesh sieve and rinse under cold running water until the water runs clear. Transfer the rice to a large saucepan and add $2^{3}/_{4}$ cups (22 fl oz/680 ml) water. Bring to a boil over medium-high heat and give the rice a quick stir to separate the grains. Reduce the heat to low, cover, and cook until the rice is tender and all the water has been absorbed, about 20 minutes. Remove from the heat, uncover, and place a clean kitchen towel over the saucepan. Cover and let the rice rest for 15 minutes.

While the rice is resting, combine the vinegar, the sugar, and 1 tablespoon salt in a small saucepan over low heat and cook, stirring to dissolve the sugar and salt, for 2 minutes. Remove from the heat and let cool to room temperature.

Transfer the rice to a wide, shallow nonreactive bowl and use a spatula to spread it to the edges of the bowl. Slowly pour in the vinegar mixture while slicing the spatula through the rice; do not stir. Cover the rice with a damp kitchen towel; do not refrigerate.

Bring a saucepan three-fourths full of water to a boil over high heat. Add the shrimp and cook just until they turn bright orange and opaque, about 3 minutes. Drain into a colander, place under cold running water, and drain again. Pat dry with paper towels. Starting at a curved edge, cut each shrimp in half horizontally.

Remove the stems from the mushrooms and discard. Thinly slice the caps. In a small saucepan over medium-high heat, combine the 2 tablespoons soy sauce, mirin, and sugar and bring to a boil, stirring to dissolve the sugar. Stir in the mushrooms, reduce the heat to medium-low, and simmer until all the liquid has evaporated, 3–4 minutes. Set aside and let cool.

Cut the cucumber in half lengthwise, then cut into strips 3 inches (7.5 cm) long and $1/_{16}$ inch (2 mm) thick. You should have about $1/_{2}$ cup (3 oz/90 g). Cut the daikon into strips of the same size. Cut the tuna and yellowtail across the grain into slices 3 inches long, 1 inch (2.5 cm) wide, and $1/_{8}$ inch (3 mm) thick.

Wet your hands with water and lift the rice into individual bowls. Use your damp hands to gently loosen the grains; the rice should not be packed. Arrange the cucumber, mushrooms, daikon, shrimp, fish, omelet, and nori on top of the rice, dividing evenly. Serve at once with the pickled ginger, wasabi, and soy sauce.

For the sushi rice

2 cups (14 oz/440 g) short-grain rice

$1/_{4}$ cup (2 fl oz/60 ml) rice vinegar

3 tablespoons sugar

Salt

12 large shrimp (prawns), peeled and deveined

8–10 dried shiitake mushrooms, rinsed, soaked in boiling water for 15 minutes, and drained

2 tablespoons soy sauce, plus extra for serving

1 tablespoon mirin

1 teaspoon sugar

$1/_{2}$ English (hothouse) cucumber, peeled

$1/_{2}$ cup (4 oz/125 g) pickled daikon

$1/_{4}$ lb (125 g) sashimi-grade tuna

$1/_{4}$ lb (125 g) sashimi-grade yellowtail

Omelet Garnish (page 273)

1 sheet toasted nori seaweed, cut into fine strips

2 tablespoons pickled ginger

1 teaspoon prepared wasabi paste

MAKES 6 SERVINGS

Stir-fried Shrimp Sambal

1½ lb (750 g) medium shrimp (prawns) in the shell

For the chile paste

2 shallots, chopped

3 cloves garlic, chopped

2 red Fresno chiles, seeded and chopped

1 teaspoon Sriracha chile sauce

½ teaspoon shrimp paste

1 teaspoon chopped palm sugar

Salt

4 tablespoons (2 fl oz/60 ml) canola oil

4½ teaspoons tamarind paste

1 tablespoon chopped fresh cilantro (fresh coriander)

MAKES 4–6 SERVINGS

A *sambal* is a chile-based condiment popular in Malaysia, Indonesia, and Singapore. Made from a variety of chiles ranging from mildly spicy to fiery hot, it is most commonly passed at the table, but it is also used as a pungent sauce in cooking to add heat and depth of flavor to a dish. This recipe calls for blending a moderately spicy *sambal* for seasoning stir-fried shrimp. Leaving the shells on the shrimp allows the tasty *sambal* to permeate the shrimp and helps keep the flesh succulent.

Using kitchen scissors, cut the shell of each shrimp along the center of its back, following the curve. Devein the shrimp, rinse well under cold running water, and pat dry with paper towels. Set aside.

To make the chile paste, in a mini food processor or mortar, combine the shallots, garlic, chiles, chile sauce, shrimp paste, palm sugar, and ¼ teaspoon salt and process or grind with a pestle until a smooth paste forms. Add 1–2 tablespoons water if needed to facilitate the grinding. Set aside.

In a large wok or frying pan over high heat, warm 2 tablespoons of the oil. Working in batches if necessary, add the shrimp, spread in a single layer, and sear until the shells are crisp and brown on the first side and begin to turn orange, 1–2 minutes. Using tongs, turn the shrimp and sear on the second side until crisp and brown, 1–2 minutes. Transfer the shrimp to a bowl and set aside.

Return the pan to high heat and add the remaining 2 tablespoons oil. When the oil is hot, add the chile paste and stir-fry until fragrant and the color turns a shade darker, 2–3 minutes. Working quickly, stir in the tamarind paste and return the fried shrimp to the pan. Stir-fry until the shrimp are well coated with the spices and heated through, about 2 minutes. Transfer to a warmed platter, garnish with the cilantro, and serve at once.

Salt-and-Pepper Shrimp

The secret to making crisp, fried, batter-coated shrimp is using a large wok or other heavy-bottomed pan over sustained, very high heat. The shrimp are then stir-fried with aromatics and a seasoning called five-spice powder, a blend that incorporates the five basic flavors of Chinese cooking: sweet, sour, bitter, savory, and salty.

In a bowl, whisk together the egg whites, cornstarch, white pepper, and 1/2 teaspoon salt until smooth. Set the batter aside.

In a small bowl, combine the green onions, ginger, garlic, and chile and stir to mix well. In another small bowl, stir together the five-spice powder, 1/2 teaspoon salt, the sugar, and 1/4 teaspoon black pepper. Set both mixtures aside.

Pour oil to a depth of 3 inches (7.5 cm) into a wok or deep saucepan over high heat and heat to 370°F (188°C) on a deep-frying thermometer. Using tongs, dip a shrimp into the batter, allowing the excess to fall back into the bowl. Slide the shrimp into the hot oil. Repeat to add 4 or 5 more shrimp to the oil; do not crowd the pan. Deep-fry until the batter is light golden brown and the shrimp just turns orange, about 30 seconds. Using a wire skimmer, transfer to paper towels to drain. Repeat to fry the remaining shrimp, allowing the oil to return 370°F and removing any browned bits of batter from the oil between batches.

In another wok or a large frying pan, warm the 2 tablespoons oil. When the oil is hot, add the green onion mixture and sauté until fragrant, about 10 seconds. While tossing and stirring constantly, add the five-spice mixture. Sprinkle the rice wine into the pan and stir-fry for just a few seconds, scraping up any browned bits from the bottom of the pan. Return the fried shrimp to the pan and stir-fry until well coated with the spice mixture and heated through. Transfer the fried shrimp to a warmed platter and serve at once.

2 large egg whites

2 tablespoons cornstarch (cornflour)

1 teaspoon ground white pepper

Salt

2 green (spring) onions, white and pale green parts, minced

2 tablespoons peeled and minced fresh ginger

3 cloves garlic, minced

1 red Fresno chile, seeded and minced

1 teaspoon five-spice powder

1/4 teaspoon sugar

Coarsely ground black pepper

Canola oil for deep-frying, plus 2 tablespoons

1 1/2 lb (750 g) large shrimp (prawns), peeled and deveined

1 tablespoon Chinese rice wine

MAKES 4–6 SERVINGS

Shrimp Curry with Coconut Milk

3 cardamom pods

2 teaspoons coriander seeds

1 teaspoon cumin seeds

$1/4$ teaspoon fenugreek seeds

3 dried red chiles, seeded

1 small cinnamon stick

2 tablespoons canola oil

4 shallots, thinly sliced

2 tablespoons peeled and grated fresh ginger

3 cloves garlic, minced

1 cup (8 fl oz/250 ml) coconut milk

1 lemongrass stalk, tender midsection only, smashed with the side of a chef's knife

Salt

$1\frac{1}{2}$ lb (750 g) large shrimp (prawns), peeled and deveined

$1/2$ teaspoon fresh lemon juice

1 tablespoon chopped fresh cilantro (fresh coriander)

1 red Fresno chile, seeded and thinly sliced

MAKES 4–6 SERVINGS

Carefully split open the cardamom pods and remove the seeds. In a small, dry frying pan over medium heat, combine the cardamom, coriander, cumin, and fenugreek seeds, the dried chiles, and the cinnamon stick. Cook, shaking the pan constantly to toast the spices evenly and prevent them from burning, until the spices are fragrant and turn a shade darker, about 2 minutes. Transfer immediately to a plate to cool.

Transfer the spices to a spice grinder or a coffee mill reserved for spices and grind to a fine powder. Set aside.

In a large wok or frying pan over medium-high heat, warm the oil. Add the shallots, ginger, and garlic and sauté until fragrant and lightly browned, 1–2 minutes. Stir in the spice powder, the coconut milk, and 1 cup (8 fl oz/250 ml) water and bring to a gentle boil. Add the lemongrass stalk and 1 teaspoon salt, reduce the heat to low, and simmer until the curry thickens and coats the back of a spoon, 10–15 minutes. Discard the lemongrass.

Just before serving, stir in the shrimp and lemon juice and simmer until the shrimp are opaque throughout, 3–4 minutes. Transfer to a warmed bowl, garnish with the cilantro and fresh chile, and serve at once.

With South India to its north and Southeast Asia to its east, Sri Lanka has developed a cuisine that marries the influences of both regions. The lemongrass in this curry hints at Thailand, Malaysia, and Indonesia, while the cumin, coriander, and fenugreek come from India. The resulting sauce for the shrimp is rich and aromatic with a hint of spice. Serve the curry with Steamed Rice (page 274).

Shrimp and Vegetable Tempura

Tempura is a classic Japanese dish of deep-fried batter-coated vegetables or seafood commonly served as part of a meal as a snack. The key to achieving the unique simultaneously fluffy and crisp coating is using a chilled batter made with ice water. It is also essential to mix the batter lightly until the dry ingredients and water are just blended. Serve the tempura immediately after cooking. Accompany it with Steamed Rice (page 274), or serve it over soba noodles, or on top of udon soup.

To make the dipping sauce, in a small saucepan, combine the dashi with $1/2$ cup (4 fl oz/125 ml) water. Add the soy sauce, mirin, and sugar and bring to a boil over medium-low heat. Add the bonito flakes, remove from the heat, and let stand for 15 minutes. Strain the sauce through a fine-mesh sieve into a serving bowl and set aside at room temperature.

Meanwhile, to make the batter, sift together the cake and rice flours, the salt, and the baking soda into a large bowl. In a separate bowl, using a fork, beat together the egg yolks and ice water until blended. Stir the egg yolk mixture into the dry ingredients just until the batter comes together.

Preheat the oven to 250°F (120°C). Pour oil to a depth of 3 inches (7.5 cm) into a wok or deep saucepan over high heat and heat to 370°F (188°C) on a deep-frying thermometer.

Using tongs or fingertips, dip a carrot piece into the batter, allowing the excess to fall back into the bowl. Slide the carrot into the hot oil. Repeat to add 4 or 5 more vegetable pieces to the oil; do not crowd the pan. Deep-fry, gently and carefully moving the tempura back and forth with a wire skimmer, until light golden brown, 1–2 minutes. Using the skimmer, transfer to paper towels to drain. Arrange the fried tempura on an ovenproof platter and keep warm in the oven while you fry the remaining vegetables. Allow the oil to return to 370°F and remove any browned bits of batter from the oil between batches.

Before dipping the shrimp into the batter, make 4 or 5 slashes about $1/8$ inch (3 mm) deep in the underside (concave side) of each shrimp to prevent them from curling while frying. Working in batches, dip the shrimp into the batter, slide into the hot oil, and deep-fry until light golden brown, 30–60 seconds. Use the skimmer to transfer the shrimp to paper towels to drain, then transfer to the platter with the vegetables.

Serve the tempura at once with the dipping sauce.

For the dipping sauce

Scant $1/8$ teaspoon dashi

3 tablespoons *each* light soy sauce and mirin

1 teaspoon sugar

2 tablespoons bonito flakes

For the batter

1 cup (4 oz/125 g) cake (soft-wheat) flour

1 cup (5 oz/155 g) rice flour

1 teaspoon salt

$1/4$ teaspoon baking soda (bicarbonate of soda)

2 large egg yolks

$1\frac{1}{2}$ cups (12 fl oz/375 ml) ice water

Canola oil for deep-frying

1 *each* carrot and zucchini (courgette), cut into pieces 4 inches (10 cm) long by $1/4$ inch (6 mm) thick

1 small sweet potato, peeled, halved, and cut into pieces 4 inches (10 cm) long by $1/8$ inch (3 mm) thick

3 oz (90 g) green beans, trimmed

5 fresh shiitake mushrooms, stems removed and caps cut in half

8 large shrimp (prawns), peeled and deveined

MAKES 4 SERVINGS

Clams with Black Bean Sauce

1/3 cup (3 fl oz/80 ml) low-sodium chicken broth

2 tablespoons light soy sauce

2 tablespoons fermented black beans, rinsed well and drained

1/2 teaspoon rice vinegar

1 teaspoon sugar

1/8 teaspoon ground white pepper

1 teaspoon cornstarch (cornflour)

2 tablespoons canola oil

1/4 cup (1 oz/30 g) minced green (spring) onions, white and pale green parts, plus 1 tablespoon

2 tablespoons peeled and minced fresh ginger

3 cloves garlic, minced

1 red Fresno chile, seeded and minced

2 tablespoons Chinese rice wine

2 1/2 lb (1.25 kg) Manila or littleneck clams, scrubbed

1 tablespoon chopped fresh cilantro (fresh coriander)

MAKES 4–6 SERVINGS

In a bowl, stir together the broth, soy sauce, black beans, vinegar, sugar, white pepper, cornstarch, and 1/3 cup (3 fl oz/80 ml) water until the cornstarch dissolves. Set the cornstarch mixture aside.

In a large wok or frying pan over medium-high heat, warm the oil. When the oil is hot, add the 1/4 cup green onions, ginger, garlic, and chile and stir-fry until fragrant, about 10 seconds. Add the rice wine and stir-fry until most of the liquid has evaporated, about 30 seconds. Stir in the black bean–broth mixture, bring to a boil, and cook for about 30 seconds.

Add the clams to the pan, discarding any that do not close to the touch. Stir-fry until the clams are well coated with the sauce. Cover, reduce the heat to medium, and cook just until the shells open, 3–4 minutes.

Sprinkle the 1 tablespoon green onions and the chopped cilantro over the clams and stir-fry until heated through, about 1 minute longer. Discard any clams that failed to open. Transfer to a warmed bowl and serve at once.

An extremely popular seasoning and an ancient cooking staple, fermented black beans have a sharp, salty, and slightly bitter flavor. Typically used in the southern region of China, the salted beans are ideal for adding depth of flavor to such dishes as stir-fried clams or other shellfish. Serve the clams with Steamed Rice (page 274) and a simple vegetable stir-fry such as bok choy with shiitake mushrooms (page 150).

Spicy Stir-fried Squid with Vegetables

The Korean peninsula is surrounded by water, and the markets overflow with an abundance of fish and shellfish, which are enjoyed pickled or crushed into a paste, stewed, steamed, or grilled. This spicy and pungent squid dish is seasoned with *kochujang*, a fermented chile bean paste that is an indispensable condiment in the Korean kitchen. Serve the squid and vegetables with Steamed Rice (page 274) and Seasoned Bean Sprout Salad (page 128).

To prepare the squid, working with 1 squid at a time, pull the head and tentacles from the pouchlike body. The innards, including the ink sac, should come away with the head. Reach into the pouch and pull out the long, plasticlike quill and discard it. Cut off the tentacles from the head just below the eyes and discard the head and innards. Squeeze the cut end of the tentacles to remove the hard, round "beak" at the base and discard it. Rinse the body inside and out under cold running water, and pull off the gray membrane that covers the pouch. Leave the tentacles whole and cut the bodies into rings 1 inch (2.5 cm) wide. Set aside.

In a bowl, stir together the garlic, ginger, soy sauce, sesame oil, chile bean paste, sugar, chili powder, and 2 tablespoons water to make a stir-fry sauce. Set aside.

In a large wok or frying pan over high heat, warm 2 tablespoons of the canola oil. When the oil is hot, add the yellow onion, carrot, and bell pepper and stir-fry until brown around the edges. Stir in the bamboo shoots and stir-fry for 1 minute longer. Transfer the vegetables to a bowl and set aside.

Return the pan to high heat and add the remaining 1 tablespoon canola oil. When the oil is hot, add the squid and stir-fry until it just begins to curl and turn opaque, 1–2 minutes. Transfer to a colander and let drain. Return the pan to high heat. When the pan is hot, return the vegetables and squid to the pan, add the green onions, and pour in the sauce. Stir-fry until the squid and vegetables are heated through and most of the liquid has evaporated, about 1 minute. Transfer to a warmed platter, garnish with the sesame seeds, and serve at once.

2 lb (1 kg) squid

3 cloves garlic, minced

1 tablespoon peeled and grated fresh ginger

2 tablespoons light soy sauce

1 tablespoon Asian sesame oil

1 teaspoon Korean chile bean paste

½ teaspoon sugar

⅛ teaspoon chili powder

3 tablespoons canola oil

1 yellow onion, thinly sliced

1 small carrot, cut into strips 3 inches (7.5 cm) long by ⅛ inch (3 mm) wide and thick

½ green bell pepper (capsicum), seeded and cut into strips 3 inches (7.5 cm) long by ⅛ inch (3 mm) wide

½ cup (2 oz/60 g) bamboo shoots, cut into strips 3 inches (7.5 cm) long by ⅛ inch (3 mm) wide and thick

2 green (spring) onions, white and pale green parts, cut into strips 3 inches (7.5 cm) long by ⅛ inch (3 mm) wide

1 teaspoon sesame seeds, toasted

MAKES 4–6 SERVINGS

Mussels with Lemongrass and Basil

2 tablespoons fish sauce

1 teaspoon fresh lime juice

1 teaspoon chopped palm sugar

½ teaspoon cornstarch (cornflour)

2 lemongrass stalks, tender midsections only

2 slices fresh galangal, each about ¼ inch (6 mm) thick

2 tablespoons canola oil

2 shallots, thinly sliced on the diagonal

3 cloves garlic, minced

1 jalapeño chile, seeded and thinly sliced on the diagonal

3 tablespoons chopped fresh Thai basil

1 teaspoon Madras curry powder

2½ lb (1.25 kg) mussels, scrubbed and debearded

MAKES 4-6 SERVINGS

In this quick and simple dish, mussels are cooked in a sauce seasoned with lemongrass and galangal, two essential aromatics in Thai cuisine. Fresh Thai basil adds a unique herbal accent with a hint of licorice. Serve the hot mussels and their sauce alone or over a bowl of warm rice noodles.

In a small bowl, stir together the fish sauce, lime juice, palm sugar, cornstarch, and ¼ cup (2 fl oz/60 ml) water until the sugar and cornstarch dissolve. Set aside.

Smash each lemongrass section with the side of a chef's knife and then cut on the diagonal into thin slices. Peel each galangal slice and then smash with the side of the chef's knife.

In a deep pot over medium-high heat, warm the oil. Add the lemongrass, galangal, shallots, garlic, chile, and 2 tablespoons of the chopped basil, and sauté until fragrant, about 15 seconds. Stir in the curry powder and the cornstarch mixture and bring the mixture to a boil.

Add the mussels, discarding any that do not close to the touch. Cover tightly and cook, shaking the pot periodically, just until the shells open, 3–4 minutes. Discard any mussels that failed to open.

Transfer the mussels to a bowl, garnish with the remaining 1 tablespoon chopped basil, and serve at once.

Shellfish in a Clay Pot

For the braising sauce

2 cups (16 fl oz/500 ml) low-sodium chicken broth

3 tablespoons rice wine

2 tablespoons light soy sauce

1 tablespoon *each* **rice vinegar and Asian sesame oil**

1 tablespoon ginger juice (page 278)

1 teaspoon sugar

1/2 teaspoon ground white pepper

1 tablespoon cornstarch (cornflour)

Salt

3 tablespoons rice wine

1 teaspoon Asian sesame oil

1/2 lb (250 g) large shrimp (prawns), peeled and deveined

6 oz (185 g) sea scallops

1/2 lb (250 g) fresh or 6 oz (185 g) dried thin, round Chinese egg noodles

1 live Dungeness crab, about 1 lb (500 g)

3 tablespoons canola oil

5 green (spring) onions, white and pale green parts, 4 cut into 2-inch (5-cm) lengths and 1 thinly sliced

3 slices fresh ginger, smashed

3 cloves garlic, smashed

MAKES 4–6 SERVINGS

To make the braising sauce, in a large bowl, whisk together the broth, rice wine, soy sauce, rice vinegar, sesame oil, ginger juice, sugar, white pepper, and cornstarch until the sugar and cornstarch dissolve. Set aside.

Submerge the bottom and lid of a large clay pot in warm water for 15–30 minutes. In a large nonreactive bowl, whisk together 1/2 teaspoon salt, 1 tablespoon of the rice wine, and the 1 teaspoon sesame oil. Add the shrimp and scallops and stir to coat thoroughly. Let marinate at room temperature for 15 minutes.

Bring a large saucepan three-fourths full of water to a boil. Stir in 1 tablespoon salt, add the egg noodles, and cook until just tender, 1–2 minutes. Drain, rinse under cold running water, and drain again. Remove the clay pot from the water, place the noodles in the bottom, and set aside.

Bring a large pot of water to a boil. Plunge the crab into the boiling water and cook for about 2 minutes. Using tongs, transfer to a colander and rinse under cold running water until cool.

Pull off the top shell and discard. Lift the tip of the triangular apron on the underside of the body, twist it off, and discard. Remove the mandibles at the face end. Pull off the feathery gills, and scrape out the gray intestinal matter from the body and discard, along with any creamy yellow liver. Rinse the body under cold running water and pat dry with paper towels. Cut the body in half lengthwise, then cut each half crosswise into 3 or 4 pieces, leaving the legs and claws attached. Using a mallet, crack the claw and leg shells at the joints and in the middle.

Preheat the oven to 425°F (220°C). In a large wok or frying pan over high heat, warm the canola oil. When the oil is very hot, add the 2-inch green onions, ginger, and garlic and stir-fry until fragrant, about 10 seconds. Add the crab pieces and toss. Add 1/4 teaspoon salt and the remaining 2 tablespoons rice wine and stir-fry until the shells begin to turn bright orange and the edges of the shells begin to brown, 7–8 minutes. Using the tongs, transfer the crab pieces to a bowl. Discard the remaining ingredients, and place the pan over medium heat. Stir the braising sauce, pour into the pan, and bring to a boil. Cook just until it begins to thicken, about 3 minutes, then remove from the heat. Pour the hot braising sauce over the noodles in the clay pot. Add the crab and any accumulated juices. Lift the shrimp and scallops out of the marinade and arrange in the pot. Sprinkle the sliced green onions on top, cover the clay pot tightly, and transfer to the oven. Braise until all of the seafood is opaque throughout, 25–30 minutes. Serve at once.

Clay pots, with a brown glazed interior and a rough unglazed exterior, have long been used by Chinese cooks for steaming and braising. Before the ingredients are prepared, the clay pot needs to be soaked so it absorbs moisture, which is released as steam during cooking. This unique technique makes the shellfish in this recipe turn out moist, tender, and flavorful. Use a large unglazed clay pot, about 3 1/2 quarts (3.5 l) in capacity, or a Dutch oven. Lobster may be substituted for the crab; boil the lobster as for the crab, halve and clean it, and cut each half into 3 or 4 pieces.

Seafood in Coconut Red Curry

This spicy and robust dry curry, combining both fresh and dried red chiles, lends itself to oily firm-fleshed fish such as sea bass or salmon, as well as shellfish. A generous amount of kaffir lime leaves contributes a distinctive citrusy floral note. An ideal accompaniment to this curry would be a refreshing Green Papaya Salad (page 123).

To make the curry paste, in a mini food processor or mortar, combine the shallots, galangal, garlic, lemongrass, cilantro stems, fresh and soaked dried chiles, lime leaves, shrimp paste, and coconut and process or grind with a pestle until a smooth paste forms. Add 1–2 tablespoons water if needed to facilitate the grinding.

In a Dutch oven or large frying pan, bring the coconut cream to a simmer over medium heat. Cook for 2 minutes. Add the curry paste and return to a simmer, stirring to dissolve the curry paste. Cook until the mixture thickens and the coconut oil separates from the cream, 2–3 minutes. Add the fish sauce, palm sugar, and lime juice and cook, stirring occasionally, until the flavors are blended, 7–10 minutes longer. Taste and adjust the seasoning.

Just before serving, cut the sea bass into pieces 2 inches (5 cm) long and $^{1}/_{2}$ inch (12 mm) wide. Cut the scallops into quarters. Peel the shrimp, leaving the tail segments intact, then devein. Stir the fish, scallops, and shrimp into the coconut curry. Simmer very gently over medium-low heat until the seafood is opaque throughout, 5–7 minutes. Be careful not to allow the liquid to come to a full boil. Stir in the lime leaves and transfer to a warmed bowl. Garnish with the cilantro sprigs and serve at once.

For the red curry paste

2 shallots, chopped

2 tablespoons peeled and chopped fresh galangal

3 cloves garlic, chopped

1 lemongrass stalk, tender midsection only, chopped

1 tablespoon chopped fresh cilantro (fresh coriander) stems

2 red Fresno chiles, seeded and chopped

3 dried red chiles, soaked in warm water for 15 minutes and drained

4 kaffir lime leaves, spines removed

$^{1}/_{2}$ teaspoon shrimp paste

1 tablespoon unsweetened flaked coconut

$1^{1}/_{2}$ cups (12 fl oz/375 ml) coconut cream

$4^{1}/_{2}$ teaspoons fish sauce

1 tablespoon *each* chopped palm sugar and lime juice

$^{1}/_{2}$ lb (250 g) sea bass fillets

$^{1}/_{2}$ lb (250 g) sea scallops

$^{1}/_{2}$ lb (250 g) medium shrimp (prawns)

3 kaffir lime leaves

2 fresh cilantro (fresh coriander) sprigs

MAKES 4–6 SERVINGS

Salted Grilled Mackerel

2 tablespoons *each* lemon
juice, lime juice, rice vinegar,
and tamari soy sauce

1 tablespoon light soy sauce

1-inch (2.5-cm) square piece
konbu

Canola oil for brushing

4 mackerel fillets,
about 6 oz (185 g) each

Salt

2 green (spring) onions

¼ daikon

MAKES 4 SERVINGS

In a small bowl, combine the lemon and lime juices, vinegar, soy sauces, and 1 tablespoon water. Wipe the *konbu* with a damp cloth, add to the bowl, cover, and refrigerate the *ponzu* sauce for at least 2 hours or up to overnight.

Preheat the broiler (grill). Line a broiler pan with aluminum foil and lightly brush with oil. Pat the fillets dry and sprinkle them liberally on both sides with 1 teaspoon salt. Arrange the fillets on the prepared pan and broil (grill) 4–6 inches (10–15 cm) from the heat source until golden brown on the first side, 2–3 minutes. Using a spatula, carefully turn the fillets and broil until golden brown on the second side and opaque throughout, about 2 minutes longer.

While the fish is cooking, cut the green onions into thin strips and peel and shred the daikon. Arrange on individual plates. Remove the *konbu* from the *ponzu* sauce and discard. Place the fillets on the plates and serve at once with the sauce.

The traditional Japanese method of generously salting and then grilling meat is called *shioyaki*. In this dish, mackerel rubbed with salt is grilled over high heat to create a crisp crust. The fish is served with a traditional *ponzu* sauce featuring lemon juice, rice vinegar, and soy sauce. Accompany the fish with Steamed Rice (page 274).

Miso-Marinated Black Cod

This dish reflects the refined simplicity of Japanese cuisine. Black cod, also known as sablefish, is marinated overnight in mild, sweet *shiro miso* and then broiled until golden brown and caramelized. The longer the fillets are marinated, the firmer and sweeter the fish becomes. Butterfish and sea bass are perfect for this dish if cod is unavailable.

In a saucepan over medium heat, combine the mirin and sake, bring to a boil, and cook for about 2 minutes. Reduce the heat to low and whisk in the miso. Add the sugar and stir until dissolved, about 1 minute. Let cool. Pour the mirin mixture into a large zippered plastic bag, add the fish fillets, and seal the bag. Turn the bag and gently massage the fillets until well coated with the marinade. Refrigerate for at least 3 hours or up to 24 hours.

Preheat the broiler (grill). Lightly oil a baking sheet. Remove the fillets from the marinade. Discard the marinade. Arrange the fillets on the prepared sheet and broil (grill) 4–6 inches (10–15 cm) from the heat source until crisp and golden brown, 2–3 minutes. Carefully turn the fillets and broil until golden brown on the second side, about 2 minutes longer. Preheat the oven to 400°F (200°C). Transfer the fish to the oven and bake until opaque throughout, about 10 minutes. Arrange the fillets on plates, garnish with the ginger strips, and serve at once.

¼ cup (2 fl oz/60 ml) mirin

2 tablespoons sake

⅓ cup (3 oz/90 g) *shiro miso*

¼ cup (2 oz/60 g) sugar

4 black cod fillets, each about 6 oz (185 g)

Canola oil for greasing

¼ cup (2 oz/60 g) pickled ginger, squeezed to remove excess moisture and cut into fine strips

MAKES 4 SERVINGS

Tandoori-Style Fish

Tandoori cooking calls for marinating fish, chicken, or lamb in yogurt and spices and then roasting the skewered fish or meat over a very hot charcoal fire in a cylindrical clay oven called a tandoor. Since home kitchens do not have tandoors, cooking the fish for this recipe over a hot grill or in a hot oven is a good alternative. Traditionally, Indian cooks have used a natural dye to color tandoori foods a vivid orange-red. The version here eliminates the red pigment.

To make the marinade, in a blender or food processor, combine the yogurt, lemon juice, shallot, garlic, ginger, chile, garam masala, turmeric, and 1 teaspoon salt and process to a smooth purée.

Pour the marinade into a large zippered plastic bag, add the fish fillets, and seal the bag. Turn the bag and gently massage the fillets until the fish is well coated with the marinade. Refrigerate for at least 1 hour or up to 2 hours.

In a large frying pan over medium heat, warm the 2 tablespoons canola oil. Add the sliced onion and sauté until crisp and golden brown, 10–12 minutes. Remove from the heat and set aside.

Prepare a charcoal or gas grill for direct grilling over high heat, or preheat the broiler (grill). Brush the grill rack or a broiler pan with oil. Remove the fish fillets from the marinade. Shake off the excess marinade and discard. Arrange the fish on the grill rack; if using a broiler, position the pan 4–6 inches (10–15 cm) from the heat source. Cook until the fish is crisp and golden brown on the first side, 4–5 minutes. Using a spatula, carefully turn the fillets and cook until golden brown on the second side, about 4 minutes longer. Move the fish to a cooler area of the grill and cover the grill, or turn off the broiler, and let the fillets continue to cook until opaque throughout, about 5 minutes.

Gently reheat the onions in the frying pan and mound three-fourths of them on a warmed platter. Arrange the fillets on top. Garnish with the remaining onions, the cilantro sprigs, and the lemon wedges. Serve at once.

For the marinade

1/2 cup (4 oz/125 g) plain whole-milk yogurt

1 tablespoon fresh lemon juice

1 shallot, chopped

3 cloves garlic, chopped

1 tablespoon peeled and chopped fresh ginger

1 jalapeño chile, seeded and chopped

2 teaspoons garam masala

1 teaspoon ground turmeric

Salt

4 sea bass or halibut fillets, about 6 oz (185 g) each

2 tablespoons canola oil, plus extra for brushing

1 large yellow onion, thinly sliced

3 fresh cilantro (fresh coriander) sprigs

1 lemon, cut into wedges

MAKES 4 SERVINGS

Steamed Fish with Green Onion, Ginger, and Sizzling Oil

2 tablespoons peeled and slivered fresh ginger

2 cloves garlic, minced

1 tablespoon light soy sauce

1 tablespoon dark soy sauce

1 teaspoon oyster sauce

1 teaspoon Asian sesame oil

1/2 teaspoon sugar

1/2 teaspoon cornstarch (cornflour)

1/8 teaspoon ground white pepper

3 tablespoons canola oil

4 sea bass or halibut fillets, about 6 oz (185 g) each

2 tablespoons canola oil

2 green (spring) onions, white part only, cut into slivers

2 tablespoons fresh cilantro (fresh coriander) leaves

MAKES 4–6 SERVINGS

Pour water to a depth of 2 inches (5 cm) into a wok or saucepan. Place a bamboo steamer basket in the wok, or fit a steamer rack in the saucepan. The water should not touch the bottom of the basket or rack. Bring the water to a boil.

In a bowl, stir together the ginger, garlic, soy sauces, oyster sauce, sesame oil, sugar, cornstarch, white pepper, and 1 tablespoon of the canola oil until the sugar and cornstarch dissolve. Place the fillets on a heatproof plate large enough to hold them in a single layer. Spoon the soy sauce mixture evenly over the fillets.

Place the plate in the bamboo steamer or on the steaming rack, cover tightly, and steam the fish over high heat until opaque throughout, about 10 minutes per inch measured at the thickest part. Remove the plate from the steamer and transfer the fillets to a platter. Spoon the sauce remaining on the plate over the fish.

To serve, in a small saucepan over high heat, heat the remaining 2 tablespoons canola oil until almost smoking. Garnish the fish with the green onions and cilantro, carefully drizzle the hot oil over the fish, and serve at once.

Throughout China, the fish is a symbol of plenty. Southern Chinese cooks believe that one of the best ways to prepare fish is by dressing it with light, delicate seasonings and steaming it until it is perfectly done. Exemplifying that approach, this recipe uses ginger and green onions to complement naturally sweet sea bass or halibut.

Fish Braised in Caramel Sauce

Sweet and salty caramel sauce, known as *nuoc mau*, is one of the cornerstones of Vietnamese cooking. The mahogany-colored sauce is made from caramelized sugar and fish sauce and is often used in stews, stir-fries, and braises like the one here, where it imparts not only a rich hue but adds depth of flavor. Light accompaniments such as Green Papaya Salad (page 123) and Sweet-and-Sour Red Onion and Cucumber Salad (page 129) pair well with this dish.

If using a clay pot, submerge the bottom and lid of the pot in warm water and let stand for 15–30 minutes.

To make the caramel sauce, in a small bowl, combine the fish sauce, soy sauce, and 1 tablespoon water. Set aside. In a small, deep saucepan over medium heat, combine the sugar, 2 tablespoons water, and the lemon juice. Stir until the sugar dissolves into a syrup. Raise the heat to high, stop stirring, and swirl the pan until the sugar turns light amber, 3–5 minutes. Remove the sugar syrup from the heat and carefully pour the soy sauce mixture into the hot syrup. Stir the mixture until the bubbles subside. Set the caramel sauce aside.

Preheat the oven to 350°F (180°C).

In a frying pan over medium heat, warm the oil. Add the shallots, ginger, and garlic and sauté until softened, 2–3 minutes. Sprinkle with ¼ teaspoon pepper, pour in the caramel sauce, and stir to blend. Reduce the heat to low, add the fish steaks, and turn to coat with the sauce.

Remove the clay pot from the water and transfer the fish and sauce to the pot or to a Dutch oven. Cover tightly, transfer to the oven, and bake for 10 minutes. Using a spatula, carefully turn the steaks, re-cover, and bake until opaque throughout, about 10 minutes longer.

Garnish the fish with the green onions and serve at once.

For the caramel sauce

2 tablespoons fish sauce

2 tablespoons light soy sauce

½ cup (4 oz/125 g) sugar

1 teaspoon fresh lemon juice

2 tablespoons canola oil

1 cup (5 oz/155 g) thinly sliced shallots

2 tablespoons peeled and minced fresh ginger

3 cloves garlic, minced

Freshly ground pepper

4 halibut or catfish steaks, about 6 oz (185 g) each

1 small green (spring) onion, white and pale green parts, thinly sliced on the diagonal

MAKES 4–6 SERVINGS

Hanoi-Style Braised Fish with Rice Noodles

In Hanoi, where this hallmark noodle dish is commonplace, catfish is partially grilled and then finished by braising at the table in an aromatic oil seasoned with turmeric, shallots, garlic, and dill. This version begins by flavoring the catfish fillets with a turmeric and lime juice marinade and then briefly braises the fish. The colorful sauce and tender fillets are then spooned over rice noodles.

In a large nonreactive bowl, whisk together 3 tablespoons of the oil, the lime juice, turmeric, 1 teaspoon salt, and ¼ teaspoon pepper. Add the catfish pieces and stir to coat thoroughly. Let marinate at room temperature for 30 minutes or cover and refrigerate for up to 1 hour.

Bring a large saucepan three-fourths full of water to a boil. Separate the strands of the noodles. Add them to the boiling water and cook for 30 seconds. Drain and transfer to a warmed serving bowl. Keep the noodles warm.

In a large nonstick frying pan over medium-high heat, warm the remaining 2 tablespoons oil. Add the shallots and sauté until translucent, about 1 minute. Add the garlic and pour the catfish with its marinade into the pan. Reduce the heat to medium-low, spread the fish in a single layer, and simmer until opaque on the first side, 3–4 minutes. Using a spatula, carefully turn the fish. Stir in the dill and cilantro and simmer until the fish is opaque throughout, 2–3 minutes longer.

To serve, pour the catfish and sauce over the noodles. Garnish with the green onions and peanuts, and serve at once with the dipping sauce.

5 tablespoons (2½ fl oz/ 75 ml) canola oil

2 tablespoons fresh lime juice

1 tablespoon ground turmeric

Salt and freshly ground pepper

1 lb (500 g) catfish fillets, cut into pieces 2 inches (5 cm) long and ½ inch (12 mm) wide

6 oz (185 g) dried rice vermicelli, soaked in hot water for 15 minutes and drained

4 shallots, thinly sliced

3 cloves garlic, minced

1 tablespoon fresh chopped dill

1 tablespoon chopped fresh cilantro (fresh coriander)

1 green (spring) onion, white and pale green parts, thinly sliced on the diagonal

1 tablespoon chopped unsalted dry-roasted peanuts

Nam Pla Dipping Sauce (page 272) for serving

MAKES 4–6 SERVINGS

Spice-Rubbed Grilled Fish

For the chile paste

**2 red Fresno chiles,
seeded and chopped**

3 shallots, chopped

**3 tablespoons peeled and
chopped fresh galangal**

**1 lemongrass stalk, tender
midsection only, smashed
with the side of a chef's
knife and chopped**

3 cloves garlic, chopped

½ teaspoon shrimp paste

**2 macadamia nuts or
blanched almonds**

Salt

**2 tablespoons canola oil,
plus extra for brushing**

1 tablespoon fresh lime juice

**1 teaspoon chopped palm
sugar**

Salt

**1 whole red snapper,
sea bass, or tilapia,
about 2 lb (1 kg), cleaned**

**1 large banana leaf,
about 12 by 16 inches
(30 by 40 cm)**

**3 kaffir lime leaves, spines
removed, thinly sliced**

1 lime, cut into wedges

MAKES 4 SERVINGS

Prepare a charcoal or gas grill for direct grilling over high heat, or preheat the oven to 450°F (230°C). Soak 3 bamboo skewers, each 8 inches (20 cm) long, in water to cover for approximately 15 minutes.

To make the chile paste, in a mini food processor or mortar, combine the chiles, shallots, galangal, lemongrass, garlic, shrimp paste, nuts, and ⅛ teaspoon salt and process or grind with a pestle until a smooth paste forms. Add 1–2 tablespoons water if needed to facilitate the grinding.

In a saucepan over medium-high heat, warm the 2 tablespoons oil. Add the chile paste and fry until fragrant and the color turns a shade darker, 2–3 minutes. Reduce the heat to low and stir in the lime juice, sugar, and ¼ teaspoon salt and simmer for 2 minutes. Remove the paste from the heat, transfer it to a large, shallow bowl, and let cool to room temperature.

Measure the fish at the thickest point. Using a chef's knife, score the fish crosswise at a 45-degree angle, making 3 equally spaced slashes about ¼ inch (6 cm) deep on each side. Wipe the banana leaf with a damp kitchen towel and place on a work surface, shiny side down, with the long side facing you. Place the fish in the bowl of chile paste and use your hands to rub the paste generously into the slits and cavity of the fish. Place the fish on top of the banana leaf horizontally and sprinkle the lime leaves on top. Drain the skewers. Fold the top and bottom portion of the leaf over the fish and secure the middle and ends of the leaf with the skewers.

Brush the grill rack with oil and place the banana leaf packet, seam side up, directly on the grill, or place the packet on a baking sheet and transfer to the oven. Cook the fish, turning the packet once, for about 20 minutes per 1 inch (2.5 cm) of thickness. Transfer the banana leaf packet to a warmed platter and unwrap the fish. Serve at once, garnished with the lime wedges.

Grilling or steaming both savory and sweet foods wrapped in banana leaves is popular in Indonesia and other countries in Southeast Asia, where banana trees are abundant. Here, the banana leaf helps keep the whole fish moist while also imparting a sweet floral fragrance. The leaves are available frozen in Asian markets and should be thawed at room temperature for several hours. A piece of aluminum foil of the same size can be substituted.

Poultry and Meat

About Poultry and Meat

Many dishes that feature pork, beef, lamb, and poultry were once considered feast foods reserved for special occasions. Simmered in rich sauces, roasted to yield crisp skins, dunked into hot pots, or covered with sweet, shiny glazes, they conveyed prosperity and celebrated abundance.

Today in Asia, meats and poultry are more widely available than they were in the past, but many dishes still call for modest amounts thinly sliced or cut into small pieces. Knives do not appear on a traditional Asian table, so large roasts are not typical centerpiece dishes. Even the suckling pig or whole chicken that anchors a celebratory dinner will be carved away from the table into bite-sized pieces. Lamb curries, beef stews, and pork rib soups feature small pieces cooked tender enough to be eaten easily with chopsticks, spoons, flatbread, or fingers.

CHICKEN AND DUCK

The custom of serving small pieces also holds true for such poultry dishes as India's chicken *tikka* (page 214), cubes of meat marinated in yogurt and spices, and Vietnam's Stir-fried Lemongrass Chicken (page 217). Both show how quickly and easily chicken takes to local flavors. Fried chicken is wildly popular in Asia, and Malaysia's spicy version (page 213) is one of the tastiest, crispiest examples. The dark meat of legs and thighs takes well to longer cooking and is ideal for dishes such as Chicken Curry with Toasted Coconut (page 210) and Red-Cooked Chicken (page 209).

Duck is appreciated for its richness and succulence. Sweet flavors are sometimes used to complement its mildly gamy character, as in Thai Green Curry with Roast Duck and Sweet Potatoes (page 221). In Goa, Indian cooks take a different tack to balance flavors, serving a hot-and-sour duck *vindaloo*. China's Five-Spice

Roast Duck (page 218) draws on a classic blend of spices—cinnamon, clove, fennel, star anise, and Sichuan peppercorn—to create a mahogany glaze on fragrant, crisp skin.

THE NUMBER ONE MEAT

Although chicken and duck are highly regarded in China, pork reigns supreme, accounting for more than 70 percent of all the meat consumed in the country. Its importance is reflected in the fact that the same word is used for both pork and meat in Chinese. Cooks roast pork to bring out its succulence, and its crisp skin is a much-desired delicacy among diners. The long, thin, cured Chinese-style pork sausage known as *lop cheong* in Cantonese adds savory sweetness to stir-fried noodles, stews, fillings for buns and poultry, rice casseroles, and steamed dishes, and cuts such as spareribs are slowly braised until the tender meat falls from the bone (page 222).

But the popularity of pork reaches beyond China. Indeed, every country in Southeast Asia offers a long menu of dishes, from the quick and easy Stir-fried Pork with Garlic (page 225) of Vietnam and the spicy charcoal-grilled pork (page 229) of the Korean peninsula to the vinegary, garlicky Pork Adobo (page 224) of the Philippines.

Even the Japanese have a favorite pork dish. *Tonkatsu* (page 227), thinly sliced, breaded, and fried cutlets that originated in the late nineteenth century, is enjoyed as an inexpensive restaurant meal by salarymen at lunchtime and families at dinnertime.

BEEF AND LAMB

Beef and lamb have played lesser, though still important roles in the Asian kitchen. Mongols swept down through China and reached as far as Vietnam, introducing beef and lamb to local tables along the way. Even today, the appearance of either meat in a dish reveals the long-reaching influence of the Muslim tribes of Central Asia.

In China's best-known party dish, Mongolian Hot Pot (page 233), thin slices of lamb, pork, or beef are cooked in hot broth at the table and served with various dipping sauces. Similar dishes have been developed in other Asian countries, such as Japan's *shabu-shabu*, traditionally thinly sliced beef cooked in dashi (broth) and served with a sesame or citrus-based *ponzu* dipping sauce.

For Vietnam's *bo nhung dam*, diners cook beef slices in a simmering broth infused with lemongrass, vinegar, and black pepper, wrap the beef in rice-paper rounds along with fresh herbs, rice noodles, and lettuce, and then dip the bundle into a pungent dipping sauce. Korean *kalbi* (page 241), grilled marinated short ribs, served with a sesame-soy dipping sauce, is another dish influenced by Mongolian open-fire techniques.

In India, Mogul rulers eschewed eating beef out of respect for their Hindu neighbors, but they depended heavily on lamb. The classic dishes of India, from *biryani* (rice and meat) to *korma* (braise) to kebabs, all feature special versions with lamb, a reflection of that legacy. *Rogani gosht*, lamb and potatoes cooked in an aromatic cream sauce with blanched almonds, is a hallmark of the Mogul kitchen. Spiced Lamb with Caramelized Onions (page 230), braised in a creamy yogurt sauce, is another of the many dishes with roots in northern India and Pakistan.

Grilled Garlic-and-Cilantro-Marinated Chicken

2 shallots, chopped

4 cloves garlic, chopped

1 tablespoon peeled and chopped fresh galangal

2 tablespoons chopped fresh cilantro (fresh coriander) stems

Freshly ground pepper

⅓ cup (3 fl oz/80 ml) coconut milk

2 tablespoons fish sauce

1 tablespoon dark soy sauce

1 tablespoon rice wine

1 tablespoon chopped palm sugar

1 tablespoon canola oil, plus extra for brushing

1 chicken, about 3½ lb (1.75 kg), halved (page 276)

Nam Pla Dipping Sauce (page 272) for serving

MAKES 4–6 SERVINGS

In a mini food processor or mortar, combine the shallots, garlic, galangal, cilantro, and ¼ teaspoon pepper and process or grind with a pestle until a smooth paste forms. Add 1–2 tablespoons water if needed to facilitate the grinding. Transfer to a bowl. Add the coconut milk, fish sauce, soy sauce, rice wine, palm sugar, and 1 tablespoon oil and stir to mix well. Pour the marinade into a large zippered plastic bag, add the chicken halves, and seal the bag. Turn the bag and gently massage until the chicken is well coated with the marinade. Refrigerate for at least 4 hours or up to overnight.

Prepare a charcoal or gas grill for direct grilling over high heat, or preheat the oven to 425°F (220°C).

Remove the chicken from the marinade and shake off the excess. Discard the marinade. Brush the grill rack with oil. Place the chicken halves, skin side up, on the grill rack directly over the coals and sear until golden brown on the first side, 4–5 minutes. Turn and grill until golden brown on the second side, 3–4 minutes longer. Using tongs, move the chicken to the side of the rack away from the direct heat. Cover and continue to cook until the juices run clear when a thigh is pierced, 20–25 minutes. If cooking in the oven, line a roasting pan with aluminum foil, place a rack on the pan, and brush the rack with oil. Put the chicken halves, skin side down, on the rack. Roast the chicken until the juices run clear when a thigh is pierced, 50–60 minutes, turning the chicken after 25–30 minutes. An instant-read thermometer inserted into the thickest part of a thigh away from the bone should register 170°F (77°C).

Remove the chicken from the grill or oven, tent with aluminum foil, and let rest for 10 minutes. Cut each half into 5 or 6 pieces, halving the thigh and breast, and transfer to a warmed platter. Serve at once with the dipping sauce on the side.

This chicken dish seasoned with typical Southeast Asian flavors has its roots in Thailand and is also a favorite in Laos. The chicken halves are customarily grilled over a charcoal fire, which adds a layer of smokiness, but roasting in the oven is an easy and convenient alternative.

Red-Cooked Chicken

Red cooking, a popular technique from eastern China, calls for simmering meat very slowly in a dark soy sauce–based poaching liquid, which imparts a rich, brownish red tinge to the cooked meat. The flavor that stands out in this chicken dish is star anise, a star-shaped spice that is sweet and aromatic with a strong licorice taste. For the most tender results, it is important to poach the chicken over very low heat; otherwise the meat may become tough.

In a Dutch oven or other deep, heavy-bottomed pot, combine the soy sauces, rice wine, vinegar, sugar, citrus zest, cinnamon, star anise, smashed green onions, ginger, and garlic. Add 5 cups (40 fl oz/1.25 l) water and bring to a boil over medium-high heat. Reduce the heat to low. Simmer, uncovered, for 20 minutes.

Meanwhile, if the giblets and neck are in the chicken cavity, remove them and reserve for another use or discard. Remove and discard any pockets of fat from the neck cavity. Place the chicken, breast side down, in the simmering liquid. Cover and reduce the heat to very low. Cook, adjusting the heat to maintain a bare simmer and skimming any foam from the surface of the liquid, for 40 minutes. Turn the chicken breast side up, re-cover the pot, and continue cooking over very low heat until the chicken is firm and opaque throughout, about 20 minutes.

Remove the chicken from the hot liquid and place the bird, cavity side down, in a colander to drain. Using a slotted spoon, remove the solids from the pot and discard. Pour off all but 1 1/2 cups (12 fl oz/375 ml) of the cooking liquid from the pot and reheat gently over medium-low heat. In a small bowl, stir together the cornstarch and 1 tablespoon water until smooth. Add the cornstarch mixture to the cooking liquid and cook, stirring, until the liquid thickens into a sauce, about 2 minutes. Swirl in the sesame oil and remove from the heat.

To serve, cut the chicken into 10–12 pieces: 2 wings, 4 breast pieces (each breast half cut in half), 2 drumsticks, and 2 thighs. If desired, cut each thigh in half. Arrange the pieces on a warmed platter, spoon the warm sauce over the chicken, garnish with the shredded green onions, and serve at once.

1 cup (8 fl oz/250 ml) light soy sauce

1/4 cup (2 fl oz/60 ml) dark soy sauce

1/4 cup (2 fl oz/60 ml) Chinese rice wine

3 tablespoons black vinegar

1/4 cup (2 oz/60 g) sugar

1 strip tangerine or orange zest, about 1 inch (2.5 cm) wide and 4 inches (10 cm) long

1 cinnamon stick

2 star anise

3 green (spring) onions, white and pale green parts, smashed with the side of a chef's knife, plus 2 onions, green parts only, shredded

4 slices fresh ginger, each about 1/4 inch (6 mm) thick, peeled and smashed with the side of a chef's knife

4 cloves garlic, smashed with the side of a chef's knife

1 chicken, 3 1/2–4 lb (1.75–2 kg)

1 teaspoon cornstarch (cornflour)

1 teaspoon Asian sesame oil

MAKES 4–6 SERVINGS

Chicken Curry with Toasted Coconut

1½ lb (750 g) skinless, boneless chicken thighs, cut into 1-inch (2.5-cm) cubes

2 teaspoons fresh lemon juice

Salt

For the spice paste

½ cup (2 oz/60 g) unsweetened flaked coconut

4 cardamom pods

4 dried red chiles, stemmed and seeded

2 tablespoons coriander seeds

1 tablespoon cumin seeds

1 teaspoon fennel seeds

¼ teaspoon peppercorns

1 star anise

½ teaspoon ground turmeric

⅛ teaspoon ground cinnamon

1 small yellow onion, chopped

2 tablespoons peeled and chopped fresh ginger

4 cloves garlic

3 tablespoons canola oil

1 teaspoon sugar

1 teaspoon tamarind paste

Salt

1 tablespoon chopped fresh cilantro (fresh coriander)

MAKES 4–6 SERVINGS

In a nonreactive bowl, combine the chicken cubes, lemon juice, and ½ teaspoon salt and stir to mix well. Let marinate at room temperature for 30 minutes.

To make the spice paste, put the coconut in a small, dry frying pan over medium heat and heat, stirring often, until lightly toasted, about 5 minutes. Pour onto a plate to cool. Carefully split open the cardamom pods and remove the seeds.

Raise the heat to medium-high and add the chiles; cardamom, coriander, cumin, and fennel seeds; peppercorns; and star anise to the pan. Toast, stirring often, until the spices are fragrant and turn a shade darker, 3–4 minutes. Transfer to a spice grinder or a coffee mill reserved for spices and grind to a fine powder. Transfer the spice powder to a blender and add the coconut, turmeric, and cinnamon. Add ½ cup (4 fl oz/125 ml) water and process to a smooth paste. Set aside.

In a blender or food processor, combine the onion, ginger, and garlic and process to a smooth paste. In a large frying pan over medium-high heat, warm the oil. Add the onion paste and sauté until it begins to brown, 4–5 minutes. Stir in the coconut-spice paste and sauté for 1 minute. Add 2 cups (16 fl oz/500 ml) water, the sugar, the tamarind paste, and 1 teaspoon salt and mix well. Bring to a boil, reduce the heat to low, and add the chicken. Return to a simmer and cook until the sauce has thickened and the chicken is opaque throughout, 20–25 minutes.

Taste and adjust the seasoning. Transfer to a warmed bowl, garnish with the cilantro, and serve at once.

This intriguing curry is from the Indian state of Goa, whose cuisine was influenced by the region's Hindu origins and by the Portuguese traders and colonists who arrived four centuries ago. A blend of eight toasted spices and chiles is combined with toasted coconut, giving a slightly sweet, nutty flavor to the braised chicken. Keep a close eye on the pan when toasting coconut, as its high fat content makes it burn easily. Serve the curry with steamed basmati rice (page 274) or Indian Flatbread (page 67).

Spicy Fried Chicken

Fried, roasted, or simmered in curry, chicken is the meat of choice in Malaysia. There is no single definitive national recipe for fried chicken—countless regional variations offer endless twists of taste. For a more intense flavor, marinate the chicken overnight. You can also roast it in the oven from start to finish: place it on an oiled rack set over a roasting pan lined with aluminum foil and bake at 450°F (230°C) for 40–45 minutes. The skin will not be as crisp, but the chicken will still be very flavorful.

Cut the chicken into 10–12 pieces (page 276). In a mini food processor or mortar, combine the shallots, ginger, garlic, chiles, soy sauce, sugar, coriander, cumin, turmeric, 1 1/2 teaspoons salt, and 1/4 teaspoon pepper and process or grind with a pestle until a smooth paste forms. Add 1–2 tablespoons water if needed to facilitate the grinding. Transfer to a large zippered plastic bag, add the chicken pieces, and seal the bag. Massage the chicken until the pieces are well coated with the marinade. Refrigerate for at least 4 hours or up to overnight.

Preheat the oven to 350°F (180°C). Pour oil to a depth of 2 inches (5 cm) into a wok or deep frying pan over high heat and heat to 370°F (188°C) on a deep-frying thermometer. Line a baking sheet with paper towels. Remove the chicken from the marinade and pat dry with paper towels. Discard the marinade. Using tongs, add half of the chicken pieces to the hot oil; do not crowd the pan. Deep-fry until crisp and golden brown on the first side, about 3–4 minutes. Turn the chicken and deep-fry until golden brown on the second side, 3–4 minutes longer. Using the tongs, transfer to the paper towels to drain. Repeat to cook the remaining chicken.

Remove the paper towels from the baking sheet and transfer the chicken to the oven. Roast until an instant-read thermometer inserted into the thickest part of a thigh away from the bone registers 170°F (77°C), 15–20 minutes. Arrange the chicken on a warmed platter, garnish with the lemon wedges, and serve at once.

1 chicken, 3 1/2 lb (1.75 kg)

2 shallots, chopped

2 tablespoons peeled and chopped fresh ginger

3 cloves garlic, chopped

3 dried red chiles, stems removed, soaked in warm water for 15 minutes and drained

3 tablespoons sweet soy sauce

1 tablespoon sugar

1 teaspoon *each* ground coriander and ground cumin

1/2 teaspoon ground turmeric

Salt and freshly ground pepper

Canola oil for deep-frying

1 lemon, cut into wedges

MAKES 4–6 SERVINGS

Spiced Grilled Chicken

For the marinade

1 cup (8 oz/250 g) plain whole-milk yogurt

1 tablespoon lemon juice

2 tablespoons peeled and grated fresh ginger

3 cloves garlic, minced

1 teaspoon garam masala

1/2 teaspoon *each* ground cumin, ground coriander, and ground turmeric

1/8 teaspoon cayenne pepper

Salt

1 1/2 lb (750 g) skinless, boneless chicken breasts

Canola oil as needed

1 yellow onion, chopped

2 tablespoons peeled and chopped fresh ginger

2 cloves garlic

1 red Fresno chile, chopped

1/4 teaspoon *each* sugar and garam masala

Pinch of cayenne pepper

1 cup (8 fl oz/250 ml) *each* tomato purée and low-sodium chicken broth

1/4 cup (2 oz/60 g) plain whole-milk yogurt

1/2 cup (4 fl oz/125 ml) half-and-half (half cream)

1 tablespoon chopped fresh cilantro (fresh coriander)

MAKES 4–6 SERVINGS

To make the marinade, in a large, nonreactive bowl, combine the yogurt, lemon juice, ginger, garlic, garam masala, cumin, coriander, turmeric, cayenne, and 1 teaspoon salt and stir to mix well. Cut the chicken into 1-inch (2.5-cm) cubes. Add to the marinade and stir to coat thoroughly. Cover and refrigerate for at least 4 hours or up to overnight.

Prepare a charcoal or gas grill for direct grilling over high heat. Soak 10 bamboo skewers, each 8 inches (20 cm) long, in water to cover for 30 minutes.

Drain the skewers. Remove the chicken cubes from the marinade and pat dry with paper towels. Discard the marinade. Thread the chicken onto the skewers, pressing the cubes together tightly. Brush the chicken and the grill rack with oil. Arrange the skewers on the rack so they are not touching one another and sear until golden brown on one side, 4–5 minutes. Turn the skewers and grill until golden brown on the opposite side, 3–4 minutes longer. Transfer to a platter and set aside.

In a blender or food processor, combine the onion, ginger, garlic, chile, and 2 tablespoons water and process until a smooth paste forms. In a large frying pan over medium-high heat, warm 2 tablespoons oil. Add the onion paste and sauté until it just begins to brown, about 5 minutes. Stir in the sugar, garam masala, and cayenne and sauté for 1 minute. Add the tomato purée and broth, reduce the heat to medium-low, and bring to a simmer. Cook, stirring often, until the sauce begins to thicken, 5–6 minutes. Reduce the heat to low and stir in the yogurt and half-and-half. Bring to a bare simmer and cook for 5 minutes to blend the flavors.

While the sauce is simmering, slide the chicken pieces off the skewers into the sauce and stir to combine. Cook until the chicken is opaque throughout, about 5 minutes longer. Taste and adjust the seasoning. Transfer to a warmed bowl, garnish with the cilantro, and serve at once.

The skewers of chicken for this mild curry, known as chicken *tikka*, are traditionally roasted in an Indian clay oven. Cooking the chicken on a grill yields equally delicious results. In India, yogurt is often used as a tenderizer, as it contains enzymes that break down and soften the proteins in meat. Here it is used as a marinade and also enriches the creamy tomato-based sauce. Serve the chicken *tikka* with steamed basmati rice (page 274) or Indian Flatbread (page 67).

Stir-fried Lemongrass Chicken

Lemongrass is one of the main ingredients in the spice paste for this classic Vietnamese stir-fry. The distinctive lemon scent and flavor permeate the chicken while it marinates for a few hours and especially after marinating overnight. For a complete meal, precede this dish with Green Papaya Salad (page 123) or Sweet-and-Sour Red Onion and Cucumber Salad (page 129) and accompany with Lemongrass and Coconut Jasmine Rice (page 112).

In a mini food processor or mortar, combine the lemongrass, shallots, ginger, garlic, chile, 1 teaspoon salt, and 1 tablespoon of the oil and process or grind with a pestle until a smooth paste forms. Add 1–2 tablespoons water if needed to facilitate the grinding. Transfer the marinade to a large zippered plastic bag, add the chicken cubes, and seal the bag. Turn the bag and gently massage the marinade into the chicken. Refrigerate for at least 4 hours or up to overnight.

In a small bowl, whisk together the soy sauces, fish sauce, vinegar, sugar, cornstarch, $1/8$ teaspoon pepper, and 2 tablespoons water to make a stir-fry sauce. Set the sauce aside.

In a large wok or frying pan over medium-high heat, warm 2 tablespoons of the oil. Add the onion and stir-fry until tender and lightly browned, 7–8 minutes. Transfer the onion to a bowl. Set the pan aside.

Remove the chicken from the marinade and pat dry with paper towels. Discard the marinade. Place the reserved pan over high heat and add the remaining 2 tablespoons oil. When the oil is hot, working in batches if necessary, add the chicken cubes and stir-fry until golden brown, 4–5 minutes.

Return the onions to the pan. Pour in the sauce and stir-fry until the sauce thickens and the chicken is opaque throughout, 1–2 minutes. Divide the chicken among individual bowls, garnish with basil leaves, and serve at once.

2 lemongrass stalks, tender midsections only, chopped

2 shallots, chopped

2 tablespoons peeled and chopped fresh ginger

3 cloves garlic, chopped

1 jalapeño chile, seeded and chopped

Salt and freshly ground pepper

5 tablespoons (2$1/2$ fl oz/ 75 ml) canola oil

1$1/2$ lb (750 g) skinless, boneless chicken thighs, cut into 1-inch (2.5-cm) cubes

1 tablespoon light soy sauce

1 teaspoon dark soy sauce

1 tablespoon fish sauce

1 teaspoon rice vinegar

$1/2$ teaspoon sugar

$1/2$ teaspoon cornstarch (cornflour)

1 small yellow onion, thinly sliced

2 tablepoons fresh basil leaves

MAKES 4–6 SERVINGS

Chile Crab

Chinese in origin, this dish is now renowned in both Singapore and Malaysia, where it is found as street food, served piping hot from a wok. The crabs are cooked twice: first they are stir-fried in a small amount of oil and then they are coated in a hearty tomato-laced sauce that is both spicy and sweet. The dish is tasty yet messy and is best eaten with your fingers, using French bread or Chinese steamed rice-flour buns to soak up the sauce. Look for the buns in Chinese bakeries or Asian markets. Large shrimp (prawns) deveined with the shells intact can be cooked in the same way.

Bring a large saucepan three-fourths full of water to a boil over high heat.

Meanwhile, to make the chile paste, in a mini food processor or mortar, combine the shallots, garlic, ginger, chiles, black beans, shrimp paste, and $1/4$ teaspoon pepper and process or grind with a pestle until a smooth paste forms. Add 1–2 tablespoons water if needed to facilitate the grinding. Set aside.

In a small bowl, stir together the tomato paste, fish sauce, soy sauce, sugar, and 3 tablespoons water to make a stir-fry sauce. Set the sauce aside.

Plunge the crabs into the boiling water and cook for about 2 minutes. Using tongs, transfer to a colander and place under cold running water until cool. Working with 1 crab at a time, pull off the top shell and discard. Lift the tip of the triangular apron on the underside of the body and twist it off and discard. Remove the mandibles at the face end. Pull off the feathery gills, and pull or scrape out the gray intestinal matter from the body and discard, along with any creamy yellow liver, known as the tomalley. Rinse the body under cold running water and pat very dry with paper towels. Using a chef's knife, chop the body in half lengthwise, then cut each half crosswise into 3 or 4 pieces, leaving the legs and claws attached. Using a mallet, crack the claw and leg shells at the joints and in the middle.

In a large frying pan or wok over high heat, warm 3 tablespoons of the oil. Put the cornstarch in a large bowl. Working quickly, add the crab pieces to the bowl and toss to coat thoroughly with the cornstarch. Transfer to a plate, shaking off the excess cornstarch. When the oil is very hot, add the crab pieces and stir-fry until the shells begin to turn bright orange and the edges of the shells begin to brown, 7–8 minutes. Using tongs, transfer the crab to a bowl.

Return the pan to high heat and add the remaining 1 tablespoon oil. Stir in the chile paste and sauté until fragrant, about 10 seconds. Return the crab to the pan and stir-fry until well coated with the chile paste. Pour in the sauce and stir-fry until most of the liquid has evaporated and the crab is opaque throughout, 4–5 minutes. Stir in the cilantro. Transfer to a platter and serve at once.

For the chile paste

2 shallots, chopped

3 cloves garlic, chopped

1 tablespoon peeled and chopped fresh ginger

2 red Fresno chiles, seeded and chopped

1 tablespoon fermented black beans, rinsed well and drained

$1/2$ teaspoon shrimp paste

Freshly ground pepper

1 tablespoon tomato paste

1 tablespoon fish sauce

1 tablespoon light soy sauce

1 teaspoon sugar

2 live Dungeness crabs, about 2 lb (1 kg) total weight

4 tablespoons (2 fl oz/60 ml) canola oil

$1/4$ cup (1 oz/30 g) cornstarch (cornflour)

2 tablespoons minced fresh cilantro (fresh coriander)

MAKES 4–6 SERVINGS

Five-Spice Roast Duck

1 Long Island duck, 3½–4 lb (1.25–2 kg), neck and giblets removed from cavity and reserved for another use

5 green (spring) onions, halved lengthwise and smashed with the side of a chef's knife

4 slices fresh ginger, each about ¼ inch (6 mm) thick, peeled and smashed with the side of a chef's knife

4 cloves garlic, smashed with the side of a chef's knife

¼ cup (2 fl oz/60 ml) Chinese rice wine

¼ cup (2 fl oz/60 ml) light soy sauce

1 tablespoon sugar

1 teaspoon five-spice powder

¼ cup (2 fl oz/60 ml) black vinegar

¼ cup (3 fl oz/90 ml) honey

Canola oil for brushing

For the dipping sauce

¼ cup (2½ oz/75 g) hoisin sauce

1 teaspoon Asian sesame oil

MAKES 4–6 SERVINGS

This version of roast duck is from China's Guangdong Province. Through an elaborate but uncomplicated three-step process, the bird is marinated, then blanched, basted, and refrigerated, and finally roasted. The sequence results in a flavorful bird with crisp skin and succulent flesh.

Remove any pockets of fat from the neck cavity of the duck. Cut off the wing tips. Place the onions, ginger, and garlic in the cavity. In a bowl, combine the rice wine, soy sauce, sugar, and five-spice powder and mix well. Transfer to a large zippered plastic bag. Place the duck in the bag and rub the marinade all over the skin and inside the cavity. Seal the bag and refrigerate overnight, turning the bag once.

In a large saucepan over high heat, bring 4 qt (4 l) water to a boil. Remove the duck from the marinade. Shake off the excess marinade and remove the aromatics from the cavity. Discard the marinade and aromatics. Put a large colander in the sink and place the duck, breast side down, in the colander. Pour half of the boiling water evenly over the duck. Turn the duck breast side up and pour the remaining water over the top. Drain the duck thoroughly, then pat dry with paper towels. Transfer to a pan just large enough to hold it.

In a small saucepan, combine the vinegar, honey, and ¼ cup (2 fl oz/60 ml) water and bring to a boil over medium-high heat, stirring to dissolve the honey. Remove from the heat. Brush the duck skin all over with the honey-vinegar mixture. Refrigerate the duck, uncovered, for 24 hours to dry out the skin.

About 30 minutes before roasting, remove the duck from the refrigerator. Preheat the oven to 450°F (230°C). Line a large roasting pan with aluminum foil. Place a V-shaped rack in the prepared pan and brush the rack with oil. Place the duck, breast side down, in the rack. Roast until the skin is golden brown, 15–20 minutes. Reduce the oven temperature to 350°F (180°C) and roast for 20 minutes. Turn the duck breast side up and continue roasting until the skin is crisp and mahogany brown and an instant-read thermometer inserted into the thickest part of a thigh away from the bone registers 170°F (77°C), 20–25 minutes longer. Transfer the duck to a carving board, and tent with aluminum foil. Let rest for 15 minutes.

To make the sauce, in a small bowl, stir together the hoisin sauce, 2 tablespoons hot water, and the sesame oil. Carve the duck into 12 serving pieces: 2 wings, 4 breast pieces (each breast half cut in half), 2 drumsticks, and 4 thigh pieces (each thigh cut in half). Arrange on a warmed platter. Serve with the dipping sauce.

Green Curry with Roast Duck and Sweet Potatoes

Thai green curry is made with a rich blend of spices, green chiles, and kaffir lime leaves. In this recipe, it flavors roast duck seasoned with Chinese spices and creamy sweet potatoes simmered in coconut milk. If you prefer not to roast a bird, five-spice roast ducks can be purchased fully cooked at Chinese delicatessens and markets. Buy a duck that weighs about 2½ pounds (1.25 kg), carve the duck, and use all the pieces in the curry. The duck is customarily left on the bone for this dish, but if you prefer, remove the meat from the bone and cut it into pieces before adding to the simmering curry.

To make the chile paste, cut each chile in half lengthwise and remove the seeds. Chop the chiles. In a small frying pan over medium heat, warm the oil. Add the chiles, shallots, galangal, and garlic and sauté until the shallots are golden brown, 5–7 minutes. Transfer to a blender or food processor and add the lemongrass, cilantro stems, lime leaves, cumin, cinnamon, cardamom, and nutmeg. Process until a smooth paste forms. Add 1–2 tablespoons water if needed to facilitate the processing. Set aside.

Carve the duck into 2 wings, 4 breast pieces (each breast half cut in half), and 4 thigh pieces (each thigh cut in half). Reserve the drumsticks for another use. Peel the sweet potatoes and cut into 1-inch (2.5-cm) cubes.

In a large frying pan over medium-high heat, warm the oil. Add the chile paste and sauté until fragrant, about 3 minutes. Stir in the coconut milk and 1 cup (8 fl oz/250 ml) water and bring to a boil. Reduce the heat to low, stir in the fish sauce, tamarind paste, lime juice, and palm sugar, and bring to a simmer. Add the sweet potatoes, return to a simmer, and cook, stirring occasionally, for 10 minutes. Gently stir the breast and thigh pieces and the wings into the curry, return to a simmer, and cook until the sweet potatoes are tender when pierced with a fork, 7–10 minutes.

Transfer the curry to a warmed bowl and serve at once.

For the chile paste

2 jalapeño chiles

2 tablespoons canola oil

4 shallots, chopped

2 tablespoons peeled and chopped fresh galangal

4 cloves garlic, chopped

1 lemongrass stalk, tender midsection only, chopped

2 tablespoons chopped fresh cilantro (fresh coriander) stems

2 kaffir lime leaves, spines removed

½ teaspoon ground cumin

¼ teaspoon *each* ground cinnamon and ground cardamom

⅛ teaspoon freshly grated nutmeg

Five-Spice Roast Duck (page 218)

2 sweet potatoes

1 tablespoon canola oil

2 cups (16 fl oz/500 ml) coconut milk

2 tablespoons fish sauce

1 tablespoon *each* tamarind paste and fresh lime juice

1½ teaspoons chopped palm sugar

MAKES 4–6 SERVINGS

Braised Pork Spareribs with Black Bean Sauce

2 tablespoons oyster sauce

2 tablespoons light soy sauce

1 tablespoon dark soy sauce

2 tablespoons Chinese rice wine

2 tablespoons fermented black beans, rinsed well and drained

1 teaspoon sugar

2 teaspoons Asian sesame oil

$1/8$ teaspoon ground white pepper

1 tablespoon cornstarch (cornflour)

Salt

$2^{1}/_{2}$ lb (1.25 kg) pork spareribs, cut crosswise into 2-inch (5-cm) pieces

5 tablespoons ($2^{1}/_{2}$ fl oz/ 75 ml) canola oil

4 green (spring) onions, white and pale green parts, minced, plus 1 green onion, shredded

3 cloves garlic, minced

1 tablespoon peeled and minced fresh ginger

1 red Fresno chile, seeded and minced, plus 1 chile, cut into thin rings

MAKES 4–6 SERVINGS

In a bowl, combine the oyster sauce, soy sauces, rice wine, black beans, sugar, sesame oil, and white pepper. Add 3 cups (24 fl oz/750 ml) water and mix well.

In a small bowl, stir together the cornstarch and $1/2$ teaspoon salt. Sprinkle the cornstarch mixture evenly over the sparerib pieces. In a large Dutch oven or other heavy-bottomed ovenproof pot over high heat, warm 2 tablespoons of the canola oil. When the oil is hot, add half of the rib pieces in a single layer and sear until crisp and golden brown on both sides, 8–10 minutes total. Transfer the seared ribs to a bowl. Add 2 tablespoons of the oil to the pot and repeat to sear the second batch of sparerib pieces.

Preheat the oven to 325°F (165°C).

Place the same pot over medium-high heat and warm the remaining 1 tablespoon oil. Add the minced green onion, garlic, ginger, and minced chile. Sauté until the onions and garlic are tender and translucent, about 3 minutes. Add the soy sauce mixture and bring to a boil. Reduce the heat to low. Return the ribs and any accumulated juices in the bowl to the pot and stir gently. Cover the pot tightly and place in the oven. Bake until the meat is very tender and almost falling off the bone, $1^{1}/_{2}$–2 hours. Stir the ribs 2 or 3 times during the braising.

Transfer to a warmed bowl or platter, garnish with shredded green onion, and chile rings, and serve at once.

Spareribs are commonly steamed and served for dim sum. In this recipe, they are slowly braised in the oven, where they become a tantalizing amber color, irresistibly rich, and extremely tender. Fermented black beans, small soybeans preserved in salt, give the stew a unique salty, sweet, and slightly bitter flavor. Be sure to rinse the beans thoroughly before using, so the finished dish is not too salty. You can ask your butcher to cut the spareribs into bite-sized pieces.

Pork Adobo

2 jalapeño chiles

8 cloves garlic, chopped

1/4 teaspoon peppercorns

Salt

2/3 cup (5 fl oz/160 ml) cider vinegar

3 tablespoons light soy sauce

2 tablespoons brown sugar

3 bay leaves

4 pork blade steaks, each about 6 oz (185 g)

2 tablespoons canola oil

MAKES 4–6 SERVINGS

Cut each chile in half lengthwise and remove the seeds. Chop the chiles. In a mini food processor or mortar, combine the chiles, half of the garlic, the peppercorns, and 1/2 teaspoon salt and process or grind with a pestle until a coarse paste forms. Add 2–3 teaspoons water if needed to facilitate the grinding. In a bowl, combine the chile paste, vinegar, soy sauce, brown sugar, and bay leaves and stir to mix well. Pour the marinade into a large zippered plastic bag, add the steaks, and seal the bag. Refrigerate for at least 4 hours or up to overnight.

In a large Dutch oven over medium-high heat, warm the oil. Add the remaining garlic and sauté until light golden brown, just a few seconds. Add the pork with its marinade to the pot, pour in 3 cups (24 fl oz/750 ml) water, and bring to a boil. Reduce the heat to low, cover, and simmer gently until the meat is deep golden brown and very tender when pierced with a fork, 1 1/2–2 hours. Discard the bay leaves. Taste and adjust the seasoning. Serve at once.

Pork adobo, the national dish of the Philippines, is considered the ultimate comfort food by many Filipinos, and by aficionados of this stew around the world. It is a braised dish with sweet-and-sour flavors that develop during slow cooking. Here, steaks cut from pork shoulder cook until the meat is moist and fork-tender.

Stir-fried Pork with Garlic

This simple stir-fry combines pork with the signature Vietnamese flavors of garlic, vinegar, soy sauce, and black pepper. Ask your butcher to cut the pork very thinly on a slicer, or freeze the pork shoulder for 30 minutes to firm it up, and then cut across the grain into thin strips. If desired, just before serving, add fresh basil leaves and stir until they wilt.

Cut the pork into pieces 2 inches (5 cm) long by 1 inch (2 cm) wide by $1/16$ inch (2 mm) thick (see note). In a large, nonreactive bowl, combine $1/2$ teaspoon of the sugar, $1/4$ teaspoon salt, and the baking soda and stir to mix well. Add the pork and stir to coat well. Let marinate at room temperature for 30 minutes.

In a bowl, stir together the broth, soy sauce, vinegar, cornstarch, remaining 1 teaspoon sugar, and $1/4$ teaspoon pepper until the cornstarch and sugar dissolve to make a stir-fry sauce. Set the sauce aside.

In a large wok or frying pan over high heat, warm the oil. When the oil is hot, add the garlic and sauté until just beginning to turn golden brown, a few seconds. Working quickly, add the pork to the pan and stir-fry until the meat is crisp and just turns opaque, about 1 minute. Stir in the sauce and sauté until it thickens, about 10 seconds. Transfer to a warmed platter and serve at once.

$1^1/2$ lb (750 g) pork shoulder

$1^1/2$ teaspoons sugar

Salt and ground pepper

$1/4$ teaspoon baking soda (bicarbonate of soda)

3 tablespoons chicken broth

2 tablespoons dark soy sauce

1 teaspoon rice vinegar

$1/2$ teaspoon cornstarch (cornflour)

2 tablespoons canola oil

4 cloves garlic, minced

MAKES 4–6 SERVINGS

Pork Cutlets with Tonkatsu Sauce

A popular dish in Japan, these pork cutlets are coated with *panko*, Japanese-style bread crumbs made from bread with the crusts removed. They are larger and have an airier texture and a longer-lasting crispness than most other types of crumbs. The cutlets are pounded so they cook evenly and quickly, helping to retain their juices, and they are served with a thick sauce seasoned with hot yellow mustard. In Japan, the breaded cutlets are also a favorite sandwich filling or are served as *katsudon*, on a bowl of steamed rice topped with egg and onion.

To make the *tonkatsu* sauce, in a small saucepan over medium heat, combine the hot water, soy sauce, Worcestershire, mirin, tomato paste, and hot mustard. Whisk until the sauce thickens and is heated through. Set aside to cool.

Place each cutlet between pieces of plastic wrap and, using the flat side of a meat pounder, pound to a thickness of $1/4$ inch (6 mm).

Put the flour, *panko*, and egg in 3 separate shallow bowls. Season the flour with $1/4$ teaspoon salt and $1/8$ teaspoon pepper. Season the pounded cutlets on both sides with $1/2$ teaspoon salt. Dredge each cutlet in the flour, shaking off the excess. Dip in the egg and then place in the *panko*, pressing on the pork to help the crumbs adhere. Place the breaded cutlets on a baking sheet until ready to fry.

In a large, nonstick frying pan over medium-high heat, warm the oil. When the oil is hot, add the breaded cutlets and fry, turning once, until golden brown, about 5 minutes per side. Transfer to paper towels to drain.

To serve, cut the cutlets into slices $1/2$ inch (12 mm) wide. Arrange on a warmed platter and serve at once with the *tonkatsu* sauce on the side.

For the *tonkatsu* sauce

$1/4$ cup (2 fl oz/60 ml) hot water

2 tablespoons dark soy sauce

2 tablespoons Worcestershire sauce

1 tablespoon mirin

1 tablespoon tomato paste

1 teaspoon prepared hot mustard

4 pork cutlets, about 6 oz (185 g) each

2 tablespoons all-purpose (plain) flour

1 cup (4 oz/125 g) *panko* or fine dried bread crumbs

1 large egg, lightly beaten

Salt and freshly ground pepper

$1/4$ cup (2 fl oz/60 ml) canola oil

MAKES 4–6 SERVINGS

Roast Pork

For the marinade

2 slices peeled fresh ginger, each about ¼ inch (6 mm) thick

3 cloves garlic

2 tablespoons hoisin sauce

2 tablespoons light soy sauce

1 tablespoon dark soy sauce

1 tablespoon Chinese rice wine

3 tablespoons honey

2 tablespoons light brown sugar

1 teaspoon tomato paste

1 teaspoon Asian sesame oil

2 lb (1 kg) pork shoulder, cut with the grain into strips 6 inches (15 cm) long by 3 inches (7.5 cm) wide by 1½ inches (4 cm) thick

1 tablespoon honey

MAKES 4–6 SERVINGS

To make the marinade, in a blender or food processor, combine the ginger, garlic, hoisin sauce, soy sauces, rice wine, honey, brown sugar, tomato paste, and sesame oil and process until a smooth sauce forms. Pour into a large zippered plastic bag, add the pork, and seal the bag. Turn the bag and massage gently until the pork is well coated with the marinade. Refrigerate for at least 4 hours or up to overnight.

Preheat the oven to 450°F (230°C). Line a large baking sheet with aluminum foil.

Remove the pork from the marinade, letting the excess fall back into the bag. Arrange the pork strips in a single layer on the prepared sheet. Roast until crisp and browned, about 15 minutes.

Meanwhile, pour the marinade into a small saucepan, add the honey, and bring to a boil over medium heat, stirring to dissolve the honey. Reduce the heat to low and simmer for 5 minutes, then remove from the heat.

Reduce the oven temperature to 350°F (180°C) and continue to roast until the pork is crisp and the glaze is shiny, 25–30 minutes longer, brushing the pork with the marinade several times. The pork is done when an instant-read thermometer inserted into the thickest part registers 160°F (71°C).

Transfer the roasted pork to a cutting board, tent loosely with aluminum foil, and let rest for 10 minutes. Cut the pork across the grain into slices about ⅛ inch (3 mm) thick and serve at once.

Cantonese barbecued pork, or *char siu*, is a shoulder cut seasoned with soy and malt sugar or honey. The traditional method is to skewer strips of marinated pork with long forks and cook them over an open fire. Similar results can be achieved by slicing the succulent meat and roasting it in a hot oven. *Char siu* is usually consumed alongside Steamed Rice (page 274) or noodles. The pork is also used in fillings for baked buns (page 80) and in fried rice. Roast pork is readily available at Chinese markets, often hanging in the window next to the roast duck and other specialty meats. If you are pressed for time, purchase it precooked for easy use in many dishes.

Spicy Grilled Pork

Pork *bulgogi* is made from thin slices of pork marinated in a mixture of seasoned soy sauce and sugar. It is typically grilled at the table, although it may also be broiled or panfried. Serve the pork as it is traditionally in the Koreas, either alongside small dishes of pickled vegetables and rice, or with lettuce leaves used to wrap each slice of cooked meat. Watch the meat carefully while it cooks on the grill, as the sugar in the marinade burns easily.

Working in batches, place the slices of pork between pieces of plastic wrap and, using the flat side of a meat pounder, pound to a thickness of $^1/_{16}$ inch (2 mm).

In a bowl, combine the onion, garlic, ginger, soy sauces, chile bean paste, sesame oil, sugar, red pepper flakes, and sesame seeds and stir to mix well. Transfer to a large zippered plastic bag, add the pork, and seal the bag. Turn the bag and gently massage the pork until the slices are well coated with the marinade. Refrigerate for at least 4 hours or up to overnight.

Prepare a charcoal or gas grill for direct grilling over high heat.

Drain the pork and onions in a colander and discard the marinade. Brush the grill rack with oil. Place the pork slices and onions in single layer on the grill so they are not touching one another and sear until crisp and brown on the first side, 2–3 minutes. Using tongs, turn the pork and onions and grill until the onions are browned and the pork just turns opaque on the second side, about 2 minutes longer. Transfer to a warmed platter and serve at once with the dipping sauce.

1$^1/_2$ lb (750 g) boneless pork shoulder, cut across the grain into slices $^1/_8$ inch (3 mm) thick

1 small yellow onion, thinly sliced

4 cloves garlic, minced

1 tablespoon peeled and grated fresh ginger

3 tablespoons light soy sauce

1 tablespoon dark soy sauce

2 tablespoons Korean chile bean paste

1 tablespoon Asian sesame oil

1 tablespoon sugar

$^1/_2$ teaspoon red pepper flakes

1 tablespoon sesame seeds, toasted

Canola oil for brushing

Korean Sesame-Soy Dipping Sauce (page 272) for serving

MAKES 4–6 SERVINGS

Spiced Lamb with Caramelized Onions

5 tablespoons (2 ½ fl oz/ 75 ml) canola oil

2 large yellow onions, thinly sliced, plus 1 small yellow onion, chopped

Salt

2 tablespoons peeled and chopped fresh ginger

4 cloves garlic, chopped

2 lb (1 kg) boneless lamb shoulder, cut into 2-inch (5-cm) cubes

1 cinnamon stick

4 cardamom pods, cracked with the side of a chef's knife

3 whole cloves

1 teaspoon ground coriander

1 teaspoon ground cumin

½ teaspoon garam masala

⅛ teaspoon cayenne pepper

½ cup (4 oz/125 g) plain whole-milk yogurt

1 tablespoon chopped fresh cilantro (fresh coriander)

MAKES 4–6 SERVINGS

In a large Dutch oven or other heavy-bottomed pot over medium-low heat, warm 2 tablespoons of the oil. Add the sliced onions and ¼ teaspoon salt. Cook, stirring occasionally, until the onions are golden brown and caramelized, 25–30 minutes. Transfer the onions to a bowl, cover, and set aside.

In a mini food processor or mortar, combine the chopped onion, ginger, and garlic and process or grind with a pestle until a smooth paste forms. Set aside.

Place the pot used to cook the onions over high heat and warm 1 tablespoon of the oil. Add half of the lamb cubes in a single layer and sear until crisp and brown on all sides, 3–4 minutes per side. Transfer the lamb to a bowl. Add 1 tablespoon of the oil to the pan and repeat to sear the remaining lamb. Transfer the second batch to the bowl and set aside.

In the same pot over medium-high heat, warm the remaining 1 tablespoon oil. Add the onion paste and sauté until beginning to brown at the edges, about 3 minutes. Add the cinnamon, cardamom, cloves, coriander, cumin, garam masala, cayenne, and 1 teaspoon salt and sauté until fragrant, about 10 seconds. Reduce the heat to low and stir in the yogurt, 1 tablespoon at a time, until the sauce is well blended, about 5 minutes. Add 2½ cups (20 fl oz/625 ml) water and return the meat and any accumulated juices in the bowl to the pan. Cover and simmer over low heat until the meat is very tender when pierced with a fork, 1½–2 hours.

Uncover the pot, stir in the caramelized onions, and continue to simmer until the sauce thickens, 7–10 minutes. Taste and adjust the seasoning. Transfer to a warmed platter, garnish with the cilantro, and serve at once.

This north Indian lamb curry is cooked slowly in a sweet, rich onion-based sauce. The style is called *dopiaza*, literally "two onions," which can refer to both the generous amount of onion used and its addition in two stages: a sautéed onion paste creates a base for the creamy yogurt sauce in which the lamb is slowly braised, and toward the end of cooking, caramelized onions are stirred in to add sweetness and a second layer of earthy flavor. The sauce is seasoned with a mixture of pungent, earthy spices, including cardamom, cloves, coriander, cumin, and garam masala.

Mongolian Hot Pot

The Asian hot pot tradition is a communal form of dining that dates back centuries. Today, a pot on a portable burner or an electric wok is used to simmer seasoned broth in the center of the table. Vegetables and noodles are cooked in the broth while diners use chopsticks to cook thinly sliced meats or pieces of seafood. To make the meat easier to slice thinly, freeze it for 30 minutes until firm.

Using kitchen scissors, cut the shells of the shrimp along the line down the center of their backs, following the curve. Devein the shrimp, rinse well under cold running water, and pat dry with paper towels. Cut the beef and pork across the grain into slices $^1/_{16}$ inch (2 mm) thick. Place the shrimp, beef, and pork in 3 separate bowls. In another bowl, whisk together the soy sauce, rice wine, sesame oil, sugar, and white pepper. Pour one-third of the soy sauce mixture into each bowl holding the meat or shrimp. Stir to mix well. Let marinate at room temperature for 1 hour, or cover and refrigerate for up to 4 hours.

To make the soup, in a large saucepan, combine the broth, soy sauce, rice wine, sugar, 1 teaspoon salt, and $^1/_8$ teaspoon pepper and bring to a boil over high heat. Reduce the heat to low and simmer the soup for 10 minutes to blend the flavors.

To serve the hot pot, set up a portable electric burner on the dining table, pour the soup into a pot or heatproof serving bowl, and place on the burner. Set each place with a soup bowl, a pair of chopsticks, and a soupspoon. Divide the dipping sauce among small bowls and place one by each place setting.

Cut the cabbage leaves into 2-inch (5-cm) squares. Cut the mushrooms into slices $^1/_4$ inch (6 mm) thick. On a chilled platter, arrange the cabbage, mushrooms, noodles, tofu, and watercress in individual mounds. Place the marinated beef, pork, and shrimp in separate serving bowls. Add the vegetables, noodles, and tofu to the soup and simmer for about 5 minutes. Pass the bowls of meat and shrimp for guests to dip into the simmering soup until cooked to the desired doneness and then place in their soup bowls. The beef and pork will cook quickly, about 1 minute for medium-rare, and the shrimp will take about 2 minutes. Using a slotted spoon, divide the vegetables, tofu, and noodles among the individual bowls. Guests can dip them in the dipping sauce or drizzle the sauce on top. When all the vegetables, meat, and shrimp are eaten, ladle the hot soup into the individual bowls to finish the meal.

$^1/_2$ lb (250 g) medium shrimp (prawns) in the shell

$^1/_2$ lb (250 g) beef sirloin

$^1/_2$ lb (250 g) pork tenderloin

3 tablespoons light soy sauce

2 tablespoons Chinese rice wine

1 tablespoon Asian sesame oil

1 teaspoon sugar

$^1/_8$ teaspoon ground white pepper

For the soup

8 cups (64 fl oz/2 l) low-sodium chicken broth

3 tablespoons light soy sauce

1 tablespoon rice wine

1 teaspoon sugar

Salt and ground pepper

Soy-Ginger Dipping Sauce (page 273)

$^1/_2$ head napa cabbage, cored

$^1/_4$ lb (125 g) fresh shiitake mushrooms, stems removed

3 oz (90 g) cellophane noodles, soaked in boiling water for 15 minutes and drained

14 oz (440 g) firm tofu, cut into 1-inch (2.5-cm) cubes

1 bunch watercress, separated into small sprigs

MAKES 4-6 SERVINGS

Warm Beef and Watercress Salad

For the marinade

1 tablespoon canola oil

3 cloves garlic, minced

1 tablespoon fish sauce

$\frac{1}{2}$ teaspoon sugar

Freshly ground pepper

1 lb (500 g) beef tenderloin, cut into 1-inch (2.5-cm) cubes

For the sauce

2 tablespoons fresh lime juice

1 tablespoon rice vinegar

1 tablespoon light soy sauce

1 tablespoon fish sauce

1 teaspoon sugar

Freshly ground pepper

$\frac{1}{2}$ small yellow onion, sliced paper-thin

1 tablespoon canola oil

2 green (spring) onions, white and pale green parts, thinly sliced on the diagonal

3 cloves garlic, minced

2 cups (2 oz/60 g) loosely packed watercress, tough stems removed

MAKES 4–6 SERVINGS

To make the marinade, in a large, nonreactive bowl, combine the oil, garlic, fish sauce, sugar, and $\frac{1}{8}$ teaspoon pepper and stir to mix well. Add the beef and stir to coat thoroughly. Cover and refrigerate for at least 2 hours or up to overnight.

To make the sauce, in a small bowl, whisk together the lime juice, vinegar, soy sauce, fish sauce, sugar, and $\frac{1}{8}$ teaspoon pepper.

Put the onion slices in a small bowl and drizzle with 1 tablespoon of the sauce. Set the onions and the remaining sauce aside.

In a large wok or frying pan over high heat, warm the oil. Add the beef and stir-fry until browned, 4–5 minutes. Add the green onions and garlic and stir-fry just until fragrant, a few seconds. Remove the pan from the heat, pour in the remaining sauce, and toss to mix.

To serve, toss the watercress with the marinated sliced onions and mound on a platter. Using a slotted spoon, spoon the beef over the greens and then drizzle the pan juices over the beef. Serve at once.

This salad of seared beef with spicy watercress and paper-thin slices of onion is popular in both Cambodia and Vietnam. Called "shaking beef" on menus in many Vietnamese restaurants in the West, the dish starts by searing cubes of beef in a hot pan, and then—true to the dish's name and to its tradition—the pan is shaken until the meat is thoroughly browned. Fresh, peppery watercress and marinated raw onions are tossed with a lime vinaigrette, and the warm beef and pan juices are poured over the salad for an effect both cooling and crisp, savory and sweet.

Stir-fried Tangerine Beef

Dried tangerine peel is the customary citrus seasoning for this classic stir-fry. This version uses the fresh fruit, both the grated zest and the squeezed juice. The beef is marinated in baking soda, which helps break down the meat fibers and gives the cooked beef a tender and velvety texture. The lightly sweet citrus sauce pairs well with Steamed Rice (page 274) and a simple stir-fried vegetable.

Cut the flank steak across the grain into slices 1/8 inch (3 mm) thick. In a large, nonreactive bowl, combine the sugar, the baking soda, and 1 teaspoon salt and stir to mix well. Add the beef slices and stir to coat thoroughly. Let stand at room temperature for 30 minutes.

To make the sauce, in a small bowl, stir together the tangerine zest and juice, rice wine, hoisin sauce, soy sauces, chile bean paste, ginger juice, sesame oil, sugar, and cornstarch until the sugar and cornstarch dissolve. Set aside.

Pat the beef slices dry with paper towels. In a large wok or frying pan over high heat, warm 2 tablespoons of the canola oil. Add half of the beef in a single layer and sear until brown on the first side, about 1 minute. Using tongs, turn and sear until brown on the second side, about 30 seconds. Transfer the meat to a colander to drain. Return the pan to high heat, warm 1 tablespoon of the oil, and repeat to sear the remaining beef. Transfer the second batch to the colander to drain.

Wipe the pan clean. Reheat over high heat and add the remaining 1 tablespoon oil. When the oil is hot, add the onion and bell pepper and stir-fry until the edges begin to brown, 3–4 minutes. Add the chile and garlic and stir-fry for 1 minute. Pour in the sauce and return the beef to the pan. Stir-fry until the beef is heated through and the sauce thickens, about 1 minute. Transfer to a warmed bowl or platter and serve at once.

1 1/2 lb (750 g) flank steak

1/2 teaspoon sugar

1/4 teaspoon baking soda (bicarbonate of soda)

Salt

For the sauce

1 teaspoon grated tangerine or orange zest

1/4 cup (2 fl oz/60 ml) fresh tangerine or orange juice

1 tablespoon Chinese rice wine

1 tablespoon hoisin sauce

1 tablespoon each light soy sauce and dark soy sauce

1 teaspoon chile bean paste

1 teaspoon ginger juice (page 278)

1/2 teaspoon Asian sesame oil

1/4 teaspoon sugar

1/4 teaspoon cornstarch (cornflour)

4 tablespoons (2 fl oz/60 ml) canola oil

1 small yellow onion, halved and thinly sliced

1 small green bell pepper (capsicum), seeded and thinly sliced lengthwise

1 red Fresno chile, seeded and thinly sliced lengthwise

2 cloves garlic, minced

MAKES 4–6 SERVINGS

Sichuan Dry-Fried Beef

1½ lb (750 g) flank steak, cut across the grain into slices ⅛ inch (3 mm) thick

1 cup (8 fl oz/250 ml) canola oil

¼ teaspoon Sichuan peppercorns

1 tablespoon chile bean paste

1 tablespoon light soy sauce

1 teaspoon black vinegar

½ teaspoon sugar

½ teaspoon Asian sesame oil

¼ teaspoon cornstarch (cornflour)

2 celery stalks, trimmed and cut into strips 1½ inches (4 cm) long by ⅛ inch (3 mm) wide

1 small red bell pepper (capsicum), seeded and cut into strips 1½ inches (4 cm) long by ⅛ inch (3 mm) wide

3 green (spring) onions, white parts only, cut into strips 1½ inches (4 cm) long by ⅛ inch (3 mm) wide

1½-inch (4-cm) piece fresh ginger, peeled and cut into strips ⅛ inch (3 mm) wide

3 cloves garlic, minced

2 tablespoons Chinese rice wine

MAKES 4–6 SERVINGS

Pat the meat dry with paper towels. Line a baking sheet with a double layer of paper towels. Pour the oil into a wok or deep frying pan over high heat and heat to 370°F (188°C) on a deep-frying thermometer. Add the beef and fry, stirring often with a slotted spoon, until it begins to turn crisp and dark brown, 3–5 minutes. Using the spoon, transfer the beef to the paper towels to drain. Pour off and discard all but 1 tablespoon of the oil left in the bottom of the pan. Set the pan aside.

Put the peppercorns in a small, dry frying pan over medium heat and cook, stirring, until lightly toasted, about 3 minutes. Transfer to a mortar, a spice grinder, or a coffee mill reserved for spices and crush with a pestle or grind to a fine powder.

In a small bowl, stir together the ground peppercorns, chile bean paste, soy sauce, vinegar, sugar, sesame oil, cornstarch, and 1 tablespoon water to make a stir-fry sauce. Set the sauce aside.

Return the pan with the reserved oil to high heat. When the oil is very hot, add the celery and bell pepper and stir-fry until lightly browned and just tender, about 2 minutes. Add the green onions, ginger, and garlic and stir-fry for 10 seconds. Pour in the rice wine and stir-fry for several seconds to evaporate the alcohol.

Stir the sauce into the pan and bring to a boil. Working quickly, return the beef to the pan and toss and stir until the beef is heated through and well coated with the sauce, about 1 minute. Transfer to a warmed platter and serve at once.

Specific to Sichuan cooking, the dry-frying method removes water from the fibers of ingredients by frying them briefly in a generous amount of oil and draining them before continuing with the recipe. In this dish, thin slices of beef are fried until crispy brown but tender within, and then added to a stir-fry of vegetables and aromatics and tossed with a tangy sauce seasoned with Sichuan peppercorns. Unrelated to black pepper or red chiles, mild Sichuan peppercorns are the dried husks of the fruit of a woody shrub that grows in the region of western China for which they are named.

Dry-Curry Beef with Coconut Milk

Festival food in Malaysia and Indonesia, this full-bodied curry resembles a slow-cooked stew. Beef, lamb, or chicken is simmered in ample coconut milk with traditional curry spices, and often the bright note of kaffir lime leaves, as in this recipe. The meat is cooked over low heat for up to 2 hours, until the liquid evaporates, the sauce is absorbed, and the coconut oil separates. During the final minutes, the meat fries in the rendered coconut oil until crisp and brown. Serve with Steamed Rice (page 274).

To make the chile paste, in a mini food processor or mortar, combine the shallots, garlic, galangal, lemongrass, chile, and lime leaves and process or grind with a pestle until a smooth paste forms. Add 2–3 tablespoons water if needed to facilitate the grinding.

In a large Dutch oven or other heavy-bottomed pot over medium-high heat, warm the oil. Add the chile paste and sauté until the paste is fragrant and turns a shade darker, 5–7 minutes.

Stir in 2 cups (16 fl oz/500 ml) water and then stir in the coconut milk, tamarind paste, palm sugar, cinnamon, star anise, cardamom pods, and 1 teaspoon salt. Bring to a boil over medium-high heat.

Add the beef and stir to submerge all of the pieces in the liquid. Reduce the heat to low and simmer, uncovered, until nearly all the liquid evaporates, the remaining sauce thickens and turns a rich, dark brown, and the meat is very tender when pierced with a fork, $1^{1}/_{2}$–2 hours. Stir occasionally to prevent the meat from sticking to the bottom of the pot.

Transfer to a serving bowl, garnish with the shredded lime leaves, and serve.

For the chile paste

3 shallots, chopped

4 cloves garlic, chopped

2 tablespoons peeled and chopped fresh galangal

2 lemongrass stalks, tender midsections only, smashed with the side of a chef's knife and chopped

1 red Fresno chile, seeded and chopped

2 kaffir lime leaves, spines removed

2 tablespoons canola oil

2 cups (16 fl oz/500 ml) coconut milk

1 tablespoon tamarind paste

1 tablespoon chopped palm sugar

1 cinnamon stick

2 star anise

3 cardamom pods, cracked with the side of a chef's knife

Salt

2 lb (1 kg) beef chuck, cut into 2-inch (5-cm) cubes

2 kaffir lime leaves, spines removed, finely shredded

MAKES 4–6 SERVINGS

Grilled Marinated Beef Short Ribs

Korean cuisine showcases many grilled meat dishes, including this smoky favorite that starts with beef short ribs. The ribs are flavored by a long stand in a sweet soy sauce–based marinade, then are seared over high heat until crispy and browned. Ask your butcher for English-style short ribs, in which the rack is sliced lengthwise to separate the ribs, and then the ribs are cut crosswise into 3-inch (7.5-cm) lengths. The ribs are cut once more, this time to split them horizontally so the marinade penetrates the meat on all sides and the ribs cook more quickly. The ribs are often served with lettuce for wrapping, steamed rice, and pickled vegetables.

Using a chef's knife, cut each short rib in half horizontally, following the edge of the bone with the knife and leaving half of the rib pieces with the bone in and leaving the other half boneless.

To make the marinade, in a large nonreactive bowl, combine the green onions, ginger, garlic, soy sauces, sesame oil, sugar, red pepper flakes, and $1/2$ teaspoon black pepper and stir to mix well.

Pour the marinade into a large zippered plastic bag, add the ribs, and seal the bag. Turn the bag and gently massage the ribs until the meat is well coated with the marinade. Refrigerate for at least 4 hours or up to overnight.

Prepare a charcoal or gas grill for direct grilling over high heat.

Remove the ribs from the marinade. Shake off the excess marinade and discard the marinade. Brush the grill rack with canola oil. Place the ribs on the rack and sear until crisp and brown on the first side, 4–5 minutes. Turn and grill until tender and a deep mahogany brown on the second side, 3–4 minutes.

Transfer the ribs to a warmed platter and serve at once with the dipping sauce.

$2^{1}/_{2}$–3 lb (1.25–1.5 kg) beef short ribs, separated and cut into 3-inch (7.5-cm) lengths (see note)

For the marinade

4 green (spring) onions, white and pale green parts, minced

2 tablespoons peeled and grated fresh ginger

5 cloves garlic, minced

3 tablespoons light soy sauce

1 tablespoon dark soy sauce

1 tablespoon Asian sesame oil

1 tablespoon sugar

$1/4$ teaspoon red pepper flakes

Freshly ground black pepper

Canola oil for brushing

Korean Sesame-Soy Dipping Sauce (page 272) for serving

MAKES 4–6 SERVINGS

Beef in Red Curry

For the red curry paste

2 red Fresno chiles, seeded and chopped

3 cloves garlic, chopped

2 shallots, chopped

1 tablespoon peeled and chopped fresh galangal

1 lemongrass stalk, tender midsection only, chopped

1 tablespoon chopped fresh cilantro (fresh coriander) stems

1 tablespoon ground coriander

1 teaspoon ground cumin

$\frac{1}{2}$ teaspoon shrimp paste

1 lb (500 g) beef tenderloin

$\frac{1}{4}$ cup (2 fl oz/60 ml) fish sauce

$1\frac{1}{2}$ tablespoons palm sugar

1 teaspoon *each* tamarind paste and fresh lime juice

2 tablespoons canola oil

1 small yellow onion, halved and thinly sliced

1 small red bell pepper (capsicum), seeded and thinly sliced

1 cup (8 fl oz/250 ml) coconut milk

1 tablespoon chopped unsalted dry-roasted peanuts

8–10 fresh basil leaves

MAKES 4–6 SERVINGS

To make the red curry paste, in a mini food processor or mortar, combine the chiles, garlic, shallots, galangal, lemongrass, cilantro, coriander, cumin, and shrimp paste and process or grind with a pestle until a smooth paste forms. Add 1–2 tablespoons water if needed to facilitate the grinding. Set aside. Cut the beef into slices $\frac{1}{8}$ inch (3 mm) thick and set aside.

In a small bowl, combine the fish sauce, palm sugar, tamarind paste, and lime juice and stir to mix well. Set aside.

Heat a Dutch oven or a large frying pan over high heat. When the pan is hot, warm the oil. Add the onion and bell pepper and stir-fry until just tender, about 5 minutes. Transfer the vegetables to a bowl and set aside.

Place the same pan over medium heat. Add the coconut milk and heat just until it begins to bubble. Stir in the curry paste, bring to a simmer, and cook for 5 minutes. Add the fish sauce mixture and simmer until the curry thickens, 7–10 minutes.

Reduce the heat to low, add the beef slices and stir-fried vegetables to the pan, and continue simmering until the beef is almost cooked through but is still pink in the center, 5–7 minutes longer. Transfer the curry to a warmed bowl, garnish with the peanuts and basil, and serve at once.

The key to fragrant Thai red curries is a homemade curry paste made from fresh red chiles, which imbue the dish with their namesake color. The paste in this typical recipe also includes garlic, shallots, galangal, lemongrass, and the indispensable shrimp paste. When raw, this paste of sun-dried, fermented ground shrimp is almost too pungent to eat, but once simmered in coconut milk with other aromatic ingredients, it gives the curry a depth of flavor and a subtle saltiness. You can make the red curry paste in quantity: transfer to a clean jar, add canola oil to cover, cap tightly, and refrigerate for up to 1 month.

Sweets and Beverages

About Sweets and Beverages

In Asia, ingredients readily cross the boundaries between savory and sweet, dessert and beverage. Playful textures and bright colors are the rule, especially in Southeast Asia. Yogurt, ghee, or coconut milk lends richness, and aromatic herbs and spices add elusive flavors.

An Asian meal typically ends with a dessert of ripe, seasonal fruit presented still in its peel. But sweets and drinks, both simple and elaborate, are regularly enjoyed between meals, often as a much-needed pick-me-up after a siesta taken to pass the hottest part of the day. For example, Filipinos always look forward to their midafternoon *merienda*, a chance to sip coffee, tea, or hot chocolate and eat *bibingka* (coconut-flavored rice cake). Or, a typical Japanese tea ceremony will pair the mildly bitter green *cha* with glutinous rice–based sweetmeats stuffed with red bean paste.

AN ECLECTIC PANTRY

Many of these time-honored snacks of East and Southeast Asia rely on an eclectic and colorful array of vegetables and legumes, including dark red adzuki beans, black beans, yellow mung beans, purple yams, cassava root, sweet potatoes, translucent tapioca and sago pearls, and thin strips of crunchy seaweed. Some sweets combine all these ingredients in a single bowl along with a cooling dose of shaved ice. Refreshing Filipino *halo-halo* and Malaysian ice *kechang* are the epitome of this exuberant approach to sweets.

The more common banana appears in batters, crepes, cakes, rolls, and fritters everywhere the fruit grows. In the Philippines, small ladyfinger bananas are wrapped in *lumpia* (egg-roll) skins and fried (page 253) to make a sweet, crispy treat. Coconut milk is another important ingredient. The meat of the ripened nut is grated, its thin milk is used for batters, and its thick cream is drizzled as a topping. Sticky Rice with Mango (page 254), Pumpkin Stewed in Sweet Coconut Soup (page 250), and Bananas and Tapioca in Coconut Sauce (page 249) all make use of its creamy richness. So, too, does *bubor pulot hitam*, sticky black rice simmered with coconut milk and palm sugar and served warm drizzled with coconut cream, a popular dish in Malaysia, Singapore, and Indonesia.

Chickpea (garbanzo) flour, nuts, and ghee (clarified butter) form the foundation of many confections in India, such as *barfi*, a dense, fudgelike sweet sometimes garnished with pistachios and silver leaf. Cardamom, rose water, and saffron are favorite flavorings throughout the subcontinent, as in the cardamom-seasoned rice pudding known as *kheer* (page 261). Another popular type of sweet is prepared by boiling milk until it is reduced to a thick, sweet, rich base for custardy ice creams, such as *kulfi* (page 264).

In China, sweet soups will sometimes cap a meal, such as the wine rice soup with sticky rice balls enjoyed in Shanghai, or the red bean soup sweetened with rock sugar eaten throughout the country.

Asian cooks have also been influenced by certain European desserts, and have married Western techniques with Eastern flavors. Examples include Vietnam's silky Coconut Crème Caramel (page 260), Japan's Green Tea Ice Cream (page 263), and the rich Egg Custard Tartlets (page 257) that are commonly part of dim sum offerings at China's teahouses.

HOT AND COLD DRINKS

Tea is drunk throughout Asia, but numerous other beverages, many of them salty, sweet, and/or spicy, are important regional specialties. In India, refreshing *lassi* makes abundant use of yogurt and sometimes milk or cream. When thinned with ice water and flavored with spices or fruit such as mango (page 271), the tangy concoction becomes a nutritious, filling beverage. In hot climates, drinks often include salt to help replace what the body loses through perspiration. India's salted *lassi*, sometimes flavored with a pinch of ground cumin, and Vietnam's salted plum limeade are two good examples.

Sweetened tea drinks usually call for long simmering of the leaves to bring out more tannin. The extra bitterness this delivers helps balance the flavors and body introduced with the addition of sugar and milk. In India, hot Spiced Chai (page 271) combines black tea, milk, jaggery (unrefined sugar), and a blend of cloves, cardamom, cinnamon, and other seasonings to create a heady spiced tea. Iced Tea (page 266), made with Thai red tea leaves, gains richness from cream and sweetened condensed milk.

To keep warm in cold northern Asia, locals typically sip hot infusions of fruits and aromatics. Citron peel, roasted corn, roasted barley, chrysanthemum flowers, and ginger (page 268) are just some of the many hot drink flavors served during the winter in China, Korea, and Japan. Some Asian countries are also known for coffee. The traditional corner coffee shop, or *kopitiam*, of Malaysia and Singapore serves the strong brew of Hokkien Chinese immigrants. In Vietnam, Iced Coffee (page 267) combines individually brewed strong, dense cups with sweetened condensed milk and ice.

Bananas and Tapioca with Coconut Sauce

Cambodian desserts exhibit a vast range of colors, flavors, and textures. Influenced by the cuisines of China, India, and Thailand, many of the country's sweets are fruit and coconut milk based. This warm pudding pairing bananas with coconut milk is a traditional street-food snack and also makes an excellent dessert to end a meal. Tapioca pearls, produced from cassava root, are starchy and bland when raw, but when cooked they take on the sweetness and richness of the bananas and coconut and become just slightly chewy.

In a large bowl, gently toss the diced bananas with the lime juice. Set aside.

In a large saucepan over medium-high heat, bring 4 cups (32 fl oz/1 l) water to a boil. Whisk in the tapioca pearls and cook, stirring occasionally, until they are no longer opaque but still have a white center, about 10 minutes. Reduce the heat to medium-low and whisk in the granulated sugar, $\frac{1}{2}$ teaspoon salt, and the coconut milk. Cook, stirring, until the sugar dissolves, 2–3 minutes.

Stir the bananas into the tapioca and simmer, stirring occasionally, until the fruit is heated through and begins to soften, 7–10 minutes. Remove from the heat and let cool to room temperature.

To make the coconut sauce, in a small saucepan over low heat, combine the coconut cream, the palm sugar, and $\frac{1}{4}$ teaspoon salt and bring to a simmer. Stir the sauce until the sugar dissolves and the cream thickens, about 5 minutes. Remove from the heat and set aside to cool.

To serve, divide the cooled tapioca among individual bowls. Top with the sauce, dividing it equally. Serve at once.

4 just-ripe finger bananas or 2 just-ripe regular bananas, cut into $\frac{1}{4}$-inch (6-mm) dice

1 teaspoon fresh lime juice

$\frac{1}{2}$ cup (3 oz/90 g) small tapioca pearls

$\frac{1}{4}$ cup (2 oz/60 g) granulated sugar

Salt

1 cup (8 fl oz/250 ml) coconut milk

For the coconut sauce

$\frac{1}{2}$ cup (4 fl oz/125 ml) coconut cream

3 tablespoons chopped palm sugar

Salt

MAKES 4–6 SERVINGS

Pumpkin Stewed in Sweet Coconut Soup

1 lb (500 g) pumpkin, butternut, or *kabocha* squash

1 pandanus leaf (optional; see note)

5 cups (40 fl oz/1.25 l) coconut milk

1/2 cup (4 oz/125 g) chopped palm sugar

Salt

MAKES 4–6 SERVINGS

Remove the skin from the pumpkin. Cut the pumpkin in half, then scoop out the seeds from each half and discard. Cut the flesh into 1/2-inch (12-mm) cubes.

Pour water to a depth of 2 inches (5 cm) into a pot. Fit a steamer rack in the pot. The water should not touch the bottom of the steamer. Bring the water to a boil over medium-high heat, add the pumpkin cubes, cover, and cook until just tender, 5–7 minutes. Set the steamer into a large bowl to drain.

If using the padanus leaf, scrape the surface with a knife, without cutting the leaf, to release the flavor. Tie the leaf in a knot. In a large saucepan over medium heat, combine the coconut milk, the palm sugar, 1/2 teaspoon salt, and the pandanus leaf (if using). Bring to a low boil over medium heat and whisk until the sugar dissolves, about 2 minutes. Gently stir the pumpkin cubes into the coconut milk and simmer until the flavor of the pumpkin and pandanus leaf infuses the coconut milk, about 10 minutes.

Remove and discard the pandanus leaf (if used), and divide the pumpkin and coconut milk among warmed bowls. Serve at once.

Pumpkin and coconut, as well as bananas and mangoes, are used frequently in Thai desserts. Here, cubes of pumpkin are cooked in coconut milk, resulting in a simple, light preparation that is really warm soup. A Thai equivalent to vanilla, pandanus leaf infuses the coconut milk with its earthy flavor. The long, shiny, pleated leaves can be found in most Asian markets.

Fried Bananas in Lumpia Wrappers

For this traditional Filipino dessert, bananas are coated in sesame seeds and sugar, enclosed in thin crepes known as *lumpia* wrappers, and then fried until crisp and golden. The wrappers, which are the Filipino equivalent of Chinese spring roll wrappers, are made from egg, wheat flour, and water. Measuring 10 inches (25 cm) in diameter, they are filled with savory as well as sweet ingredients and are sold in the frozen-food section of most Asian markets. The wrapped bananas can be assembled in advance, covered with plastic wrap, and refrigerated for up to 2 hours before frying. Small bananas, appropriately called finger bananas, are sold in many Asian and Latin markets.

In a bowl, combine the brown sugar and sesame seeds. Set aside. If using finger bananas, cut each banana in half lengthwise. If using regular bananas, cut each in half lengthwise, then cut each half in half crosswise. In a bowl, combine the banana pieces and lime juice and stir gently to coat the bananas.

To assemble the bananas, working with 1 wrapper at a time, place it on a work surface; keep the other wrappers covered with a slightly damp kitchen towel to prevent them from drying out. Place a banana piece, flat side down, on the bottom third of the wrapper. Lightly brush the edges of the wrapper with the beaten egg. Sprinkle the banana with 1 teaspoon of the sugar-sesame mixture. Fold the wrapper away from you and over the banana, encasing it. Tuck in the sides and continue wrapping the banana until you have a tight roll. Brush the seam with the beaten egg, press the edges firmly to seal, and place on a plate.

Pour canola oil to a depth of 2 inches (5 cm) into a wok or deep frying pan over high heat and heat to 370°F (188°C) on a deep-frying thermometer. Line a baking sheet with a double layer of paper towels. Using a spatula, slide 4 or 5 banana rolls into the hot oil; do not crowd the pan. Deep-fry, turning once, until crisp and golden brown, about 4 minutes total. Using a wire skimmer or slotted spoon, transfer the rolls to the paper towels to drain. Allow the oil to return to 370°F before cooking the remaining rolls.

Cut the rolls in half. Transfer to a warmed platter. Using a fine-mesh sieve, dust the rolls with the confectioners' sugar. Serve at once.

¼ cup (3½ oz/105 g) firmly packed brown sugar

2 tablespoons sesame seeds, toasted

4 just-underripe finger bananas or 2 just-underripe regular bananas

1 teaspoon fresh lime juice

8 round *lumpia* wrappers or spring roll wrappers, thawed

1 large egg, beaten

Canola oil for deep-frying

1 tablespoon confectioners' (icing) sugar

MAKES 8 ROLLS

Sticky Rice with Mango

2 cups (14 oz/440 g) glutinous rice

²⁄₃ cup (5 fl oz/160 ml) coconut milk

¹⁄₃ cup (3 oz/90 g) granulated sugar

Salt

For the coconut sauce

1 cup (8 fl oz/250 ml) coconut cream

¹⁄₂ cup (4 oz/125 g) chopped palm sugar

1 tablespoon unsweetened flaked coconut

2 ripe mangoes

MAKES 4–6 SERVINGS

A staple in northern Thailand, sticky, or glutinous, rice has an appealing chewy texture. It is served with savory foods such as curries and grilled meats and is used in desserts like this popular combination of mango and a rich coconut sauce, sold by street vendors and found in most restaurants.

Place the rice in a large fine-mesh sieve and rinse under cold running water until the water runs clear. In a large saucepan over high heat, bring 6 cups (48 fl oz/ 1.5 l) water to a boil. Pour the rice into the boiling water, turn off the heat, and let the rice stand for 30 minutes. Pour water to a depth of 3 inches (7.5 cm) into a pot. Line a steamer insert with a double layer of cheesecloth (muslin) squares; the cheesecloth should be larger than the diameter of the steamer. Place the insert in the pot. The water should not touch the bottom of the steamer. Drain the rice, place it in the lined steamer, and drape the excess cheesecloth loosely over the rice. Cover the pot and steam the rice for 20 minutes. Carefully remove the cheesecloth packet, line the steamer with another oversized double layer of cheesecloth, and invert the rice onto the steamer. Drape the excess cheesecloth over the rice and steam for 15 minutes longer.

In a small saucepan, combine the coconut milk, the granulated sugar, and ¹⁄₈ teaspoon salt. Bring to a simmer over low heat and stir until the sugar dissolves, 2–3 minutes. Transfer the cooked rice to a large bowl and gradually pour in the coconut milk mixture while gently mixing with a spatula. Cover with plastic wrap and let stand at room temperature for at least 30 minutes or up to 3 hours. Do not refrigerate the rice.

To make the coconut sauce, in a small saucepan, combine the coconut cream and palm sugar. Bring to a simmer over low heat and stir until the sugar dissolves, 2–3 minutes. Set aside to cool.

Put the coconut in a small, dry frying pan over medium heat. Cook, stirring often, until lightly toasted, about 5 minutes. Pour onto a plate to cool. Stand each mango on a narrow side. Positioning a sharp knife slightly off center, cut the flesh from one side of the pit, then cut the flesh from the other side. Peel the halves and cut the flesh into thin slices. Trim the flesh from the pit and cut into thin slices. Scoop out the rice and divide among individual plates. Using a fork, poke several holes into the top of each mound of rice. Drizzle with the coconut sauce. Garnish with the sliced mangoes and toasted coconut. Serve at once.

Egg Custard Tartlets

Sweet, bright yellow custard tartlets are found in Chinese bakeries or on the menu of dim sum restaurants. Introduced to Hong Kong in the 1940s, they most likely evolved from Portuguese egg tarts or are an adaptation of English custard tarts. The dough for these flaky pastries is customarily made from lard. This version uses butter and a bit of cream cheese for a more forgiving, airy dough.

To make the dough, in a bowl, whisk together the flour, sugar, and salt. In a large bowl, using a mixer on medium speed, beat the butter and cream cheese until well combined, about 1 minute. Add the dry ingredients and the ice water and beat on medium speed until the dough forms large clumps. Scrape down the sides of the bowl and then turn the dough out onto a lightly floured work surface.

Form the dough into a cylinder 12 inches (30 cm) long. Cut the cylinder crosswise into 12 equal pieces. Have ready 12 tartlet pans each 3 inches (7.5 cm) in diameter and 1–1 1/2 inches (2.5–4 cm) deep. Press each piece of dough evenly into the bottom and up the sides of a pan. Place the lined pans on a baking sheet and refrigerate until the dough sets, at least 1 hour or up to overnight.

Preheat the oven to 325°F (165°C). Lightly prick the bottom of each dough-lined pan with a fork, and bake on the baking sheet until light golden brown, 15 minutes. Let cool on the baking sheet for 10 minutes.

To make the filling, in a saucepan over medium heat, combine the milk and 2 tablespoons water. Bring to a boil, then remove from the heat. In a bowl, whisk together the egg yolks, egg whites, sugar, salt, and lemon juice until the mixture is well combined, 1–2 minutes. Whisking continuously, gradually pour the hot milk mixture into the eggs in a slow, steady stream. Stir in the vanilla. Pour the custard through a fine-mesh sieve into another bowl or a large pitcher.

Pour the custard into the baked tartlet shells, filling each to within 1/8 inch (3 mm) of the rim. Bake until the centers are just set, 15–20 minutes. Do not let the custard brown. The custard filling will puff up, but will flatten when the tartlets cool. Remove the tartlets from the oven and let stand on the baking sheet until they are cool to the touch, then serve.

For the dough

1 1/4 cups (6 1/2 oz/200 g) all-purpose (plain) flour

2 tablespoons sugar

1/4 teaspoon salt

6 tablespoons (3 oz/90 g) unsalted butter, at room temperature

3 tablespoons cold cream cheese

2 tablespoons ice water

For the filling

1/3 cup (3 fl oz/80 ml) whole milk

3 large egg yolks

2 large egg whites

1/3 cup (3 oz/90 g) sugar

Pinch of salt

1 teaspoon fresh lemon juice

1/2 teaspoon vanilla extract (essence)

MAKES 12 TARTLETS

Fried Pancakes with Spiced Syrup

1½ cups (7½ oz/235 g) all-purpose (plain) flour

½ cup (2½ oz/75 g) rice flour

2 tablespoons sugar

½ teaspoon baking powder

⅛ teaspoon salt

⅓ cup (2½ oz/75 g) plain whole-milk yogurt

⅛ teaspoon ground saffron

For the spiced syrup

2 cups (1 lb/500 g) sugar

1 teaspoon fresh lemon juice

½ teaspoon ground cardamom

⅛ teaspoon ground saffron

1 tablespoon rose water

Canola oil for deep-frying

MAKES 4–6 SERVINGS

Believed to have originated in northern India, these sweet treats, called *jalebi*, are served warm or cold by street vendors. The pancakes are similar in concept to American funnel cakes: the batter is deep-fried and then soaked in sugar syrup. They are somewhat chewy and have a sweet coating of syrup flavored with rose water and cardamom. The batter is formed into concentric circles by using a plastic bag with a hole cut in one corner, as here, or a plastic squeeze bottle.

In a large bowl, whisk together the flours, sugar, baking powder, and salt. In a small bowl, whisk together the yogurt, the saffron, and ¾ cup (6 fl oz/180 ml) warm water. Add the wet ingredients to the dry ingredients and whisk until the batter is smooth. Cover the batter and let stand at room temperature for 1 hour.

To make the spiced syrup, in a large saucepan, combine the sugar, the lemon juice, and 1½ cups (12 fl oz/375 ml) water. Bring to a simmer over low heat and cook, stirring, until the sugar dissolves, 3–4 minutes. Raise the heat to medium-high and boil until the mixture begins to thicken and turn syrupy and registers 220°F (105°C) on a candy thermometer. Remove from the heat and stir in the cardamom and saffron. Let the syrup cool to room temperature and stir in the rose water.

Pour canola oil to a depth of 1 inch (2.5 cm) into a large, shallow frying pan over medium-high heat and heat to 360°F (185°C) on a deep-frying thermometer. Line a baking sheet with a double layer of paper towels. Transfer the batter to a zippered plastic bag and cut off a bottom corner to make a ¼-inch (6-mm) opening. Gently squeezing the bag, pour an even flow of batter into the hot oil, forming a single layer of coiled concentric circles 5–6 inches (13–15 cm) in diameter. Repeat to form 1 or 2 more cakes; do not crowd the pan. Fry the pancakes until they are crisp and light golden brown, 1–2 minutes. If necessary, turn the pancakes with a spatula to cook them evenly. Using a wire skimmer, transfer to the paper towels to drain. Allow the oil to return to 360°F between batches. You should have 12 pancakes.

Just before serving, while the pancakes are still warm, bring the spiced syrup to a gentle simmer over low heat. Remove the pan from the heat, immerse 2 or 3 pancakes in the syrup, and let soak for several seconds. Using the skimmer, remove the pancakes and carefully shake off the excess syrup. The pancakes should absorb some of the syrup but should stay slightly crisp. Transfer the pancakes to a warmed platter and serve at once.

Coconut Crème Caramel

For the caramel

¹/₂ cup (4 oz/125 g) sugar

¹/₂ teaspoon fresh lemon juice

For the custard

1 cup (8 fl oz/250 ml) whole milk

1 cup (8 fl oz/250 ml) coconut milk

1 teaspoon vanilla extract (essence)

4 large eggs, beaten

¹/₃ cup (3 oz/90 g) sugar

Salt

MAKES 6 SERVINGS

To make the caramel, place the sugar, the lemon juice, and ¹/₂ cup (4 fl oz/125 ml) water in a deep saucepan over medium heat. Using a wooden spoon, stir the sugar until it dissolves, about 2 minutes. Stop stirring and raise the heat to high. Let the sugar come to a vigorous boil and then cook, swirling the pan occasionally, until the sugar turns light caramel in color, 5–6 minutes. Quickly remove from the heat and carefully pour the hot syrup into six ¹/₂-cup (4–fl oz/125-ml) ramekins. Tilt each ramekin to coat the bottom and halfway up the sides. If the caramel in the saucepan begins to harden, warm it over low heat to achieve the desired consistency. Place the ramekins in a deep roasting pan. Set aside.

Preheat an oven to 325°F (165°C).

To make the custard, in a large saucepan over medium-low heat, combine the whole milk, coconut milk, and vanilla and bring almost to a boil, 3–4 minutes. Meanwhile, in a large bowl, whisk together the eggs, the sugar, and ¹/₈ teaspoon salt until blended. Whisking continuously, gradually pour the hot milk mixture into the eggs in a slow, steady stream. Pour the custard through a fine-mesh sieve into each ramekin, filling it three-fourths full.

Place the pan of filled ramekins in the oven and pour hot water into the pan to reach halfway up the sides of the ramekins. Bake the custards until a knife inserted in the center of a custard comes out clean, 25–30 minutes. Carefully remove the ramekins from the pan and let cool to room temperature. Cover the ramekins with plastic wrap and refrigerate for at least 4 hours or up to overnight.

To serve the crème caramel, run a knife around the inside edge of each ramekin to loosen the custard. Invert a dessert plate over the ramekin and invert both the plate and the ramekin. When the custard releases, the caramel will spill over the custard. Serve at once.

In this Vietnamese version of a French classic, coconut milk is used in lieu of cream, resulting in a rich dessert with a delicate coconut flavor. Considered a contemporary rather than traditional dessert, the custards are usually served after a formal meal. They can be made a day in advance and refrigerated until ready to serve.

Cardamom-Spiced Basmati Rice Pudding

This traditional Indian rice pudding, known as *kheer*, is made by slowly boiling fragrant basmati rice in milk sweetened with sugar. The pudding is often spiced with cardamom and saffron, which add a delicate earthy flavor. *Kheer* is an essential dish on the menu of many Hindu and Muslim feasts in South Asia. Although traditionally made with rice, it can be prepared with other grains and even vermicelli noodles. The pudding obtains its sweetness and creaminess from the slow cooking of the rice, so be patient while stirring and reducing the milk on the stove top over low heat.

Gently crack each cardamom pod with the side of a chef's knife.

In a large saucepan over medium heat, combine the milk, the rice, the sugar, and ¼ teaspoon salt. Add the cardamom pods and bring to a boil.

Reduce the heat to medium-low and simmer, stirring occasionally with a wooden spoon, until the rice is tender and the milk is reduced to about 5 cups (40 fl oz/ 1.25 l), 60–80 minutes. The pudding will be the consistency of pancake batter.

Remove the pan from the heat and discard the cardamom pods. Stir in the saffron and half of the almonds, pistachios, and raisins and mix well to combine.

Serve the rice pudding warm or cold, spooned into small bowls and garnished with the remaining almonds, pistachios, and raisins.

8 cardamom pods

8 cups (64 fl oz/2 l) whole milk

½ cup (3½ oz/105 g) basmati or jasmine rice

½ cup (4 oz/125 g) sugar

Salt

Pinch of saffron

2 tablespoons chopped blanched almonds

2 tablespoons chopped unsalted roasted pistachio nuts

3 tablespoons golden raisins (sultanas)

MAKES 4–6 SERVINGS

Green Tea Ice Cream

Matcha green tea powder is a popular ingredient for Japanese desserts. Made of finely ground dried green tea leaves, it is rich in green tea essence without the bitterness. The powder also infuses the ice cream with its beautiful hue. If time allows, make the ice cream at least a day in advance to allow the flavors to develop.

Put the green tea powder in a small heatproof bowl, add the boiling water, and mix well. Set aside to cool to room temperature.

In a large saucepan over medium heat, combine the cream and milk and bring almost to a boil, 2–3 minutes. Meanwhile, in a large bowl, whisk together the egg yolks, the sugar, and 1/8 teaspoon salt until pale and creamy, 2–3 minutes.

Whisking continuously, gradually pour the hot cream mixture into the eggs in a slow, steady stream. Pour the egg mixture into the same saucepan and cook over low heat, stirring constantly with a wooden spoon, until the custard is thick enough to coat the back of the spoon and leaves a clear trail when a finger is drawn through it, 5–6 minutes. Remove from the heat and pour through a fine-mesh sieve into a bowl. Stir in the green tea mixture and mix well.

Place the bowl in a larger bowl partially filled with ice cubes. Stir the custard while it cools and thickens, 5–6 minutes.

Pour the custard into an ice-cream maker and freeze according to the manufacturer's instructions. Transfer the ice cream to a freezer-safe container and freeze until firm, at least 4 hours or up to overnight, before serving.

3 tablespoons matcha green tea powder

1/2 cup (4 fl oz/125 ml) boiling water

1 cup (8 fl oz/250 ml) heavy (double) cream

1 1/2 cups (12 fl oz/375 ml) whole milk

3 large egg yolks

1/2 cup (4 oz/125 g) sugar

Salt

Ice cubes

MAKES 1 QT (32 FL OZ/1 L)

Ice Cream with Pistachios, Cardamom, and Rose Water

8 cardamom pods

3 cups (24 fl oz/750 ml) heavy (double) cream

3 cups (24 fl oz/750 ml) whole milk

½ cup (4 oz/125 g) sugar

Salt

1 teaspoon rose water

3 tablespoons chopped blanched almonds

3 tablespoons chopped unsalted roasted pistachios

MAKES 1 QT (32 FL OZ/1 L)

Gently crack each cardamom pod with the side of a chef's knife. In a large saucepan over medium heat, combine the cream and milk and bring almost to a boil, 2–3 minutes. Reduce the heat to low, add the cardamom pods, and simmer, stirring occasionally to prevent a skin from forming, until the mixture is reduced by half, 45–50 minutes.

Pour the milk mixture through a fine-mesh sieve into a large bowl and discard the cardamom pods. Return the mixture to the same saucepan, add the sugar and ⅛ teaspoon salt, and simmer over low heat, stirring, until the sugar is dissolved, about 2 minutes. Return the mixture to the large bowl and stir in the rose water, almonds, and 2 tablespoons of the pistachios.

Place the bowl in a larger bowl partially filled with ice cubes, and stir the mixture while it cools, 10–15 minutes. Pour the mixture into a freezer-proof container, cover with plastic wrap, and freeze overnight.

Let the ice cream stand for a few minutes before serving in individual bowls. Garnish with the remaining pistachios.

In Pakistan, a frozen treat called *kulfi* is served for dessert or is a snack purchased from street vendors. Unlike true ice cream, it does not have eggs and is poured into a mold and frozen rather than aerated by a machine. This version is infused with cardamom and rose water, an essence distilled from rose petals. Other ingredients commonly used to flavor this dense frozen dessert are mango and saffron. *Kulfi* should be eaten a little soft and melting around the edges.

Iced Tea

½ cup (½ oz/15 g) Thai red tea leaves (see note)

½ cup (4 fl oz/125 ml) half-and-half (half cream)

⅓ cup (3 fl oz/80 ml) sweetened condensed milk

2 tablespoons sugar

2 cups (16 oz/500 g) crushed ice

MAKES 4 SERVINGS

In a saucepan over medium heat, bring 4 cups (32 fl oz/1 l) water to a boil. Add the tea leaves, turn off the heat, and let steep for 5–7 minutes. Strain the tea through a very fine-mesh sieve or a sieve lined with cheesecloth (muslin) into a heatproof pitcher. Let cool to room temperature.

Meanwhile, in a measuring pitcher, whisk together the half-and-half, condensed milk, and sugar until the sugar dissolves.

To serve, divide the crushed ice among 4 tall glasses. Pour the sweetened milk over the ice, dividing it evenly. Slowly fill the glasses with the brewed tea, keeping the tea separate from the milk. Provide long spoons for stirring the milk and tea together before drinking.

In Thailand, this signature drink is prepared by brewing Thai red tea leaves with star anise, cinnamon, and vanilla. The cooled tea is combined with ice and sweetened milk to make a refreshing, creamy drink. When the bright orange-brown tea is carefully poured on top of the milk and ice, it creates an attractive layered appearance. Thai red tea leaves premixed with spices can be found at many Asian markets.

Iced Coffee

In Vietnam, the local dark-roast coffee is brewed with a small metal drip filter into a cup containing ice and condensed milk. If you cannot find Vietnamese coffee, brew ground French-roast beans.

Using a drip coffee machine or a French press, brew the finely ground coffee with 3 cups (24 fl oz/750 ml) water.

To serve, spoon 2 tablespoons condensed milk into each of 4 tall glasses. Place the glasses on small saucers and fill the glasses with ice cubes. Pour ³/₄ cup (6 fl oz/ 180 ml) of the brewed coffee over the ice cubes in each glass. Provide long spoons for stirring the coffee and condensed milk together before drinking.

1 cup (7 oz/220 g) finely ground dark-roast coffee (see note)

8 tablespoons (4 fl oz/ 125 ml) sweetened condensed milk

Ice cubes

MAKES 4 SERVINGS

Ginger Tea with Honey

2 teaspoons pine nuts

2-inch (5-cm) piece fresh ginger

2 cinnamon sticks, plus 4 sticks for garnish

4 tablespoons (3 oz/90 g) honey

MAKES 4 SERVINGS

Place the pine nuts in a dry frying pan and toast over medium heat, stirring frequently, until they are just golden, about 2 minutes. Immediately pour onto a plate to cool.

Peel the ginger, then cut into slices about ¼ inch (6 mm) thick. Smash the slices with the side of a chef's knife to release their flavor.

In a large saucepan over medium heat, combine the ginger slices, the 2 cinnamon sticks, and 5 cups (40 fl oz/1.25 l) water. Bring to a boil over medium heat and cook for 2 minutes. Reduce the heat to low and simmer, uncovered, for 30 minutes. Remove from the heat.

To serve, strain the tea through a fine-mesh sieve into warmed cups. Stir 1 tablespoon honey into each cup and garnish with the toasted pine nuts, dividing them evenly. Place a cinnamon stick in each cup and serve at once.

For centuries, ginger has been revered in Asian cultures for its powerful healing properties. Ginger tea, an important beverage in Korean medicine, is believed to prevent colds and aid digestion. Korean teas are often made from many ingredients other than tea leaves, such as dried fruits, grains, and roots or rhizomes like ginger. When choosing fresh ginger for this tea, look for heavy rhizomes that have smooth, light brown skin and a hard surface.

Mango Lassi

Similar in consistency to a milkshake, this yogurt beverage combines yogurt with fresh fruit, blended with ice to make a cold, frothy refreshment. Other popular flavorings are lemon and rose water, or cumin and saffron for a less sweet variation. Use frozen mangoes, or fresh pineapple or bananas, if fresh mangoes are unavailable.

Stand each mango on a narrow side on a cutting board. Positioning a sharp knife slightly off center, cut the flesh from one side of the pit in a single piece, then cut the flesh from the other side. Peel the mango halves. Trim the flesh from the pit. Chop all the mango flesh.

Place the mango flesh, yogurt, lemon juice, sugar, cardamom, and salt in a blender. Add the ice cubes and purée until smooth, 30–60 seconds. Taste and adjust the flavor with sugar.

Pour into 4 tall glasses and serve cold.

2 ripe mangoes

2½ cups (20 oz/625 g) plain whole-milk yogurt

1 teaspoon fresh lemon juice

¼ cup (2 oz/60 g) sugar

¼ teaspoon ground cardamom

Pinch of salt

1½ cups (12 oz/375 g) ice cubes

MAKES 4 SERVINGS

Spiced Chai

Chai is the word for "tea" in many parts of the world. Spicy milk tea, or *masala chai*, is strong black tea brewed with a mixture of aromatic spices and sweetened with hot milk and sugar. It is a centuries-old beverage that has played an important role in India. Be sure to select a strong black tea for steeping, such as Nilgiri, Assam, or Darjeeling from India or Ceylon from Sri Lanka. *Masala chai* can also be served over ice.

Gently crack the cardamom pods with the side of a chef's knife. Remove the seeds and discard the pods. In a mortar, a spice grinder, or a coffee mill reserved for spices, combine the cardamom, cinnamon stick, peppercorns, and cloves and crush with a pestle or grind to a coarse powder.

Transfer the spice powder to a large saucepan and add the milk and 1 cup (8 fl oz/250 ml) water. Bring to a boil over medium heat, then reduce the heat to low and simmer, uncovered, for 10 minutes. Stir the tea leaves and sugar into the milk mixture, cover, and steep the *chai* over low heat for 5 minutes, or until it reaches the desired strength. Remove from the heat.

Strain the *chai* through a fine-mesh sieve into warmed cups. Serve at once.

5 cardamom pods

1 cinnamon stick

4 peppercorns

4 whole cloves

3 cups (24 fl oz/750 ml) whole milk

⅓ cup (⅓ oz/10 g) tea leaves (see note)

½ cup (4 oz/125 g) sugar

MAKES 4–6 SERVINGS

Basic Recipes

From China to Indonesia, Japan to India, accompaniments are integral to Asian cuisines. Dipping sauces are used to season myriad dishes. Chutneys and *raita* provide a refreshing contrast to spicy curries. Rice steamed until tender and fluffy is a staple across the continent.

Nuoc Cham Dipping Sauce

1 red Fresno chile, seeded and chopped

3 cloves garlic, chopped

1½ tablespoons sugar

¼ cup (2 fl oz/60 ml) fish sauce

3 tablespoons fresh lime juice

1 tablespoon rice vinegar

1 small Thai chile, thinly sliced into rings

In a mini food processor or mortar, combine the chopped chile, garlic, and sugar and process or grind with a pestle until a smooth paste forms. Transfer the chile paste to a small bowl and stir in the fish sauce, lime juice, vinegar, and 2 tablespoons warm water. Garnish with the sliced chile. The dipping sauce can be covered and refrigerated for up to 4 days.

Makes about ⅓ cup (3 fl oz/80 ml)

Tamari-Sesame Dipping Sauce

3 tablespoons tamari soy sauce

2 tablespoons rice vinegar

½ teaspoon Asian sesame oil

1 teaspoon minced green (spring) onion

¼ teaspoon sugar

In a small bowl, whisk together the soy sauce, vinegar, sesame oil, green onion, and sugar until the sugar dissolves. Stir in 1 teaspoon warm water. Refrigerate for up to 4 days.

Makes about ⅓ cup (3 fl oz/80 ml)

Chile-Soy Dipping Sauce

¼ cup (2 fl oz/60 ml) light soy sauce

2 tablespoons rice vinegar

2 teaspoons *each* Asian sesame oil and chile paste

2 teaspoons minced green (spring) onion

1 teaspoon sugar

In a small bowl, whisk together the soy sauce, vinegar, sesame oil, chile paste, green onion, and sugar until the sugar dissolves. Stir in 2 tablespoons warm water. Refrigerate for up to 4 days.

Makes about ½ cup (4 fl oz/125 ml)

Korean Sesame-Soy Dipping Sauce

¼ cup (2 fl oz/60 ml) light soy sauce

1 tablespoon Asian sesame oil

1 green (spring) onion, minced

2 cloves garlic, minced

½ teaspoon chili powder

¼ teaspoon sugar

1 tablespoon sesame seeds

In a small bowl, whisk together the soy sauce, sesame oil, green onion, garlic, chili powder, and sugar until the sugar dissolves. Stir in 1 tablespoon warm water and the toasted sesame seeds. Refrigerate for up to 4 days.

Makes about ⅓ cup (3 fl oz/80 ml)

Nam Pla Dipping Sauce

1 red Fresno chile, seeded and chopped

3 cloves garlic, chopped

1 tablespoon sugar

¼ cup (2 fl oz/60 ml) fish sauce

3 tablespoons fresh lime juice

1 tablespoon rice vinegar

2 tablespoons warm water

1 tablespoon grated carrot

1 small Thai chile, thinly sliced into rings

In a mini food processor or mortar, combine the chopped chile, garlic, and sugar and process or grind with a pestle until a smooth paste forms. Transfer the chile paste to a bowl and stir in the fish sauce, lime juice, vinegar, and 2 tablespoons warm water. Garnish with the grated carrot and sliced chile. Refrigerate for up to 4 days.

Makes ⅓ cup (3 fl oz/80 ml)

Sweet-and-Sour Dipping Sauce

3 tablespoons tomato ketchup

1 tablespoon black vinegar

1 teaspoon dark soy sauce

½ teaspoon *each* Asian sesame oil and sugar

1 teaspoon cornstarch (cornflour)

In a small saucepan over medium heat, combine the ketchup, vinegar, soy sauce, sesame oil, sugar, cornstarch, and ⅓ cup (3 fl oz/80 ml) water and stir to mix well. Bring to a gentle boil and cook, stirring constantly, until the sauce thickens, about 2 minutes. Remove from the heat. Refrigerate for up to 1 week.

Makes about ⅓ cup (3 fl oz/80 ml)

Soy-Ginger Dipping Sauce

3 tablespoons light soy sauce

2 tablespoons dark soy sauce

2 tablespoons black vinegar

1 tablespoon Asian sesame oil

1 teaspoon chili oil

1 teaspoon Sriracha chile sauce

2 green (spring) onions, white parts only, minced

2 cloves garlic, minced

1 teaspoon peeled and grated fresh ginger

2 teaspoons sugar

In a small bowl, whisk together the soy sauces, vinegar, sesame oil, chili oil, chile sauce, green onions, garlic, ginger, and sugar until the sugar dissolves. Stir in 3 tablespoons warm water. The dipping sauce can be covered and refrigerated for up to 4 days.

Makes about 3/4 cup (6 fl oz/180 ml)

Lime Dressing

2 tablespoons seeded and chopped jalapeño chile

3 cloves garlic, chopped

2 tablespoons chopped fresh cilantro (fresh coriander) stems

1 tablespoon chopped fresh mint

Freshly ground pepper

1/4 cup (2 fl oz/60 ml) fish sauce

2 tablespoons fresh lime juice

1 teaspoon rice vinegar

1 teaspoon chopped palm sugar

In a mini food processor or mortar, combine the chile, garlic, cilantro, mint, and 1/8 teaspoon pepper and process or grind with a pestle until

a smooth paste forms. Add 1–2 teaspoons water if needed to facilitate the grinding. Transfer the garlic paste to a large bowl and whisk in the fish sauce, lime juice, vinegar, and palm sugar. The dressing can be covered and refrigerated for up to 4 days.

Makes about 1/2 cup (4 fl oz/125 ml)

Roasted Beef Broth

3 lb (1.5 kg) beef bones

1 large yellow onion, quartered

5 cloves garlic

4 slices fresh ginger, each about 1/4 inch (6 mm) thick, peeled

2 parsnips, peeled and cut into 2-inch (5-cm) chunks

6 star anise

5 whole cloves

1 cinnamon stick

Salt

Preheat the oven to 450°F (230°C). Place the beef bones, onion quarters, garlic, and ginger in a roasting pan. Roast, turning the bones once, until mahogany brown in color, about 1 hour.

Transfer the contents of the pan to a stockpot. Add 3 qt (3 l) water and bring to a boil over high heat. Boil for 5 minutes. Reduce the heat to medium-low and skim off any foam that rises to the top. Add the parsnips, star anise, cloves, cinnamon, and 1 tablespoon salt, cover partially, and cook until reduced to 2 qt (2 l), 1 1/2–2 hours. Strain the broth through a fine-mesh sieve set over a bowl and let cool to room temperature. Discard the solids. Refrigerate the broth for at least 4 hours or up to overnight. Skim the fat from the top of the broth and discard. The broth can be covered and refrigerated for up to 4 days.

Makes about 2 qt (2 l)

Malaysian Chile Paste

2 red Fresno or serrano chiles, seeded and chopped

3 shallots, chopped

2 cloves garlic, chopped

1 lemongrass stalk, tender midsection only, chopped

1 tablespoon peeled and chopped fresh galangal

1 tablespoon chopped fresh cilantro (fresh coriander) stems

1 teaspoon ground turmeric

1/2 teaspoon shrimp paste

In a mini food processor or mortar, combine the chiles, shallots, garlic, lemongrass, galangal, cilantro, turmeric, shrimp paste, and 2 tablespoons water and process or grind with a pestle until a smooth paste forms. The chile paste can be covered and refrigerated for up to 4 days.

Makes about 1/2 cup (4 oz/125 g)

Omelet Garnish

2 large eggs

Salt and freshly ground pepper

1 teaspoon canola oil

In a small bowl, beat the eggs with 1/8 teaspoon salt and a pinch of pepper until thoroughly combined.

In an 8-inch (20-cm) nonstick frying pan over medium heat, warm the oil. Pour in the egg mixture and cook just until the edges begin to set, 2–3 seconds. Using a rubber spatula, stir the mixture in a circular motion until it thickens slightly, about 10 seconds. Using the spatula, pull the cooked egg in toward center, then tilt the pan so that the uncooked egg runs to the edges. Repeat until the omelet is just set but still moist on the surface, about 20 seconds.

Use the spatula to slide the omelet onto a cutting board. Let cool for about 5 minutes. Cut the omelet in half and stack the halves, then slice into strips about 1/8 inch (3 mm) wide.

Makes about 2 cups (8 oz/250 g)

Cucumber and Tomato Relish

2 tablespoons fresh lemon juice

1/4 teaspoon sugar

1/4 teaspoon cumin seeds, toasted and ground

Pinch of cayenne pepper

Salt

1 small yellow onion, minced

1 large English (hothouse) cucumber, peeled and cut into 1/4-inch (6-mm) dice

1 tomato, seeded and cut into 1/4-inch (6-mm) dice

In a nonreactive bowl, whisk together the lemon juice, sugar, cumin, cayenne, and 1/2 teaspoon salt. Add the onion, cucumber, and tomato and toss to mix well. Cover and refrigerate for at least 4 hours or up to overnight before serving. The relish can be covered and refrigerated for up to 4 days.

Makes 2 cups (12 oz/375 g)

Steamed Rice

2 cups (14 oz/440 g) basmati, jasmine, sticky, or other long-grain white rice

Place the rice in a fine-mesh sieve and rinse thoroughly under cold running water. Drain well.

If cooking the rice on the stove top, transfer the rice to a 2–3-qt (2–3-l) heavy-bottomed

saucepan and add 3 cups (24 fl oz/750 ml) water. Bring to a boil over medium heat, stir once, and then reduce the heat to low. Cover the pan with a tight-fitting lid and cook the rice, undisturbed, for 20 minutes. Remove from the heat and let stand, covered, for 10 minutes. Fluff the rice with a fork before serving.

If using a rice cooker, rinse and drain the rice as directed, then place in the rice cooker bowl with 3 cups water and cook according to the manufacturer's instructions.

Makes 4 cups (20 oz/625 g)

Fried Shallots

1 cup (8 fl oz/250 ml) canola oil

3 large shallots, cut into slices 1/8 inch (3 mm) thick

In a saucepan over high heat, heat the oil to 370°F (188°C) on a deep-frying thermometer. Using a spatula, slide the shallots into the hot oil and fry, stirring occasionally, until crisp and deep golden brown, 2–3 minutes. Using a slotted spoon, transfer to a plate lined with paper towels to drain.

Makes 1 cup (3 oz/90 g)

Tamarind Chutney

1/2 cup (4 oz/125 g) tamarind paste concentrate

1/4 cup (2 oz/60 g) plus 1 tablespoon sugar

1 1/2 teaspoons cumin seeds, toasted and ground

1 teaspoon peeled and grated fresh ginger

1/2 teaspoon fresh lemon juice

1/8 teaspoon cayenne pepper

Salt

In a saucepan over low heat, combine the tamarind paste concentrate, the sugar, and 3/4 cup (6 fl oz/180 ml) water. Bring to a simmer and cook, stirring, until the sugar dissolves, 2–3 minutes.

Stir the cumin, ginger, lemon juice, cayenne, and 1/2 teaspoon salt into the tamarind mixture, return to a simmer, and cook for 5 minutes longer. Remove from the heat and let the chutney cool to room temperature before serving. The chutney can be covered and refrigerated for up to 4 days.

Makes 1 1/4 cups (10 fl oz/310 ml)

Cilantro Chutney

1 1/2 cups (2 1/2 oz/75 g) coarsely chopped fresh cilantro (fresh coriander)

4 green (spring) onions, white and pale green parts, chopped

1 jalapeño chile, seeded and chopped

1 tablespoon peeled and grated fresh ginger

1 clove garlic

3 tablespoons fresh lemon juice

Salt and freshly ground pepper

In a blender or food processor, combine the cilantro, green onions, chile, ginger, garlic, lemon juice, 1/2 teaspoon salt, and 1/8 teaspoon pepper. Add 2 tablespoons water and process to a smooth purée, stopping to scrape down the sides of the jar or bowl as needed. Taste and adjust the seasoning. Serve at room temperature. The chutney can be covered and refrigerated for up to 4 days.

Makes 1 1/2 cups (12 fl oz/375 ml)

Mint Chutney

1½ cups (2 oz/60 g) firmly packed
fresh mint leaves

4 green (spring) onions, white and pale
green parts, chopped

1 jalapeño chile, seeded and chopped

1 clove garlic

3 tablespoons fresh lemon juice

½ teaspoon sugar

½ teaspoon garam masala

Salt

In a blender or food processor, combine the
mint, green onions, chile, garlic, lemon juice,
sugar, garam masala, and ¼ teaspoon salt.
Add 2 tablespoons water and process to
a smooth purée, stopping to scrape the sides
of the jar or bowl as needed. Taste and adjust
the seasoning. Serve at room temperature.
The chutney can be covered and refrigerated
for up to 4 days.

Makes 1¼ cups (10 fl oz/310 ml)

Chile Sambal

8 red Fresno chiles

4 shallots, chopped

6 cloves garlic, chopped

1 teaspoon sugar

Salt

3 tablespoons canola oil

1 tablespoon fresh lime juice

½ teaspoon shrimp paste

In a mini food processor or mortar, combine the
chiles, shallots, garlic, sugar, and ½ teaspoon
salt and process or grind with a pestle until
a smooth paste forms. Add 1–2 tablespoons
water if needed to facilitate the grinding.

In a small frying pan over medium-low heat,
warm the oil. When the oil is hot, add the chile
paste and fry until bright red and very fragrant,
about 1 minute. Reduce the heat to low and stir
in the lime juice and shrimp paste. Simmer until
the sauce begins to thicken, 5–7 minutes.
Serve at room temperature. The sambal can
be covered and refrigerated for up to 2 weeks.

Makes 1 cup (8 fl oz/250 ml)

Raita

1 small cucumber, peeled, seeded,
and minced

Salt

2 cloves garlic, minced

1 cup (8 oz/250 g) plain low-fat yogurt

2 tablespoons fresh lemon juice

½ teaspoon ground cumin

⅛ teaspoon ground white pepper

2 tablespoons minced fresh cilantro
(fresh coriander) leaves

Place the minced cucumber in a fine-mesh
sieve, sprinkle with 1 teaspoon salt, and let
drain for 30 minutes. Pat the drained cucumber
dry with paper towels.

In a mortar or on a cutting board, using a pestle
or the side of a chef's knife, grind or mash the
garlic with ½ teaspoon salt to form a smooth
paste. In a bowl, combine the garlic paste,
yogurt, lemon juice, cumin, white pepper, and
cilantro. Fold in the drained cucumber. Taste
and adjust the seasoning. The *raita* can be
covered and refrigerated for up to 2 days.

Makes 1½ cups (9 oz/280 g)

Pickled Carrots and Daikon

2 cups (16 fl oz/500 ml) rice vinegar

½ cup (4 oz/125 g) sugar

Salt

1 red Fresno chile, thinly sliced into rings

1-inch (2.5-cm) piece fresh ginger,
cut into 4 or 5 thin slices

2 cloves garlic, thinly sliced

1 large carrot, cut into strips
3 inches (7.5 cm) long by
¼ inch (6 mm) wide and thick

1 small daikon, peeled and cut into
strips 3 inches long by ¼ inch (6 mm)
wide and thick

In a saucepan over medium heat, combine
the vinegar, the sugar, 1 tablespoon salt, and
½ cup (4 fl oz/125 ml) water and bring to a boil.
Cook, stirring occasionally, until the sugar and
salt dissolve, about 4 minutes. Add the chile,
ginger, and garlic to the vinegar mixture and
remove from the heat. Let the pickling liquid
steep until it cools to room temperature, then
strain and discard the solids.

Pour 6 cups (48 fl oz/1.5 l) water into a large
saucepan and bring to a boil over medium-
high heat. Add the carrot and daikon strips
and cook for 5 minutes. Drain the vegetables
in a colander and let stand for 15 minutes.

Pat the vegetables dry with paper towels and
pack into a clean glass jar. Pour the cooled
pickling liquid over the vegetables to cover
and seal with a tight-fitting lid. Refrigerate the
pickled vegetables for at least 4 days before
serving. The vegetables, lightly covered, can
be stored in the refrigerator for up to 1 month.

Make 2 cups (8 oz/250 g)

Glossary

BAMBOO SHOOTS Beneath towering bamboo trees, the tips of cone-shaped shoots push through the ground twice a year. The exuberant spring growth has firmer flesh and a more assertive flavor than the slim, sweet, delicately textured shoots of winter. Both types are widely available halved or sliced, then preserved in brine in cans or jars. For the best quality, look for whole peeled preserved shoots sold in bulk, submerged in large tubs of water, at Asian markets. To improve their flavor, soak preserved shoots in warm water for 10 minutes and then drain well before using. Fresh shoots, still whole and unpeeled, occasionally appear in the produce aisle. After paring away the dark sheath and trimming all the fibers at the base, cut fresh bamboo shoots in half lengthwise and boil for 30 minutes in lightly salted water to leach away their natural bitterness. Store in the refrigerator in an airtight container with cold water to cover for up to 1 week.

BLACK VINEGAR Also known as Chinkiang or Zhejiang vinegar, this thick, glossy, dark vinegar has a complex flavor with a hint of wood smoke. Black vinegar may be fermented from glutinous rice, wheat, millet, or sorghum, depending on the region in China where it is produced, and the best bottles are aged for several years to deepen their flavor. Balsamic vinegar, which has a similar flavor, serves well as a substitute.

BONITO FLAKES Known as *katsuobushi* in Japan, these paper-thin shavings from dried, smoked, and cured fillets of bonito tuna play an essential role in Japanese cuisine. They flavor clear dashi soup stock and are used as a garnish for salads, rice, and noodles.

CARDAMOM The small pods of the tropical cardamom plant, native to the Malabar coast of southwestern India, encase tiny, black, highly aromatic seeds. South Asian cooks use the spice generously, adding ground seeds or crushed whole pods to drinks, sauces, soups, curries, and rice dishes. Bright green pods are preferable to the white ones, which have been bleached and thus diminished in flavor.

CHICKEN Descended from the jungle fowl of India and Southeast Asia, chicken is one of the most frequently served foods at Asian tables. The best-quality chickens have firm, plump flesh and pale skin free of bruises. Buy whole birds when possible, as they are easy to cut into pieces and their trimmings can be used to make flavorful, homemade stock.

To prepare a whole chicken for cooking, remove the giblets and neck from the cavity, reserving them for another use or discarding. Remove any pockets of fat from the neck and tail cavities. If a recipe calls for chicken halves, place the bird, breast side down, on a cutting board. Using poultry shears and beginning at the neck opening, cut along both sides of the backbone. Remove the backbone, reserving it for stock or discarding. Turn the bird breast side up, flatten it slightly, and cut in half along the breastbone.

To divide a whole bird into serving pieces, use poultry shears to cut through the skin between each thigh and the body. Bend the leg back to loosen the thighbone from its joint, then cut through it to remove the entire leg. To separate the thigh from the drumstick, locate the joint by following the thin line of fat between them. Cut through the joint to separate the pieces. Turn the bird's body to access each wing. Move each wing to locate the joint connecting it to the body, and then cut through the joint to free the wing. Cut along both sides of the backbone and remove it. Cut through the center of the breast to split it in half, and then cut each breast crosswise into 2 pieces. Prepared in this manner, a whole chicken will yield 10 pieces. For 12 pieces, cut each thigh in half.

CHILE BEAN PASTE When fermented and puréed with chiles, garlic, and spices, soybeans create a thick paste with a strong, salty-hot flavor. Known as *lat chu jeung* in China or *kochujang* in Korea, chile bean pastes are essential to the boldly flavored sauces of the Sichuan and Hunan provinces.

CHILE PASTE Many different types of purées made from chiles are used throughout China, Korea, and Southeast Asia as condiments at the table and as staple ingredients in the kitchen. They range from thin *sambals* of fresh chiles to thick pastes ground from dried or pungently fermented chiles. Salt or vinegar may be added as a preservative, and other ingredients such as garlic, dried shrimp, tamarind, fried shallots, or grated ginger contribute multiple layers of flavor and texture.

CHILES Hundreds of chile varieties thrive in Asia, from the rare and fruity Kashmir chile of northern India to the tiny, intensely hot bird's-eye chile of Thailand. Variations in color, texture, sweetness, and heat level of chiles help define local flavors. The cuisines of Korea, Thailand, Indonesia, Sri Lanka, and the provinces of Sichuan and Hunan in China are famous for their abundant use of hot chiles, and on nearly every table throughout Asia they are offered in some form—flakes, powder, oil, paste, pickled, or fresh slices. To lessen the heat of fresh chiles, halve them lengthwise with a paring knife, then scrape away the seeds and the pale membranes.

Fresno A mild to hot chile that is about 3 inches (7.5 cm) long. Less fleshy than the jalapeño, red Fresno chiles generally come to market in late summer and autumn.

Jalapeño A popular fresh chile that can range from mild to fiery hot. The thick-walled jalapeño tapers 2–4 inches (5–10 cm) to a blunt tip and is usually green in color, though riper, sweeter red chiles are seasonally available.

Serrano This fresh chile up to 2 inches (5 cm) long is sold in its green or ripened red form. Green serranos in particular tend to be hot.

Dried red These thin, pointed, bright red chiles are similar to dried *árbol* and dried cayenne, which can be used as substitutes. To lessen their heat, trim the stem and shake out the seeds.

CHILI OIL This clear, red oil infused with the spicy heat of dried chiles is especially popular as a condiment in China. Some versions include flakes of roasted chile, fermented black beans, or toasted sesame oil for richer flavor.

To make chili oil, heat 1/2 cup (4 fl oz/125 ml) canola oil over low heat until it begins to ripple. Stir in 3 tablespoons red pepper flakes, remove from the heat, and let cool. Cover and let stand for 24 hours. Pour the oil through a fine-mesh sieve into a glass bottle with a cork or screw top, close tightly, and store in a cool, dry place for up to 3 months.

CHILI POWDER Ground chiles blended with various spices, seeds, and other aromatic ingredients are popular condiments in Japan and Korea. *Shichimi togarashi*, Japanese for seven-flavor chile pepper, has a complex flavor with a touch of spicy heat.

CILANTRO The fresh coriander plant, also known as cilantro or Chinese parsley, is one of the most common herbs in the world. Its thin, woody root and long stems add depth of flavor to Thai, Malaysian, and Indonesian curries, and its lacy leaves garnish dishes throughout Asia. With its distinct citrus and mint tones, cilantro plays a central role in chutneys and dips.

COCONUT MILK AND COCONUT CREAM
Coconut palm trees thrive throughout tropical Asia. Pressed from the grated meat of the ripened nut, coconut milk lends sweetness and richness to sauces, soups, desserts, and drinks. Look in Asian markets for canned or frozen coconut milk. Stir canned coconut milk well before adding to recipes, and thaw the frozen completely before using.

Rich in natural fats, the cream of the coconut rises to the top of the milk when undisturbed. In Southeast Asia, the thick cream is used as a topping on desserts, as a cooking fat for aromatic ingredients, and as a finishing swirl of richness in curries and sauces. To settle coconut cream for measuring, place an unopened can of coconut milk in the refrigerator and let stand for at least 4 hours. Open the can, being very careful not to shake or invert it. The cream will be floating in a solid layer on top of the milk. Spoon out the amount of cream required, transfer any unused coconut milk or cream to a clean container, and refrigerate for up to 1 week. Do not confuse this cream with the small cans of sweetened coconut cream used for making mixed drinks; the two are not interchangeable.

CURRY POWDER In South Asia, dried spices are roasted, ground, and then blended into complex mixes, known as masalas, to flavor sauces. The spice mixes vary by region and dish, from mild and aromatic korma to assertively spicy vindaloo, and many cooks prefer to prepare their own unique blend. In the West, prepackaged curry powder labeled "Madras" refers to a commonly available mixture that is brightly colored yellow with turmeric. This version is also the standard for Indian-inspired dishes in Japan, China, and Southeast Asia.

DAIKON Popular throughout Asia, this long, snowy white radish is especially important in China, Japan, and Korea, where it comes to the table in some form nearly every day. In soups and long-cooked stews, its pungent flavor becomes sweet and mild.

DASHI Essential to Japanese cuisine, dashi is traditionally made by infusing *konbu* seaweed and dried fish, such as bonito flakes, in hot water to make a clear, delicate stock. Today a convenient form of instant dashi, concentrated and dried into granules, is available in most Asian and specialty markets. To prepare, stir 1/8 teaspoon of the dashi granules in 1 cup (8 fl oz/250 ml) hot water until dissolved. Look also for premeasured, self-contained dashi packets, resembling large tea bags, that require only a few minutes of gentle simmering.

EGGPLANT Native to southern India, eggplant (aubergine) grows in a wide range of shapes and colors. The tiny, round, white ones in Thailand give the vegetable its name, though much more widely used are the long, thin, lavender variety of Japan and the hefty, dark purple globe eggplant more common in the West. It is a versatile vegetable that takes well to stir-frying, deep-frying, braising, baking, grilling, and pickling. When selecting eggplant, look for ones boasting smooth, shiny skin free of blemishes and a stem that is still fresh and green.

FERMENTED BLACK BEANS This staple of Chinese pantries is made from dried soybeans that have been cooked, salted, and fermented until black in color and slightly soft in texture. Some versions are flavored with aromatics such as anise or tangerine peel. Before using, rinse them well and drain. A recipe may call for adding the beans whole to a dish or mashing them with sugar, ginger, garlic, or chiles before stirring into a sauce or marinade.

FISH SAUCE Salted and packed in large vats, anchovies give off an amber, pungently flavored liquid known as fish sauce, one of the most important seasonings in Southeast Asia. Called *nam pla* in Thailand, *nuoc mam* in Vietnam, and *patis* in the Philippines, it is used much like soy sauce as a basic seasoning for meat, poultry, and seafood. It also adds savory flavor to soups and sauces, serves as the base of dipping sauces, and is sprinkled on food at the table.

FIVE-SPICE POWDER This classic Chinese spice mixture is an aromatic blend of ground fennel, clove, cinnamon, Sichuan peppercorn, and star anise. It appears frequently in marinades, glazes, and long-cooked stews, and it also comes to the table mixed with coarse salt as a dipping condiment for roasted meats.

GALANGAL A distant relative of ginger, galangal is used in Southeast Asian kitchens to add bright flavor to soups and curry pastes. The most common variety has a pale, creamy, smooth skin with dark striations that must be peeled before using. If the fresh root is unavailable, look for glass jars with slices preserved in brine.

GARAM MASALA A dried spice mixture made popular in northern India's Mogul court, garam masala typically includes cinnamon, fenugreek, cumin, peppercorns, and cardamom. It now appears in curries throughout India and Southeast Asia. Cooks also sprinkle it as a finishing spice on dishes just before serving.

GHEE Known as *usli ghee* in India, this Asian version of clarified butter involves gently simmering the fat to remove all its moisture. In the process, the ghee develops an amber color and unique, nutty flavor. Clarification also increases its smoke point to allow higher heat frying and extends the butter's storage life at room temperature, an important aspect of cooking in tropical regions.

To make ghee, melt 8 oz (250 g) unsalted butter in an uncovered heavy-bottomed saucepan over medium-low heat. When the butter is melted, raise the heat to medium and simmer until the clear fat separates from the milk solids, about 15 minutes. When the butter stops crackling, signifying that all its water content has evaporated, reduce the heat to low and continue simmering gently until the butter takes on an amber color and has a nutty aroma, 10–15 minutes. Take care not to scorch the milk solids, or they will become unappealingly bitter. Remove the pan from the heat and let stand, uncovered, until the butter is cool. Carefully pour or spoon out the clear fat that floats to the top, transferring it to clean glass jars and making sure to leave behind the dark residue. Discard the residue. Cover the jars tightly and refrigerate for up to 6 months or freeze for up to 1 year.

GINGER The fresh rhizome of the ginger plant is one of the most important aromatic ingredients in Asian cooking. Gently crushed for simmering stocks, ground into wet pastes, finely minced for savory fillings, or thinly shredded for dipping sauces, ginger appears in some form at nearly every meal. Buy the freshest and youngest ginger possible, choosing plump, firm roots with a smooth, shiny peel. Refrigerate for up to 2 weeks wrapped in a dry paper towel inside a plastic bag and peel before using. Lightly pickled ginger serves as a palate cleanser in Japan and a garnish for salads and noodle dishes in Southeast Asia.

GINGER JUICE Delicate sauces, dressings, and soups often call for ginger juice. Pressed from finely grated ginger, the liquid carries the rhizome's vivid flavors without adding fibrous texture or clouding clear stocks and sauces. The younger the ginger, the more juice it will give.

To make ginger juice, peel fresh ginger. Using a ginger grater or a mini food processor, grate or mince the ginger into a bowl. Using your hands, squeeze the grated or minced ginger to extract as much juice as possible, discarding the solids or reserving for another use. Approximately 2 tablespoons grated ginger will yield about 1 tablespoon ginger juice.

HOISIN SAUCE This popular thick, dark sauce flavored with five-spice powder is a classic table condiment and is also used in cooking.

KAFFIR LIME LEAVES With their distinctive double leaves and knobby-skinned fruit, kaffir lime trees grow throughout the tropical regions of South and Southeast Asia. The leaves contribute a flowery aroma when infused whole in stocks and sauces. Finely shredded, they garnish soups, salads, and curries. If the leaves are large, remove the center spine by tearing it gently away from each leaf.

KIMCHI Korean cuisine is famous for its spicy and pungent kimchi, a type of fermented pickle, usually napa cabbage, that is flavored with salt, chiles, green (spring) onions, and ginger. Once buried in ceramic crocks to keep through long winters, the pickle is now widely available in glass jars in most supermarkets. It is a ubiquitous side dish on Korean tables.

KONBU In the seas surrounding the islands of Japan grow a wide variety of seaweed, each highly nutritious and rich in savory flavors. The most common, harvested from the cold water of the northern regions, is the dark green, large-leafed *dashikonbu* that is widely available dried in Asian markets. It should never be washed, as much of its flavor resides on its surface. Wipe gently with a damp cloth and avoid cooking for more than 10 minutes.

LEMONGRASS With their long, flat leaves and woody stems, lemongrass stalks resemble sturdy, pale green onions. The citrusy flavor and fragrance are essential to the complex dishes of Southeast Asia, where the aromatic herb is ground into curry pastes, infused into soup broths, and finely shaved into fresh salads. To prepare lemongrass, remove the outer layers from the stalk and trim away the green leaves and root end, leaving about 6 inches (15 cm) of the tender, ivory-colored midsection. Lay on a cutting board and bruise well with the side of a chef's knife, then slice or chop.

LENTIL, RED The oldest in the lentil family, this small and brightly colored legume has been a part of Indian cuisine for more than 4,000 years, where it is most commonly simmered into a thin purée or soup flavored with spices and herbs.

MIRIN A sweetened rice wine used specifically for cooking rather than drinking, mirin adds body and gloss to Japanese glazes, dressings, and sauces. Look for bottles listing only rice wine and sugar as ingredients.

MISO Salting, fermenting, and inoculating whole soybeans with rice mold results in miso, a richly flavored and nutrient-dense paste that is essential to Japanese cuisine. Varying widely in color and robustness of flavor, miso is stirred into sauces and glazes and appears daily at the table in soup. *Shiro* refers to a type of miso that has a pale color and a sweet, delicate flavor.

MUNG BEAN SPROUTS Crisp, white mung bean sprouts contribute freshness and texture to many Asian dishes, especially soups, salads, stir-fried noodles, and filled rolls. To keep them as fresh as possible, immerse in a container of cold water and store in the refrigerator for up to 3 days.

MUNG BEANS, DRIED YELLOW Dried mung beans are simmered into smooth soups, puréed into crisp batters, or fried and sprinkled whole as garnish from India to Indonesia. Sweetened, the beans appear in fillings, puddings, desserts, and sweet snacks throughout Southeast Asia. Look for split and dried mung beans, called *moong dal* in Indian markets

or labeled "green bean" (for the bright green covering that is polished away) in Chinese or Vietnamese markets.

MUSHROOMS Asian cuisine highlights an astonishing array of mushrooms. Rare *matsutake*, bite-sized straw mushrooms, and crunchy tree ears are just a few that you can find in Asian and specialty produce markets. Store fresh mushrooms in paper bags in the refrigerator.

Enoki Delicate, white winter mushrooms that have slender stems and tiny, round caps. Their pleasantly crunchy texture is best highlighted with minimal cooking, and in Japan, enoki are especially popular when heated briefly in soups or hot pot. They grow in light clumps that can be separated by trimming away their solid base and gently fanning their stems.

Shiitake Also often known as Chinese black mushrooms, brown, flat-capped shiitakes are typically cultivated on oak logs. The mushrooms are widely available both fresh and dried. The latter, much appreciated for their smoky, meaty flavor and chewy texture, require reconstituting before use.

NOODLES Eaten as often as rice in many Asian countries, noodles can be made from a wide variety of grains. Traditionally, wheat noodles were enjoyed in cool, northern countries, and rice noodles were the staple of warmer, southern regions. Today, noodles of all colors, flavors, and textures have become popular throughout Asia.

Buckwheat soba A firm bite, square-cut profile, and brownish purple color distinguish these Japanese noodles, usually prepared simply with clear broth or thin dipping sauces.

Cellophane Also known as mung bean, bean thread, or glass noodles. Made from mung bean starch, these translucent, firm noodles hold up well to braising and stir-frying. Soak in warm water for 30 minutes and drain before using.

Egg A wide range of fresh and dried noodles are made from wheat and eggs, from thin threads to wide, flat ribbons. Fresh, chewy, thick, round egg noodles are a specialty of Shanghai.

Rice Especially popular in southern China and Southeast Asia. Thin vermicelli and wider *banh pho* noodles, available both fresh and dried, have a delicate texture that is enjoyed in brothy soups. Silky ribbons cut from fresh rice noodle sheets are stir-fried or simply steamed.

Sweet potato starch Similar to cellophane noodles, these clear and chewy Korean noodles are the basis for soups and stir-fries.

Udon Thick, substantial noodles made of wheat flour and popular in Japan as the foundation for soups and other dishes.

NORI SEAWEED A flat, dark green wrapper made from pressed, dried, and roasted algae. In Japan and Korea, sheets of nori are used to enclose popular foods such as rice balls, *maki* rolls, and other savory treats eaten by hand. Nori is also seasoned with salt and sesame oil to accompany rice or thinly shredded to garnish soups and salads. Sheets of nori, lightly toasted to bring out their flavor, are widely available.

OYSTER SAUCE A staple in Cantonese cooking, this thick, dark brown sauce was traditionally made from oysters, water, and salt. The sauce's salty-sweet flavor adds richness to braises and stir-fry sauces, and the sauce appears often at Chinese tables as a simple topping for dark greens or crisp vegetables.

PALM SUGAR Similar to packed brown sugar in appearance and dark maple syrup in flavor, palm sugar is boiled down from the sap of palm trees and then shaped into solid cones, cubes, or disks. Its complex flavor, which varies regionally, is essential to savory as well as sweet dishes throughout Southeast Asia. With a sharp knife, remove the desired amount from the molded sugar and then chop before measuring. Dark brown sugar can be used as a substitute.

RICE Most varieties of rice fall into two general categories. Long-grain rice, which grows well in warmer climates, has dry, elongated grains when cooked; many varieties are famous for their nutty or floral aromas. Short-grain rice, which thrives in the colder clime of northern Asia, has short, plump grains that are moist and glossy.

Basmati A long-grain rice served at special occasions in India, Pakistan, and other South Asian countries. Basmati stars in festive rice dishes such as *biryani* and *pullao*.

Jasmine A favorite in Thailand and Vietnam, this fragrant long-grain rice is named for the tropical flower whose aroma it evokes when cooked.

Sticky Also known as sweet or glutinous rice, varieties of this rice include both long and short grain as well as a range of colors from white to red to black. The extra-starchy rice is used throughout Asia for desserts and fillings.

RICE FLOUR Ground into a fine powder, long-grain rice lends crispness and lightness to fritters, crepes, pancakes, and Japanese tempura. Look for small plastic bags of rice flour in Asian markets. Take care not to confuse the long-grain rice version with glutinous rice flour, which will result in a translucent, dense, chewy dough.

RICE-PAPER WRAPPERS Known as *banh trang* in Vietnam, rice paper wrappers are thin, dried sheets that, when moistened, become translucent wrappers. Large rounds enclose cooked meat or seafood, lettuce, and fresh herbs. Smaller rounds, filled with minced shrimp (prawns) and pork, are used in fried spring rolls.

RICE VINEGAR This mildly flavored vinegar, most often made now from rice wine lees, is widely used in China and Japan. Less acidic and sharp than distilled white vinegar, it blends well into salads and light sauces. Depending on the region and the brand, it may range from crystal clear to pale gold in color, with the latter generally having more flavor. Avoid varieties with salt or other flavorings, and look instead for unseasoned rice vinegars.

RICE WINE A spirit distilled from glutinous rice, Chinese rice wine adds depth to marinades, sauces, soups, and classic red-cooked braises. For the best flavor, choose rice wine from Shaoxing that has been aged for at least 5 years, or substitute with good-quality dry sherry.

ROSE WATER Known as *gulab jal* in India, where it was a favorite ingredient in Moghul court cuisine, this dilute distillation of red rose petals lends its flowery fragrance to many desserts and drinks such as *kheer*, *kulfi*, ice cream, syrups, and sweet *lassi*. Orange flower water or a small amount of pure almond extract may be used in its place.

SANSHO PEPPER Ground from the pods of the Japanese prickly ash tree, *sansho* pepper has an aromatic flavor that blends exceptionally well with other spices, especially in *shichimi togarashi* mixtures. Ground *sansho* carries a gentle numbing sensation rather than the sharp heat of chiles and is traditionally used to complement grilled chicken and eel.

SESAME OIL, ASIAN With its dark amber color and its rich, nutty flavor, oil pressed from roasted sesame seeds serves as a key ingredient in Chinese, Korean, and Japanese food. Not to be confused with clear, refined sesame oil used for cooking, roasted sesame oil is best used in small amounts in marinades, fillings, dipping sauces, and salad dressings.

SESAME PASTE This thick paste, made from darkly toasted sesame seeds, serves as the base for a wide range of dipping sauces in China, Korea, and Indonesia. It is also the central flavoring for spicy Sichuan *dan dan* noodles. Much like natural peanut butter, its oil will separate and rise in the jar; stir well before using. Roasted almond butter is a better substitute than Middle Eastern tahini, which has a much lighter color and flavor.

SESAME SEEDS Tiny, pointed sesame seeds have a nutty flavor and a delicate texture much appreciated in China, India, Japan, and Korea. Hulled, white sesame seeds coat deep-fried foods and appear in marinades. A second type, known as tan sesame seeds, has a slightly darker color and stronger flavor. The sweetened paste of black sesame seeds is a popular filling in Chinese desserts and snacks. The best flavor and texture comes from toasting sesame seeds just before using.

To toast sesame seeds, heat a small, dry frying pan over medium heat. Add the seeds and cook, stirring occasionally, until golden brown, 4–5 minutes. Transfer immediately to a plate to cool. Take care not to scorch them, or they will turn bitter in flavor.

SHRIMP PASTE Similar to anchovies, shrimp paste is salted, fermented, and ground shrimp, the pungent flavor of which lends complex flavor to savory dishes throughout Southeast Asia. Known as *mam tom* in Vietnam, *kapi* in Thailand, and *belacan* in Malaysia, shrimp paste can vary widely from a moist, light gray paste to a dark brown, solid, dry brick.

SOY SAUCE A fundamental seasoning in China, Japan, and Southeast Asia, soy sauce is a dark, salty liquid made from soy beans fermented with a small amount of wheat to develop complex, meaty flavors. The highest quality soy sauces are made from only whole beans, wheat, and water and then are aged in barrels. Different types of soy sauces include light soy (not to be confused with "lite" or reduced-sodium soy sauce), the basic version stocked in most Chinese kitchens for its lighter color and saltier flavor, and dark soy, a darker version often used in braises, glazes, and heartier sauces. A thick, sweet soy sauce with molasses flavor, known as *kecap manis*, is popular in Indonesia and Malaysia.

SOYBEAN PASTE One of the oldest seasonings in the world, from which soy sauce was later developed, fermented soybeans become intensely rich and savory in flavor as they age and mellow into a paste. Soybean paste lasts indefinitely when packed into ceramic crocks or glass jars. Look for pastes made from whole beans for a fuller, rounder flavor.

SRIRACHA CHILE SAUCE Named for a town in the south of Thailand, Sriracha is a bright red, smoothly textured chile sauce. Its hint of sweetness makes it a popular condiment at the table and a versatile ingredient in the kitchen.

TAMARI SOY SAUCE This variation on soy sauce is made without wheat. A specialty of Japan, it complements the flavors of sashimi especially well. Regular soy sauce is often mislabeled as tamari, so be sure to check the ingredient list for only soybeans, salt, and water to ensure true tamari.

TAMARIND PASTE The long fruit pods of the tamarind tree are a staple of India and Southeast Asia. Extremely sour when green, tamarind fruit ripens to a sweet-tart flavor. Both green and ripe forms are used as a souring agent in soups and sauces. Tamarind is most commonly available dried and pressed into a block or puréed into a convenient concentrate. Soak the dried fruit in water and then strain, discarding the seeds and fibers. The most convenient form is a dark, thick concentrated paste that can be stirred directly into other liquids.

THAI BASIL Its purple stems and its gentle anise flavor distinguish Thai basil from Italian sweet basil. Popular in Thailand and Vietnam, whole leaves garnish soups, curries, and spicy stir-fries.

TOFU Delicate, creamy, and highly nutritious bean curd, or tofu, is made by boiling and straining soybeans to make soy milk, then coagulating the milk with mineral compounds. There are many varieties that fall generally into two different styles: a silken Japanese version and a more coarsely textured Chinese tofu. The smoothness of soft, silken tofu is best highlighted in soups and appetizers. Firm, extra-firm, and pressed tofu can be cut into cubes and stir-fried, or crumbled and mixed into fillings. To store tofu, immerse it in a container of cold water and refrigerate for up to 1 week, changing the water daily.

WAKAME Fronds of this abundant seaweed are popular in Japan, where they are sliced thinly for tossing in vinegary salads or cut into small squares to float in miso soup. There are many varieties of wakame, ranging from light green to deep brown in color. Generally, the darker the color, the more pronounced its savory flavor. Look for small packets of dried wakame in Japanese markets or natural-food stores.

WASABI PASTE An aromatic cousin of horseradish, the bright green root of the wasabi plant thrives in Japan's mountain streams. The root is traditionally grated into a paste to accompany sushi and sashimi. In the West, wasabi appears most commonly in tubes as a prepared paste or in small tins as a fine powder. Mix the powder with a very small amount of water and then let stand for 10 minutes so the paste thickens and develops flavor.

WATER CHESTNUTS One of the auspicious vegetables of Chinese legend, the water chestnut is a corm, or the rounded stem of a type of grass that grows in water. Beneath its dark brown peel lies pale, crisp, starchy flesh with a sweet flavor. Whole and sliced water chestnuts are commonly available in cans. Simply rinse in cold water and drain well before using. When buying fresh water chestnuts, choose firm ones with smooth skins. Peel them with a sharp paring knife, immersing them in water as you work to prevent discoloration.

WONTON WRAPPERS Rolled thinly from a dough of wheat flour, egg, and water and then cut into squares or rounds, wonton wrappers are commonly filled with minced shrimp (prawns), pork, tofu, or vegetables. The resulting dumplings can be boiled, steamed, panfried, or deep-fried. Japanese-style *gyoza* require the thinnest rounds. Thick rounds, often labeled for pot stickers, are ideal for panfried dumplings and hearty Korean *mandu* dumplings. Thin, square wrappers make delicate wontons for clear soup or for deep-fried appetizers.

YARD-LONG BEANS Related to cowpeas, the aptly named yard-long bean is a thin, crinkly, dark green pod that can grow to lengths exceeding 24 inches (60 cm). Firmer and drier than standard green beans, yard-long beans are used widely in China, India, and Southeast Asia. Their crunchy, dry texture holds up well to braising, stir-frying, and deep-frying. Cut into short lengths, the beans are also enjoyed raw in salads and fresh vegetable platters in the highlands of Southeast Asia.

Index

OXMOOR HOUSE INC.

Oxmoor House books are distributed by Sunset Books
80 Willow Road, Menlo Park, CA 94025
Telephone: 650-321-3600 Fax: 650-324-1532
VP and Associate Publisher Jim Childs
Director of Marketing Sydney Webber

Oxmoor House and Sunset Books are divisions of
Southern Progress Corporation

WILLIAMS-SONOMA, INC.
Founder & Vice-Chairman Chuck Williams

WELDON OWEN INC.
Executive Chairman, Weldon Owen Group John Owen
CEO and President Terry Newell
Senior VP, International Sales Stuart Laurence
VP, Sales and New Business Development Amy Kaneko
Director of Finance Mark Perrigo
VP and Creative Director Gaye Allen
VP and Publisher Hannah Rahill
Associate Publisher Amy Marr
Associate Creative Director Emma Boys
Art Director Peter Antonelli
Designers Diana Heom and Rachel Lopez Metzger
Managing Editor Judith Dunham
Editor Donita Boles
Production Director Chris Hemesath
Color Manager Teri Bell
Production Manager Michelle Duggan
Photographers Tucker + Hossler
Food Stylist Erin Quon
Food Stylist's Assistants Jeffrey Larsen and Victoria Woollard

ACKNOWLEDGMENTS
Weldon Owen would like to thank the following people for
their generous support in producing this book: Carrie Bradley,
Kami Bremyer, Ken DellaPenta, Lauren Hancock, Marlies Lee,
Marlene McLoughlin, Tym Meeker, Gentaro Nakamura,
Leigh Noe, Kathryn Shedrick, Sharon Silva, Julia Tom,
Lisa Weiss, and Dawn Yanagihara.

THE ESSENTIALS SERIES
Conceived and produced by
WELDON OWEN INC.
415 Jackson Street, San Francisco, CA 94111
Telephone: 415-291-0100 Fax: 415-291-8841

In Collaboration with Williams-Sonoma, Inc.
3250 Van Ness Avenue, San Francisco, CA 94109

A WELDON OWEN PRODUCTION
Copyright © 2009 Weldon Owen Inc.
and Williams-Sonoma, Inc.

First printed in 2009
10 9 8 7 6 5 4 3 2 1

ISBN 13: 978-0-8487-3268-4
ISBN 10: 0-8487-3268-5

Printed by SNP-Leefung
Printed in China